The Virtual Dimension

edited by John Beckmann

The Virtual Dimension

Architecture, Representation, and Crash Culture

PRINCETON ARCHITECTURAL PRESS   NEW YORK

Supported in part by the Graham Foundation for Advanced Studies in the Fine Arts.

IMAGES ON PAGES II-VII:

ENIAC COMPUTER

1945: The primary reason to build the ENIAC was a need for faster calculations. The Army required new firing tables for its guns, and each new table itself required between two and four thousand individual trajectories. A person with a desk calculator could compute one trajectory in about twelve hours. The ENIAC could do the same problem in just thirty seconds.

The ENIAC was invented by John Mauchly and J. Presper Eckert Jr., and when it was completed it contained 17,468 vacuum tubes, about seventy thousand resistors, ten thousand capacitors, six thousand switches, and fifteen hundred relays. It was 100 feet long, 10 feet high, and 3 feet deep. Numbers were entered into the ENIAC by turning rotary switches and via punch cards. It weighed 30 tons and covered 15,000 square feet of floor space.

The ENIAC's clock speed was 100,000 pulses per second, or 0.1 MHz. Today desktop computers run at well over 300 MHz.

Photographs courtesy University of Pennsylvania School of Engineering and Applied Science

CREDITS

xiv, xv, xvi: Photographs by Edgerton Germeahausen and Grier, Inc. (EG&G) for the Atomic Energy Commission. 26: Photograph by Patrick Demarchelier courtesy *Harper's.* 61–2: *Cyberforce* 2, no. 21 (May 1996). *Cyberforce* is tm and copyright Top Cow Productions, Inc., 1996, all rights reserved. 78–83: Courtesy D'Amelio Terras. 178: Courtesy UPI/Corbis-Bettman. 188–93: Courtesy Julie Saul Gallery. 333-334, 338 top: T. Figallo. 336 left: K. Nozawa. 336 right: M. Mutschlechner. 337: S. Hunter. 338 bottom: M. Kitagawa. 339: T. Shinoda.

PUBLISHED BY

Princeton Architectural Press

37 East Seventh Street

New York, NY 10003

02 01 00 99 98   5 4 3 2 1

FIRST EDITION

COVER PHOTOGRAPH, COVER AND BOOK DESIGN: Sara E. Stemen

Special thanks to Eugenia Bell, Caroline Green, Clare Jacobson, Therese Kelly, Mark Lamster, and Annie Nitschke of Princeton Architectural Press —Kevin C. Lippert, publisher

Printed and bound in the United States

For a free catalog of books published by Princeton Architectural Press, call toll free 1.800.722.6657 or visit www.papress.com

Library of Congress Cataloging-in-Publication Data

The virtual dimension : architecture, representation, and crash culture / edited by John Beckmann. — 1st ed.

    p. cm.

   ISBN 1-56898-120-1 (alk. paper)

   1. Architecture—Technological innovations.

  2. Architectural design—Data processing.

  3. Architectural practice. I. Beckmann, John.

NA2543.T43V57 1998

720'.1'05—DC21   97-24469

                     CIP

Contents

Acknowledgments

For the interzone nomads of space-time:

William S. Burroughs, Gilles Deleuze + Félix Guattari

I WOULD LIKE to thank the following people who in innumerable ways have made this book possible. First, to all of the brilliant contributors without whom this book would not be what it is, Margaret Janik for being my mirror, Stephen Perrella for his cantankerous late-night phone calls, Marcos Novak for his initial pivotal discussions, Chris Romero and Brian Kralyevich of Oscillation Digital Design Studio for an excellent job on an aggregate that we just couldn't get off the ground, Mark C. Taylor for being réal throughout, Kevin Clark for being the pusher, Emmylou Harris/Daniel Lanois, Lucinda Williams, and the McGarrigles for keeping me company, The Graham Foundation for Advanced Studies in the Fine Arts for their generous support, Kevin Lippert for his encouragement, Mark Lamster for the arduous task of editing this beast, Sara Stemen for her design, and the entire staff at Princeton Architectural Press, my parents Margaret and Norman Beckmann who undoubtedly were sent from heaven, and finally to my daughter Kyra who is pure sunshine.

I would also like to thank the following companies for letting me test drive some of their stuff: Alias/Wavefront Inc., Apple Computer Inc., Autodessys Inc., Diehl Graphsoft Inc., Engineered Software, Graphisoft U.S. Inc., Microsoft/Softimage Inc., Pixar Inc., Silicon Graphics Inc., Strata Inc., Yonowat S.A.

The end of the spectacle brings with it the collapse of reality into hyperrealism, the meticulous reduplication of the real, preferably through another reproductive medium such as advertising or photography. Through reproduction from one medium into another the real becomes volatile, it becomes the allegory of death, but it also draws strength from its own destruction, becoming the real for its own sake, a fetishism of the lost object which is no longer the object of representation, but the ecstasy of the degeneration and its own ritual extermination: the hyperreal.

—Jean Baudrillard, *Symbolic Exchange and Death*

Nevada proving ground—complete destruction of house no.1

located 3,500 feet from ground zero, from the 17 March 1953

atom blast at Yucca Flat. The only source of light was that

from the bomb.

Merge Invisible Layers

JOHN BECKMANN

If we release the silicon mosquito from the silicon chip, it flies off and we cannot find it again, it's very small, like dust.

HIROFUMI MIURA, A PROFESSOR OF MECHANO-INFORMATICS AT THE UNIVERSITY OF TOKYO[1]

I WALK AROUND the city streets for days on end. I have come to see the world in wire-frame, always from multiple points of view: from plan, elevation, section, and sometimes from a birds-eye perspective. I calculate the number of polygons, the needed texture maps, camera paths, and the radiosity factors required to construct and animate any given scene. I study the subtleties in light—its shimmering, almost hallucinatory mosaic refracting off intersecting planes of concrete, mirror, and glass, against the crush of urban landscape, amid the splinters of a broken sky.

For years I've resided in the branch-shaped housing sector on Wernher von Braun Boulevard. It's the one with the Booleaned windows, the endless Bezier curves, the multiple light extrusions, and the numerous means of escape. Some might call them entrances. Ramps like shoots, crisscrossing warped staircases, balconies pried open with spines extending out in all directions. Nevertheless, it is a home, it is my home of, and to, pure information.

A cathedral of light, if you will, of prefabricated carbon-fiber and lightweight synthetic thermal resins; equipped with stereo-immersive walls and motion sensors that respond via a bodynet to my ever shifting loci of desires and needs; continuously morphing by means of mu brainwave emissions into twisted algorithmic forms that are never in repose. It is a writhing psychic vessel of my disembodied senses and multiple hovering eyes, a taut mirror to both the inner and outer vectors, of surfaces within surfaces that unfold toward infinity.

My body is one and several. I change identity with the click of a keystroke. Shifting from male to demure Lolita, to a frolicking strawberry shortcake—I put a spell on you. You download a virus. I download cyberfeminist cut-ups, as information travels at one-trillion-bits-per-second through optical fiber. Autonomous intelligence filters (bots) seek and replicate all the electrons fit to transmit via the datamesh called the Internet. My self-replicating agents return home like omnivorous Pac-Men from an ever expanding digital killing field with the desired bytes and bits in tow. I have gone full-circle searching for some arcane piece of information—a piece to complete the fractal puzzle. The doubling, or interleaving of reality, is a squeamish electromechano affair between the virtual and the real. I experience a split. I'm looping the loop on a slippery thrill ride, incessantly riding on the "go-go" in-between. The psychic spin: my spirit whirls. That real-time streaming of potentialities, which has thoroughly kicked butt, like a schism break mechanism or Gaussian blur. That old hat "line of fright" has got me under its spell. Freeze frame. Instant replay. Cutting and pasting. Dragging and clicking. Forever coding in the margins. It's a feeding frenzy for virtual avatars. I sense that it's somehow too late, that I preach to the scan-converted, to those who will never become lost.

Let's go to the video tape...

THE GAP (NOT THE STORE)

At the beginning of his authoritative work, *A History of Civilizations*, Fernand Braudel wrote that "Civilizations, vast or otherwise, can always be located on a map...to discuss civilization is to discuss space, land and its contours."[2] Now there is no map, and any remaining geographical contours are significantly blurred or have officially collapsed. Multinational corporations (some significantly larger than many countries) and the blind market forces of late capitalism have fabricated a borderless accelerated space based solely around the transformation, manipulation, and flow of capital. Silently, the world has slipped out from under us as we dreamt our televised dreams, our souls shanghied by a culture of greed that is adrift on a reality that has become severely overexposed. We now confront a reality that has become psychically overstuffed; a mad accumulation of reality that is bifurcating between the real as we know it, and the teleschizoid assemblages that we have yet to fully formulate.

To speak of, or to even attempt to visualize form now, one must contemplate its antithesis. Meta-attributes have replaced physical attributes: metaquery, metacontent, metasymbols, and metaplace. Though the dream is seemingly at hand, this electronic reality exists remotely—in the netherworld of earth orbiting satellite links, communication servers, the Internet and intranets, and so on. We have, in effect, fallen outside of ourselves, as the once hard distinction between remote and local stages become even further dispersed, and the exposure intervals between time and space, inside and outside, mind and body, imaginary and real are no longer quantifiable factors.

This current transitory condition floats on a heuristic logic of its own making, as the real becomes thoroughly interleaved with the artificial. We "surf" on the flows of a hypernothingness state; hemophiliacs in search of some image clotting machine, careening around the outermost edge of a teflon coated information vortex; like junkies in need of a quick sensory fix. Finally, we have arrived at the manifest destination: the eternal return—like a snake devouring its own tale. In topology, this would be equivalent to a self-intersection on a nonorientable surface. A Klein bottle cannot be embedded in three-space, but it can be immersed there.

2:14:37 AM. Any representation of reality is tantamount to the ultimate user dungeon.

The virtual dimension has triggered a decisive cognitive rupture with the very notion and relevance of the Newtonian conception of space. It is a profoundly radicalized break. A break that in many respects is analogous to the space Brunelleschi and others opened up in the fifteenth century by developing the language of linear perspective. Perspectival law fixed the viewer in one place. Centuries later, perspective (a singular point of view) eventually gave way to analytical cubism (all-at-once, multiple, and simultaneous points of view), as developed by Picasso and Braque. Cubism was the first art movement that was synchronous with the multidimensionality that characterized the new scientific theories of relativity formulated by Einstein and Bohr.

With the development of immersive and augmented environments we have indeed reached a strange new plateau in the human condition, as we rapidly transit from analog to digital modalities. These are zones of pure simultaneity, absolute simulation, instability, and instant electronic transmission. All representations of the physical, if desired, can be removed—no vanishing point and no horizon. The once stable laws of time and space have been effectively rendered null and void; entropic delirium slips across the curvatures of time. Space is no longer something one moves through—space now moves through us.

In other words, in case you've had your sensor buried somewhere deep within the bowels of the earth, we have already gone virtual: the limits of the physical realm have been eclipsed by the digital. Advanced technologies have not only caught up with reality, they have in many ways surpassed it. We are inhabitants of the ether: the constellations of the visible world have merged with the screen. In a century immersed in the magic of technological acceleration, the very scaffoldings of perception have become transparent to our willful gaze.

ACTIVEMATRIX

° Biometrics: The EyeDentification 2001 retinal scanning terminal from EyeDentify recognizes an individual's retinal vascular pattern in less than five seconds.[3] On 20 May 1996, Illinois Governor Jim Edgar announced that the state had launched the nation's first retinal eye scanning project to identify eligible welfare clients and prevent fraud.[4]

○ On November 11, 1997 the Brazilian artist Eduardo Kac implanted an identification microchip with nine digits into his ankle and registered himself with a databank in the United States via the Internet. "Replacing the traditional branding with a hot iron, the microchip—a transponder tag—is used to identify and recover lost or stolen animals."[5] Implanting the chip in Kac's ankle intentionally referenced the fact that the ankle has traditionally been a part of the body that has been chained or branded.

○ Naked City: The Federal Aviation Administration will begin testing the use of a full-body 360 degree holographic imaging system at a United States airport. The system, developed by Pacific Northwest, uses millimeter waves to quickly generate a naked image of the scannee. Pacific Northwest is hot at work on developing x-ray specs using the same holographic technology.

○ Nanomusic: The world's smallest guitar (about the size of a single human cell) carved out of crystalline silicon has been made at Cornell University to demonstrate a new technology that could have a variety of uses in fiber optics, displays, sensors, and electronics. If plucked—by an atomic force microscope, for example—the strings would resonate, but at inaudible frequencies.[6]

○ Mind over Cursor: Scientists at the New York State Department of Health in Albany recently showed that it is possible for a person using brain wave control alone to move a computer cursor around a display screen. Dr. Jonathan Wolpaw, who heads the group, is looking for differences that can be used by a disabled subject to communicate with the outside world without moving or speaking. The system looks at natural mu brainwave emissions, fluctuations from the part of the brain called the sensorimotor cortex. A computer applies a mathematical technique called a Fourier transform to detect and measure the signal a subject attempts to transmit along these fluctuations. A subject is presented with a computer screen divided into quadrants, with the cursor starting out in the center. The experimenter randomly picks one of the four general directions, and by force of will, the subject tries to move the cursor in that directions to one of the four corners of the screen. Similar techniques may one day allow an airplane pilot to operate certain controls merely by thinking, and an Air Force program at the Wright-Patterson Air Force Base is already engaged in such experiments.[7]

° ImmersaWork: A tele-immersive networked application is being developed for the coming Internet 2 by the National Tele-Immersion Initiative. "An initial network of at least four Tele-Immersion sites will be put in place. Each of these will have a "telecubicle"....A telecubicle is an office that can appear to become one quadrant in a larger shared virtual office space. Four telecubicles can be joined in virtual space so that each forms a quadrant of a larger virtual whole. The desk surfaces line up to form a large table in the middle of the virtual shared room. Virtual objects and data can be passed through the walls between participants, and placed on the shared table in the middle for viewing.[8]

° Low-Earth Orbiting Satellites: Teledesic Corporation, backed by Microsoft's Bill Gates and cellular telephone tycoon Craig McCaw, promises to launch an "Internet in the Sky" by the year 2002. As planned today, the system would use 288 satellites in geosynchronous orbit. Teledesic claims that its customers will be able to download data at a speedy 28 megabits-per-second—one thousand times faster than an ordinary telephone connection, from anywhere in the world.[9] If you were to connect the dots between the satellites they would resemble a huge dome encasing the globe.

The Global Positioning System (GPS), consisting of twenty-four operational satellites in six sidereal orbital planes, encircles the earth and can pin-point our precise physical whereabouts with startling accuracy. Every square meter of the globe has been mapped and digitized by high-altitude photography. Consequently, it has become increasingly impossible in our surveillance-ridden society to even get lost: "The last bit of Earth unclaimed by any nation-state was eaten up in 1899. Ours is the first century without terra incognita, without a frontier."[10]

This progressive and continual derealization of nature has led to a scientific reterritorialization of the world itself. Our bodies, from the cellular, to the subcellular, to the molecular level, are in effect becoming crystalline. Researchers at IBM can manipulate single atoms, various nanotechnology research teams have successfully bonded gold with DNA (an accomplishment that may lead to new forms of electrical conduction). Medical surgeons will routinely wield remote-control scalpels and perform telepresence operations. And when the Human Genome Project is completed by 2005, our entire genetic blueprint will fit onto the side of a single CD-ROM, and the genetic foundations of any biological question will be a major step closer to being significantly decoded. These are some of the misfortunes (or little miracles) of the present age. They exist as parameters of artifice, as mass dissolves into data in the boundless age of the MetaMillennium®.

[ESC]

Television and computer screens have become my replacement windows on the world. Their flickering vistas do not offer me apertures of transcendence, or even escape. Ultimately, I'm led back to my monstrous and ever hyperaccelerating self, which floats in a digital ouroboros as information traveling at the speed of light devours itself as quickly as it can be produced. The postcapitalist-schizo is an accumulating production machine that whirls in the "real-time" digital casino of short-term interest rates, leveraged buyouts, and skyrocketing corporate profit margins. By adding I have eradicated function, as I participate in constructing a veritable electroMERZ. Stop in at the drive-thru McDonald's on the way to the Seremetyevo Airport 1, on the way to...

2:34:23 AM. I'm witness to some of the symptomatic signs of an adrenaline rush as I give up the ghost, as virtual rigor mortis kicks in, and digital ectoplasm spews from my carpal tunnel-ridden hands.[II]

[Section Deleted]

RELOADING...

MetaModernity™ and the death of the future began in Hiroshima on 6 August 1945, at exactly 8:15 in the morning. In a brilliant flash the temperature of the air reached 3,000–4,000 degrees Celsius. The shadows of the living were rayographed onto the surface of the earth by heat rays hotter than anything previously imagined. The sheer incomprehensibility of this massive obliteration of human life has set the hive mind reeling to this day. To move on from the psychic paralysis of that catastrophe is now the ultimate goal of any "user-friendly" condition, post-"Little Boy" blues.

GROUND CONTROL TO MAJOR TOM

When the first images of Earth taken by American astronauts were fed back to us, that vivid image of our planet as a lonely orb floating in the vastness of space reinforced our growing perception of human beings as a single distinct race. It gave us a narcissistic vision of wholeness and reinforced our belief in the utopian expansiveness of unlimited technological progress. Man on the moon: the looking glass effect. It was mankind's first global out-of-body experience. Reality itself was pulled inside out. It was a staggering accomplishment. This "impossible event" coincided with tremendous social upheavals taking place back on Spaceship Earth: political assassinations, the drug and sexual revolutions, the women's liberation movement, race riots in San Francisco and Detroit, student marches in Europe and the United States, the Vietnam War, and so forth. It was a time of swift and overwhelming change as chthonic fissures rippled through every strata of society.

The utopian dreams of the Space Age collapsed in a mere 73 seconds when the Challenger crew plummeted to their deaths in a fiery crash as millions of school children looked on in disbelief. This stillborn disillusionment with "getting off" Spaceship Earth has forced us to rechannel our desires. It is no longer possible to blast our problems into deep space.

But we are hastily taking them into cyberspace. At AlphaWorld, one of the first VRML (virtual reality modeling language) communities, settlers have already formed the first gang, called The Order, a name taken from the neo-Nazi group in the race-war novel *The Turner Diaries*. "Its members have discovered how to use aliases on line and then, using other people's names, have cursed and taunted some settlers. Russ Freelander, who is one of the few AlphaWorld settlers with the power to destroy structures, has occasionally gone out to The Order's headquarters at coordinates 666 North, o West to erase profanity. The Order has fought back by erecting a castle and a wall on which they post insults against Freelander and demands for freedom of expression."[13]

To venture into cyberspace with your own personality is insufficient. You need to cultivate multiple yous, avatars, and partial derivatives. You need to construct a new surface, a new territory, on which to project your desires.

DEVELOPING AN ON-LINE PERSONALITY

Have you ever wanted to develop an on-line personality? This seminar will give you the opportunity to take an approach for creating a character for the Internet. You will learn how to successfully promote your character and what is and is not believable. Topics include: historical overview; what is an on-line personality?; what makes for a good on-line personality and for believable characters?[13]

[Cut to a slow-motion panning shot of some Germans selling chunks of the Berlin wall to Japanese tourists.] The Wall is gone, though its presence, its trace, still remains. Ask any German.

USE IT OR LOSE IT:

A billion-dollar fitness industry now caters to our alienation and obsession with inertness and the art of staying in place: Stairmasters, treadmills, bicycling machines, rowing machines, and so forth. As electrons replace the physical need for "being there," and as our bodies are required for less and less manual labor, it becomes readily apparent that the trend in our culture toward excessive exercise is not merely a passing fad. We unconsciously intuit the need to keep our bodies strong and healthy. As the regime of invisible technologies takes logistic grip, we are developing an even more obsessive appetite for sculpting and morphing our physical selves. Not just through exercise but through the indiscriminate use of plastic surgery. We crave to shape skin and bone as effortlessly as we manipulate pixels on our screens. Perhaps it's not strictly narcissism at work, but a latent drive in the species to avoid utter extinction, a denial of our own mortality.

[I leave my home seduced by the horizon of the distant, but my body accelerates into obsolescence. I have no place—or that place is everywhere. This absence of place has created binary encoded spaces of death. Not frozen, but seamlessly enfolded. An erosion of trajectories, like an ancient wound. I draw a thousand lines across the void.]

THE GREAT MOTHER

The anarchic Internet, a bastion of antiquated Cold War-era technology when fused with LEO satellite technology will become our collective exonervous system, the perfect host organism as "the network itself has become the computer," the "Great Mother," capable of storing and relaying all the knowledge and information we can throw at it. It will eventually wrap Spaceship Earth like a vast Borgesian library of the absurd. A Dewey Decimal System based on the binary reduction of zeros and ones. "If you could only see what I've seen with your eyes."[14] We generate content now just to watch it die. We get off on the *petite meta-morte* in the temporal space of the chronic surface, amid the illusion of a global community.

William Gibson, the writer who coined the term "cyberspace," recently wrote: "Post-industrial creatures of an information economy, we increasingly sense that accessing media is what we do. We have become terminally self-conscious. There is no such thing as simple entertainment.

We watch ourselves watching Beavis and Butt-head, who are watching rock videos."[15]

Is it no surprise that as the dawn of the nonlocalised MetaMillennium® nears, "the more fluently we manage to reproduce ourselves, and our worlds, the more fleeting seems our embrace"?[16] Metascenes…duplicates of duplicates ad infinitum…we already don't really see, we scan, as the vortex-like datamesh delivers a mirage of information-as-knowledge to our retinas at warp speed.

GIMME A VIRTUAL JESUS

In the summer of 1995, the first retail store selling VR equipment opened its doors in Indianapolis. Virtually Yours is wedged between a pizza parlor and a laundromat in a small shopping center on the city's northeast outskirts. A businessman who stumbled upon the store when he and his son went out for pizza saw the potential for education…he asked Virtually Yours to supply expertise and equipment to Sunship Ministries as a marketing tool for getting developing countries to welcome them. "[We] could let people interact with a virtual Jesus."[17]

Holographic VR and haptic telepresence environments emerge as the inevitable extension of our screen-driven selves. No longer content to experience the idea of nothingness, we now want to inhabit it directly, like a luminous presence spiraling out of thin air. In our increasingly artificial cocoons, we acclimate to the Hertzian light that replaces natural daylight. Our newly founded digital reflection is not merely a limit, but rather a rite of passage, a transition into what Hakim Bey has called "a temporary autonomous zone," as we shift seamlessly between "the real" and ever more illusionary worlds. We suffer from a boundary loss that is screen-like by nature—amorphous—and hangs silently on a binary code that sublimely replicates death. Slow death delivered by zeros and ones on the Home Shopping Network simulator channel.

The gratifications and excitement of upward mobility threaten to abandon us to the unraveling inner spaces of our own psychic rootlessness, just as our "culture of bits" threatens to absorb the space where we take place. And this disappearance, for all intents and purposes, has already happened.

Technology has always evoked new representations of reality. Paul Virilio has asserted that the creation of virtual images is a crash site: "Cyberspace is an accident of the real. Virtual reality is the accident of reality itself.... It no longer occurs in matter, but in light or in images...thus, the accident is in light, not in matter. The creation of a virtual image is a form of accident. This explains why virtual reality is a cosmic accident. It's the accident of the real."[18]

Perversely, the advent of the virtual, or "the accident of the real," comes just in time to prop up our sagging belief systems. Culturally imbedded protocols, signs, referents, are endlessly being recycled with the hope that some overlooked freak mutation will somehow catch fire again. Elvis meets_____, meets_____.

Perhaps it is a nostalgic look back on a future that simply didn't take place, that we so desperately yearn for. Even at Disney World, former home to "imagineering" the future, has thrown in the futurist towel. "The new Tomorrowland begins with Jules Verne and ends with Buck Rogers."[19] Clearly, the "Magic Kingdom" would have a hard time pitching a diorama with multiple mommies and their cloned kids. At Tomorrowland, the future has sadly turned back in on itself—a kind of "back to the future" approach is being substituted in its place. It is "a reflection of the ennui that many Americans, at century's end, feel about the chips and bits in which they are immersed."[20]

To this effect, VR offers up a lightscape, a mirror thrust up through our television screens, enabling a vision quest for our waking discontents and its burden of impossible dreams. Telepresence and remote-sensing technologies allow us to become at once actors and spectators, transmitters and receivers, the spinning Janus face—in the teeming universal hive mind we now call cyberspace.

What is the surroundsound of one astral hand clapping in the frenzied aisles of consumerism? It is the tumultuous condition: the equivocal stare of chance upon transferring your consciousness to the ElectroMonad™.

METAPHORIC VESSELS AND THE TOPOLOGIES
OF INDIFFERENCE: ADJUST TO NEW PARAMETERS
AND CONSTRUCT DIRECTLY

Architecture is now invisible, and organizing information is referred to as architecture. The instrumentalized surface of the interface is an architecture that lies suspended between silence and the virtual. An electronic inscription of our extended and blurred bodies, incised onto an event horizon of no escape. An epoch tossed into a wormhole in the ether. The hyperatrophied mortal coil long since forgotten recedes into the network. Forever a gaze with no center. A gaze that is beyond identity, beyond body—that offers itself up as pure acceleration. Dilated organs without bodies perhaps, not bodies without organs. The distributed home bo(d)y$^{©}$.

Architecture must inevitably hemorrhage in this seismic mix. It must flow out in other less predictable directions. New spatial aggregates will require multiple escape routes. A single door for entering and exiting will no longer suffice. "Riemannian spaces…amorphous collection of pieces that are juxtaposed but not attached to each other." Pure patchwork with an infinite porosity of structure, like a sponge.[21]

Formerly, architecture hoarded forms by creating variations of closure. Freezing the mobility of relations of the in-between by storing an energy that now can only circulate. It attempted to capture some sort of spatio-temporal event within a formal framework, an anthropomorphic diagram, an envelope of recursive cell-like boundaries that mirrored our conception of the cosmos, and our place within it.

The very development of architectural theory can be likened to the spread of an image virus, memes that tend to explode out of an emergent set of embedded and acceptable codes or systems. In other words, they emerge out of a collectivist soup and are disseminated through various professional journals, style magazines, and coffee table books. The mark of a great architect today is judged more by the loud thump their new book makes when it hits the boardroom table then by their contributions toward the betterment of society. Doesn't the product of architecture in our culture exist as yet another form of corporate branding, like the latest pair of Nikes stitched up in Indonesia? Architectural evolution seems to have no foresight, it gropes from one path of dependence to the next. Architecture moves with the velocity of a slug through its own waste matter. Will we soon have a trip-hop architecture, an illbient-itecture, a gangsta-tecture, ad infinitum?

3:15:11 AM. The (phant_ms) of architecture haunt me, like an uninterrupted sequence of points projected onto the surface of some warped parabola. With no beginning and no end, a Moebius strip that cannibalizes itself. An immutable feedback with a single razor-sharp edge. Spatial organizations that are all links and no thresholds. A space that aspires to death, yet anticipates nothing, constantly retreating. A space that is always becoming the paradoxical other, constantly superpositioning itself on the whole, an organization that craves totality like a virus or a burst of lightening.

As the developmental logics of contemporary architecture are being conceived increasingly more for the display of audiovisual information than for the framed location of real bodies, a mode of built environments, as overwhelming as the datameshes that they seek to ground, is now being jettisoned globally.

What then is the fate that awaits architecture when it no longer requires a roof, structure, walls, windows, or staircases and becomes reduced to a screen for advertising? When the reversal, doubling, or unfolding of an interior for an exterior takes place? When the former reflexive relationships between exterior and interior disclosures become severed, spaces where gravity itself has been abruptly dislocated, vast infinitely morphing fields/screens of the convulsive marvelous, as we point and click our way through spatial membranes like lab rats in an infinite hyper-Pavlovian maze?

Information as decoration? Karrie Jacobs has ironically observed: "Some would argue that screens, whether they show video images or computer data, are appearing on building walls because they dispense information. I suspect the screens (and their cousins, the news zippers) proliferate because they represent the look of information…TV sets adorn buildings all over town, and still there's nothing to watch."[22]

We are witness to the emergence of architecture and its "chromed" double, an architecture that casts no shadows. An electro-shadow-less architecture made by vampires for vampires, forever condemned to live a soulless immortality in front of the flickering phosphorescent glow of computer displays as cities crumble around them. An architecture without the presence of angels in the global space of temporalized flows? The birth of an inbred couture culture groomed to watch space, rather than to directly participate in it?

It is perhaps at this interval; where the sublimity of nature has been overwhelmed by the infinity of information, where information itself has become elevated to a new form of religion, that new kinds of spatial figures will begin to take into account tectonic strategies, whereby structures are conceived in a more profound way than mere collage, or the manipulation of historical fragments. Bed becomes chair becomes table becomes wall becomes room becomes building becomes infrastructure. Continuous like film, an architecture based on duration and flow, from the actual to the virtual, and from the virtual to the actual. Of projected and transmitted surfaces within surfaces—kernels within kernels that forever unravel and surprise. An approach to building and conceptualizing space that is in tandem to the hyperlink, metaballs, blobs, and your latest plug-in. I suggest exploring a geometry of the uncanny surface, of polymorphous porosity, of the topological configuration of the in-between. Extend out from the middle and move toward the ripples at either edge of infinity. Move beyond three-space. Take a bite out of time, push the simultaneous and the porous. Analog method—students take note: fabricate your next architectural model in poured latex (as a negative), and hang it out to dry. Stick your arm deep down into the malignancy of the thing—like those psychic surgeons in Manila, and pull it inside out like a sock. Pull the floors through the roof, the walls through the light apertures. Now start taking pictures of your ambitious creation from various angles, plans, elevations, etc. Have the photographs developed. Stack them neatly on top of one another.

Slice an arch through them from one edge to the other. Place the sectioned images in sequence, in order of the directional cut. You now have a nice working diagram of simultaneity. Begin constructing your program from this new picture of space-time.

The primary task at hand is to illicite new movements toward the virtual by tripping up repetition, purging habit and reason, and encouraging difference. The virtual, and this is a point worth clarifying, lies outside the actual—it exists as a force, not a space. It operates and acts on another plane, in nother dimension. It is a continuous unfolding on the road to becoming other. Fold follows fold.

Alternatively, and by contrast, new digital methods for creating and programming space will undoubtedly be developed based upon advances in AI (artificial intelligence) research, such as neural-net computers similar to the kind already in place at NASA's Langley Research Center. Neural-nets consist of many control systems, or nodes, interconnected like neurons in the brain. Each node assigns a weight, or value, to inputs from the other nodes. By changing values, the neural-net can change the way it responds. A NASA project, being designed with the collaboration of Lockheed Martin and the Mississippi State University, for the "Waverider" Mach 5 airplane is a prime example of this approach. The "Waverider" prototype incorporates a radical solution—the plane can teach itself to fly.

This same sort of thinking will be used to generate provocative new forms. Assemblages that will not rely upon the random egocentric mutterings and musings of the designer. Building designs will in fact "self-assemble." You program in the variables (history, program, site, budget, style), model and render it in UrSpace™, and bingo! A resin model pops out like a piece of toast from an STL (stereo lithography) machine—you've got a slick little project. You could even program in a certain amount of indeterminacy, chaos, or Euler characteristics, if that's your trip, and hedge the topological envelope. Go ahead, make a name for yourself, you futurist!

1. Quoted in Andrew Pollack, "Tiny Toyota Utilizes New Advances In Micro-machine Technology," *New York Times*, 18 November 1996.

2. Fernand Braudel, *A History of Civilizations*, trans. Richard Mayn (New York: Penguin Books, 1995), 9.

3. Rayco Securities World Wide Web site, http://www.raycosecurity.com/access/EyeDentify.html. For general information on the field of biometrics see National Computer Security Association's Biometric Information World Wide Web site, http://www.ncsa.com/cbdc/cbdc-l.html.

4. State of Illinois World Wide Web site, http://www.state.il.us/Gov/press/fraud.htm.

5. Arlindo Machado, "A Microchip Inside the Body," Nettime list, 22 February 1998.

6. Cornell Science World Wide Web site, http://www.news.cornell.edu/science/July97/guitar.ltb.html. For information on the field of Nanotechnology, see Nanothinc World Wide Web site, http://www.nanothinc.com/index.html.

7. Malcolm W. Browne, "How Brain Waves Can Fly a Plane," *New York Times*, 7 March 1995. See also, Jonathan R. Wolpaw and Dennis J. McFarland, "Multichannel EEG-Based Brain-Computer Communication," *Electroencephalography & Clinical Neurophysiology* 90 (1994): 444–9.

8. National Tele-Immersive Initiative World Wide Web site: http://io.advanced.org/tele-immersion/

9. Teledesic Corporation World Wide Web site, http://www.teledesic.com

10. Hakim Bey, *T.A.Z.: The Temporary Autonomous Zone, Ontological Anarchy, Poetic Terrorism* (New York: Automedia, 1991).

11. Repetitive Strain Injury has emerged as the leading occupational injury in America, accounting for well over three hundred thousand new cases each year, according to the Bureau of Labor Statistics.

12. "Evolution of Virtual Universe Echoes Reality, Warts and All," *New York Times*, 7 February 1996.

13. Pratt Institute, fall 1997 course catalog, New York, 19.

14. Dialog spoken by the playback tape dealer Lenny Nero (Ralph Fiennes) from the film *Strange Days*.

15. William Gibson. "The Net is a Waste of Time," *New York Times Magazine*, 14 July 1996, 31.

16. Hillel Schwartz. *The Culture of the Copy: Striking Likenesses, Unreasonable Facsimiles* (New York: Zone Books, 1996), 20.

17. Barnaby J. Feder. "Selling Virtual Reality, in Indiana," *New York Times*, 7 August 1995.

18. Louise Wilson. "Cyberwar, God and Television: Interview with Paul Virilio," *CTheory* (1995), World Wide Web site, http://www.ctheory.com/a-cyberwar_god.html

19. Beth Dunlop, quoted in Seth Schiesel, "Once-Visionary Disney Calls the Future a Thing of the Past," *New York Times*, 23 February 1997. "The new Tomorrowland begins with Jules Verne and ends with Buck Rogers."

20. Ibid.

21. Gilles Deleuze and Félix Guattari, *A Thousand Plateaus*, trans. Brian Massumi (Minneapolis, MN: University of Minnesota Press, 1987), 485.

22. Karrie Jacobs. "Video Killed the Gargoyle," *New York Magazine* (17 February 1997), 24–7.

Flesh Space

STAHL STENSLIE

PRESENT CYBERSPACES ARE pristine and monosensory. They disembody the user through glossy cheap polygons and sensorially insulting bitrates. Rarely is the virtual dimension mixed with bodily fluids and designed as a holistic, multisensory body experience. And why should the stirring hot bits of cyberspace remain within the interface? If the virtual dimension is to impress its users beyond the shallow (monosensory) surface of current interface technologies— and immerse users in what the hype promises—a direct, corporal link is required. Future communication will go beyond the interface as we know it. Not into an absurd "uploading of the body" or the disappearance of the body in information, but rather in the re-emerging of the body as interface; an unpredictable, unreliable, unstable, and emotional interface, susceptible to hormonal flux and biological decay, but with a "fuzzy" logic guaranteeing information digestion/exchanges in bit rates higher than any contemporary, "logic" interface.

Presently the interface restricts our experience. Visual simulations give us only a small window into the virtual dimension. If (visual) simulations function as convincing experiences, it is predominantly due to the phenomenon of consensual hallucinations; the participants agree to believe in the mediated illusions. The cognitively induced deception of perception is a useful phenomenon for visual simulations, but why not extend the psychophysical relationships between the real and virtual worlds and mold deadly and sensuous phenomena into the virtual dimension? A rock thrown at you in VR is not a rock until it hits your head and hurts.

Solve et Coagula is primarily an attempt to give birth to a new life form: half digital, half organic. Through a multisensory interface the installation networks the human with an emotional, sensing, and artificially intelligent creature; it mates man with a machine turned human and everything that goes with it: ecstatic, monstrous, perverted, craving, seductive, hysterical, violent, and beautiful.

WIRING MAN AND MACHINE

Technologically it is extremely hard to link man and machine in a nonobtrusive way. Present tactile technologies rely on mechanical stimulation of the body through the use of small vibrators, pneumatic devices, heat-pads, electrical currents. Manipulation techniques are comparatively coarse, and they will remain so until wetware like biochips, brain/nerve implants, gentech and nanotech appear.

The *Solve et Coagula* project wires the user and the machine through a lightweight body suit, a head-mounted display with a headtracker, a microphone and a three-dimensional audio interface. The bodysuit is equipped with 128 effectors (tactile outputs), pressure sensitive joints, and two handheld pressure pads. The effectors, which provide tactile stimulus are specially built vibrators pressed against the body by the bodysuit. Some are attached to strings to distribute the vibrations in various ways. The strength of the effectors' output is variable. They are placed around the whole body and in such positions that they cover both the most touch sensitive and touch significant zones.

The artificial intelligence expresses emotions and touches users through the triggering of the effectors in various patterns. It embraces the user, giving the human component a feeling of its different virtual bodies rendered real.

TACTILE FLESH

The bodysuit conveys a range of pull-push sensations that impress the user with a sense of the creature's bodily presence. The sensory resolution measured in number of effectors is low compared to the millions of nerve endings beneath every square centimeter of skin. However, through the vast number of possible touch-combinations, the project has developed a body manipulative touch language of high complexity. It creates feelings ranging from the pleasurable to the painful, modeling moving objects, tactile shapes and textures.

The creature senses the user and extracts his or her emotional state through voice analyses and body tracking (pressure, position of view, and movement). The aim of mapping the user is to seduce the user's senses and manipulate him or her according to the dynamics of the human-machine life form.

CODED FLESH

The sensory bandwidth of a human is about 11-million bits-per-second. With emotional interface technology at this bandwidth, flesh can be coded. As networks grow and become preferred environments in which to socialize and interact, the private/social sphere will expand and we will grow familiar with communication on more intimate levels. Tactile communication will be included as it naturally belongs to the expressive toolbox of human communication. As the resultant emotional interfaces provide higher bandwidth and resolution, sexuality might even become a better metaphor for social interaction than speech. Sensually corporeal, communication will go beyond the shallow surface of the visual interface and definitively attract more attention. And attention is an attractive resource on a Web with millions of sites.

Introducing flesh into the virtual dimension will
change the paradigm of computing and communication. By breaking down the sensory border
between man and machine, the virtual dimension
can be rendered real. Its future interface will not
only be multisensory, it will be emotional.

"A body only exists to be other bodies."
—William S. Burroughs

from *Electronic Revolution* (Cambridge, England: Blackmoor Head Press, 1971).

"Space," "Being," and Other

Fictions in the Domain of the Virtual

FRANCES DYSON

WHEN THE PHILOSOPHER Martin Heidegger writes that "the essence of modern technology is by no means anything technological," the issues he raises are fundamentally ontological, dealing with the "being" of being human as much as the being of technology.[1] This link between two "essences"—the human and the technological—is articulated in the popular discourse on cyberspace: cyber theorists refer to cyberspace as a "mode of being," and to the cybernaut as a new kind of human. What lubricates this coupling is a peculiar blend of rhetoric and discourse through which "reality" and "space" are affixed to the terms "virtual" and "cyber" as attributes. That these attributes constantly map and regulate perceptions of new communications technologies such as the Internet and the "information superhighway," and new media forms such as virtual reality (VR), reveals at the same time a sophisticated marketing strategy, a good deal of confusion, and a persistent desire to reformulate what counts as existence so that it will apply with equal gravity to the virtual realm, philosophically and culturally situating it beyond any possibility of doubt.[2] Thus the "ontology" of cyberspace does not imply the being of some thing or another, rather it signals the attempts to assign being as an attribute to these new forms of media and communications.[3] It signals, in other words, a rhetorical maneuver, a play within the field of metaphor, fantasy, and what William Gibson, in coining the terms "cyberspace," identifies as "consensual hallucination."

Being is a complex assignation: it must take account of the critiques of Western metaphysics that have been erupting for the last twenty odd years, yet at the same time establish a ground within that metaphysics in order to argue the ontological status of virtuality. As a central metaphor within the notion of being, "space" provides a means of negotiating such a dilemma, having sufficient ambiguity to enable the discourse to drift between a cornucopia of real and mythic spaces, between for instance, the "space of the screen," the "space of the imagination," "outerspace," "cosmic space," and literal, three-dimensional physical "space." The power of "space" lies in the possibilities it implies: immersion, habitation, "being-there," phenomenal plenitude, unmediated presence, all fall within its domain. Without "space" there can be no concept of presence within an environment, nor, more importantly, can there be the possibility for authenticity that "being-in-the-world" allows. Heidegger aside, many proponents of virtuality recognize nonetheless that authentic being, "being-there," generates what is possibly the last bastion of hope against the fear and cynicism that pervades late-twentieth-century culture, transforming the gloss of technological progress into another form of toxic overlay. Where a distrust of print and broadcast media—especially television—signals a general critique of representation, virtuality claims to have superseded the mediation of the screen and the passivity/control of the televisual apparatus. Where an excess of computation and simulation—deposited via the cold glare of the ATM screen and the fake frills of ersatz home and apple pie—has produced a fear of the loss of the real, virtuality provides the warm glow of cyber companionship and the physicality of interactive environments. Where anxiety about the reductive and quantitatively determined representations of science seem to coalesce in the binary logic of the computer, virtuality situates itself within the new terrains of artificial intelligence (AI), chaos theory, and biotechnology, as part of a generalized scientific shift that would return the organic to the mechanistic, the "body" to the mind.

This essay examines the metaphors of space, architecture, embodiment, and being as they manifest in the rhetoric of virtuality and materialize in the virtual environments and subjectivities of millennial culture. It does so by looking first at precedents in the built and media environment that have helped establish a discourse of immateriality upon which the rhetoric of virtuality depends; second, at the reformulated metaphysics summoned to prove, or at least rationalize, what are essentially ontological and epistemological claims; third, at the neofuturist and ocularcentric mechanisms that support the idea of an immersive space in virtual environments; fourth, at the appropriation of architectural metaphors that concretize the spatial metaphor, and finally, at the incorporation of embodiment as a means of confirming the authenticity, the "being" of cyberspace.

PRECEDENTS TO IMMATERIALITY.

While represented as an entirely new phenomenon, the virtual environment, or cyberspace, is not without its historical precedents, nor is it independent of the particular cultural predispositions that have assisted its establishment. The past thirty years have seen the proliferation of "non-places": the bland shopping malls, indistinguishable airports, megalithic office blocks, gated communities, theme parks, old-worldly villages, and managed and coifed "wilderness" areas that, functioning as signs rather than places, immerse the user in a self-conscious form of ritual bearing little relation to any actual time or location. Alongside the built environment, the global reach of television networks saturates world screens with a homogenous stream of images, sounds, rhythms, flows, nuances of light, color, and location that create the background to a predominantly North American content.[4] Cultural difference is absorbed, and an intense uniformity is produced via the rigorous programming that commercial interests demand. Even before the virtual landscape, the flat terrain of the screen has standardized an interface that, in its broadest sense, forges a relationship between the eye and how it sees—constructing a viewer that is "screen based" above and beyond the particular screens (television, computer, or the stereoscopic "eyesuckers" of VR) that are watched.

In the familiar characterizations of cultural discourse, screen culture inhabits neither place nor ground: it is fragmented and dislocated, it operates on a surface that is ephemeral and mediated, it has a four second attention span. With the accouterments of telecommunications—faxes, modems, mobile phones, beepers—these tendencies are amplified.[5] The ever-expanding, continuously on-call individual, becomes another kind of interface, for ever screening, filtering, ignoring, accepting, and repressing the plethora of inputs, information and demands for action that absorb his or her private space and individual time. While this appropriation of personal time and actual place may once have been viewed as a surreptitious lengthening of working hours and (mostly) unremunerated use of an individual's major asset—the home, for work purposes—it is now applauded as evidence of the collapse of borders, the process of globalization that is manifested on a national and individual level as everyone becomes his or her own small business. Reflecting trends in poststructuralist theory, this exchange between the individual and the electronic media and telecommunications environment is discursively represented as the achievement of a polymorphous, multiplicitous, heterogeneous subjectivity, a "liquid identity," a "post" human freed from the bonds of the autonomous subject for whom exchange and hybridity mean death.[6] Subjectivity is performed as a new kind of text while the body becomes a permeable surface, adorned with signs and riddled with the inscriptions and prescriptions of culture. Even the genetic structure is at base a complex but decipherable code, or so genetic research tells us. In this context, the hinge between cyber and space conveniently slides between the sometimes embarrassing ontological claims of some enthusiasts and the postmodern "body-as-text" for which corporeal presence and ontological status are no longer an issue. As Katherine Hayles points out, this belief in the body-as-text runs across theoretical discourse within the humanities, information theory, and information technologies.[7] Cyberspace is established as an "other" place to enact the deconstructed self: a self whose multiplicity and ambiguity is continually reinforced as the body seems to increasingly inhabit the dematerialized world that technology creates.[8]

The new postmodern subject, barely distinguishable from its prostheses, existing in flows of information, suspicious that—as some technophiles claim—matter is nothing but data after all, enters a new theoretical order. Seeing, and the poststructuralist framework dominated by the mediated image, is replaced by being, and the supposedly unmediated experience of immersion. Despite the fact that most cyber experience occurs via the screen, or more contemporaneously, as flows of data, the body-as-text elides the distinction between the screen and its viewer by ignoring the actuality of the screen and elaborating instead the metaphor of virtual "space." The "as if you are there" is truncated to a "you are there." One is in cyberspace, not watching it, one is a navigator, a netizen, not a viewer. This shift is in line with modernist ambitions of eliding the gap between signifier and signified, viewer and viewed, real and representation. In the high modernism of virtual rhetoric this ambition travels with its own ideology: the "being-in" of cyberspace is a deliberate move away from the trope of the viewer as witness to the world, as discerning judge of quality and truth as inherently separate from the environment. The subject-object distinction is not allowed to interfere with the cybernaut's mythic immersion in what is often represented as a mystical space. The era of the consumer gives way to the era of the virtual world citizen: the former exercises the right to choose (marginally) while the latter takes an oath of allegiance, allowing it to exist in a particular space, to be. No wonder, then, that Microsoft software opens with icons of socialist realism, often depicting young men in patriotic fervor marching forward into the future. The shift from a mode of manipulating representation to manipulating ontology requires absolute devotion.

That the flickering, two-dimensional screen scanning nothing more than digitally stored information could be described in terms of space and embodiment is not so surprising given the trajectory of Western thought: since Plato, existence has been identified with objects, objects with discrete units, and units with data. Each of these terms allows for the introduction of the next, reinforces and validates its antecedents and becomes a criterion for both being and knowledge. The relationship formed between these terms has been profoundly articulated by Heidegger, whose critique of modern technology is perhaps most relevant in this age of the global digital. Drawing on pre-Socratic philosophy, Heidegger writes of the "monstrous transformation" that occurs in modern philosophy whereby existence, being, is thought of in terms of "beings," and as a result of this reduction beings are experienced as objects.[9] With being so easily located and objectified, a phenomenon can be reduced to its abstract properties, such as its quantities, volumes, location, and these can be represented as fixed, unchanging, and ever subject to the indubitable laws of physics and mathematics. This kind of "representational" thinking, as Heidegger calls it, leads to a process of "enframing"—the reduction of matter to quantifiable, measurable and predictable terms. Matter is thought of as a "standing reserve," a set of measurable resources ready and waiting for exploitation. The human species becomes the "orderer of the standing reserve"—the measure of all things and as a result "encounters existence as his [sic] construct."[10]

The parallels between digital technologies and Heidegger's concept of "enframing" are all too obvious—indeed technologies like VR can be seen as the logical outcome of a process that began with the Cartesian grid and has continued to be ever further refined, abstracted, and imposed upon the perception of the world.[11] Just as the Renaissance map or diagram reduced the three-dimensional world to a two-dimensional representation, displaying it as given, "there" to be explored, colonized, and eventually carved up into real estate, VR reduces this two-dimensional set of co-ordinates to a numerical series composed of just two binaries. Ironically, it is only through such an intense reduction that the infinite horizons of the "virtual real estate" now covering the Internet, or the virtual frontier now replacing the dream of (outer)space exploration, can be produced.

FROM SEEING TO BEING

Of course, habitation is the issue here. While it is generally accepted that one cannot live in a map, the virtual "environment" (which is in reality no more than a scene) is always described as if there is some inhabitable territory "behind" it. The two-dimensional screen is not seen as an abstraction of some real territory, rather the screen "fronts" a piece of machinery (the computer) that is most often imagined as another world subtended by a landscape of circuitry that the user zooms over. That the screen is able to evoke such strong connections to territories and spaces is a testament to the power of film and television. However, beyond the screen there is the long history of Western ocularcentrism, a history that coincides with the conflation of being with objects. This coincidence rests on the belief that, of all the attributes of objects, visibility and extension are primary, thus vision and the occupation of space are deeply implicated in the constitution of existence. Associating seeing with Being has significantly shaped the development of Western thinking: it has made sight the dominant sense; it has furnished an epistemology with a range of prohibitions against knowledge derived from the other senses; it has been fundamental to the construction of a subjectivity where the eye and the subject coincide—where vision, abstracted, becomes the ground for all objectivity, certainty, and inspiration. With the eye an extension of the mind, and the mind divorced from the body, the actuality of sight has been transformed into an ideology:[12] the individual becomes the center of its world, always looking outward with its gaze—god-like—scanning, naming, and colonizing the universe.

With modernism, vision extends its grasp, appropriating the future as a territory unique to the very concept of modernity. "Looking ahead" literally and metaphorically, is encouraged, "looking back" prohibited. And in a very Western move, the future has been placed "in front" of the individual, whereas everything else—including the "meat" existing from the head down—is cast "behind us."[13] Indeed, the more that looking ahead is equated with progress, enlightenment, and a technologically aided evolution, the more a focus on the past is considered regressive, "backward," going against not only the telos of Western civilization but the species itself. In the technology of VR, frontality and futurity coalesce in a simulation of frontality's other—phenomenal immersion—by literally closing the gap between the eye and the screen. This is accomplished not by "moving into" the screen as the rhetoric of immersion suggests, but rather by bringing the stereoscopic screens so close that the eyes are enclosed in a total vision of images. At the same time, the interactive component of VR allows the virtual scene to change as the head moves, while the standard navigational device—the data glove—allows the user to point to the direction they want to go, which then changes the scene to simulate their movement toward that place. Moving forward thus becomes an expression of progress and an amplification of the dominance of vision.[14] At the same time, subjectivity is collapsed into a single point of view: the virtual world is nothing other than what is, literally, in front of the user; space is defined not only as what is to be seen, but what is to be navigated and in a sense constructed by the viewer.[15] This kind of interactivity and virtual landscape navigation is rapidly moving onto the Net, giving cyberspace the appearance and feel of being not just a place to inhabit, but a place to navigate, to move forward through, and in the process, to command and control.

ARCHITECTURAL METAPHORS: LAWS FOR OBJECTS AND LAWS FOR HUMANS

From "space" we move to built space and the discourse of architecture. Architecture implies space and habitation, and as a metaphor, removes cyberspace and computing from its most obvious and unwanted corollary—television and the information networks of telecommunications. Having fully accepted and internalized the legitimacy of "space" as an attribute of virtuality, designers, artists, philosophers, and architects have been debating what these virtual spaces might be, how they might be constructed, and (tellingly) what kind of laws they might obey. An early writer on the architecture of cyber-space, Michael Benedikt, speculates that cyberspace "will require constant planning and organization," that it will need "structures" that will have to be "designed" by "cyber architects" who are "schooled in computer science and programming (the equivalent of construction), in graphics, and in abstract design."[16] Benedikt begins his discourse on the principles of cyberspace by arguing that the logics, physics, and metaphysics that apply to discussions of real space also apply to virtual space: "A central preoccupation of this essay will be the sorting out of which axioms and laws of nature ought to be retained in cyberspace, on the grounds that humans have successfully evolved on a planet where these are fixed and conditioning of all phenomena."[17]

For certain physical laws to be violated, for certain axioms to apply, there needs to be not just a symbolic equivalence between the physical and the virtual, but an ontological equivalence. Thus, "digital-space" is made commensurate with "real-space," and not only physical axioms, but also meta-physical axioms are sustained, ensuring that the same epistemological system governing Western thought will continue to operate. For instance, there is the "Principle of Exclusion"—roughly equating to the law of identity—whereby two identical objects cannot share the same space at the same time.[18] The "Principle of Maximal Exclusion" ensures that a space will be designed that minimizes the violations of the Principle of Exclusion—that is, a space will be designed where objects have a place, a time, a trajectory of movement, etc.

After renaming such age old maxims that define ostensible real-ity, Benedikt is pleased and surprised to find that his principles in fact operate in reality—further evidence of the naturalness of cyberspace, of its pseudo-physicality. But Benedikt's principles pertain not only to logic or physics: in shaping the realism of virtual worlds he coins the "Principle of Indifference," based on the maxim that "the felt realness of any world depends on the degree of its indifference to the presence of a particular 'user' and on its resistance to his/her desire."[19] In the same way that narrative in realist cinema unfolds with-out the consent of the viewer—producing a voyeur—cyberspace must produce a voyager—a subject who moves into a space that is already there, pre-existent, with its own restrictions, its own "reality." Allied to the "Principle of Indifference" is the "Principle of Transit," whereby "travel between two points in cyberspace should occur phenomenally through all intervening points, no matter how fast,…and should incur costs to the traveler proportional to some measure of the distance."[20] This kind of detail seems to contradict the rhetoric of infinite freedom and transcendence to the immaterial that has been associated with cyberspace. Why must distance and travel literally drag in cyberspace? Could it be that limits, principles, restrictions, and laws create a sense of comfortable confinement? Or does the continuous presence of obstacles produce the kind of obsessive drive exhibited by game playing or religious devotees? Whatever the quest, this pseudo mystical space promises a plenitude that can only be reached through a continuous investment in technology (the hardware and software through which cyberspace is accessed) and an unrelenting devotion to its development or "evolution"—that is, to the future within which this plenitude will be revealed.[21]

Metaphors of cities and organisms, of electronic spheres that blanket the earth like ozone, of spiritual influences that are pulling humans toward a higher, technologically refined plane, all fit within the trope of an independent world. Cyberspace is represented as an entity that is more than the sum of its parts. Its chips, circuits, and cables do not match its higher evolutionary and phenomenological level, the level of human thought and art. For Benedikt cyberspace is more than a space, it is "a place and a mode of being."[22] As such, cyberspace prompts humans to "be" differently. Often couched in evolutionary terms, the inhabitants of cyberspace are described as developing nonphysical qualities, qualities that pertain to their non-embodiment, and that suit the demands of virtual architecture and virtual physics. Yet for Benedikt, virtual humans, like virtual spaces, must also be subject to laws. For instance, the "Principle of Personal Visibility" ensures that users can be seen by other users, although an individual user may choose not to see others. Not only must one be seen, but users must all see the same thing. This is the "Principle of Commonality" which recommends that "virtual places be "objective" in a circumscribed way for a defined community of users."[23] Even in this immaterial space, one must satisfy the main guarantor of existence—visibility—and one must be "accountable" to "objective" reality. With its laws for virtual objects and virtual subjects, cyberspace becomes a mirror of the real—the physical, social, economic and ideological world that we currently inhabit.

If realism has long since ceased to monopolize electronic media, why, in this twenty-first-century "geography of the imagination," has it returned with such insistence? As an image-based and interactive digital simulation of an environment—virtual reality—or even as a text based MUD (multi-user domain) or MOO (MUD object oriented), cyberspace ceases to have the same relationship of necessity to the physicality it represents.[24] Yet time and again virtual environments are filled with structures that resemble those found in the physical world, and while there may be exceptions to this in more artistic projects, one still finds the simulation of physicality—of texture mapping and surface rendering—a high priority in virtual design. Certainly, the predictable forms of virtual environments—with navigational interfaces, MUDs and MOOs are generally premised on a basic structure of four walls with an entry—reflect an intolerance for differently configured spaces. Does the surprisingly banal physicality and the incessant imposition of Renaissance perspective of most virtual environments simply reflect an ingrained conservatism, a lack of imagination on the part of these cyberpioneers? Or could it have something to do with the appropriation of the concept of "architecture" itself, the desire to consolidate the "being-in" and "being-there": the "reality" of the virtual that immediately comes to mind when architectural structures are represented. In this regard, the discourse of architecture is a good accomplice, in that, like the rhetoric of virtuality, it denies the gap between representation and reality, insinuating a "presence" and naturalness where in fact only mediation exists. As the architect Peter Eisenman points out, the "natural" in architecture is in fact a product of convention; however, this convention is extremely difficult to articulate because of the way that sign and referent, meaning and object collapse. A wall, for instance, both realizes and symbolizes its function as an object that holds things up: "...in architecture there will always be the presence of walls, walls that are both icon and instrument."[25] If there need not

be walls in cyberspace, then wherein lies the "naturalness," the indexical relationship between thing and representation that cyberadvocates insist distinguishes this form of media from any other? For the discourse of architecture,
like that of metaphysics, to act as a ground for the virtual, for cyberspace to justify its appropriation of "space," "immersion," and "reality," the gap between
icon and instrument, representation, and reality must be concealed at all
costs.[26] Ironically, the attempt to deny processes of representation, to capture
the thing-in-itself, involves an appeal to neo-Platonic notions of ideal
essences; the abstract, necessary, and unchanging forms that, as Andrew Benjamin points out, endure "within an ontology and temporality of stasis"[27]—a
far cry from the infinite speed and motion that the idea of cyberspaces con-
jures. Using the term architecture, and invoking the structure it implies, can
therefore be seen as part of a larger strategy for legitimating "cyberspace" as a
scientific domain: supported by the laws and structures of architecture, cyberspace becomes an object of knowledge tied to metaphysics—and in this sense
also a fiction, a "consensual hallucination."

VIRTUAL EMBODIMENT: FROM "YOU ARE IN" TO "YOU ARE"

If stasis is inherent in the concept of architecture, in a further
irony, it is exactly stasis that is produced in the physical correlate of the virtual
sphere. Despite all the fanciful flights through walls and over cyberscapes that
are part of the reportage of VR, the physical environment is characterized by
an unhealthy lack of movement and change, and the repetition of this ideal
"doctrine of being" is often manifest in repetitive strain injury incurred by the
user. Despite the relative stillness of the body in both VR and at the computer
terminal, its physical movements are nonetheless important to register interactivity, and therefore, "immersion." Thus the participation of the user's body,
whether it be through body movements in VR or via pointing and clicking a
mouse, often warrants a recognition of that corporeality in the design of cyberspace, such as a virtual hand, to show that the user really is "physically" entering the space. Via such limited movement the user's actual embodiment
becomes another component of the mechanism for simulating immersion-in-

a-space, with the user's own body providing the here-and-now being, while the simulated environment stands in as the "there." Doubting either term in this equation is tantamount to doubting one's existence—an activity not encouraged in the hyperindividuated, omnipotent "go get 'em" fare of most virtual scenarios.[28] But like architecture, the body that is implicated in this mechanism is a body in scare quotes, a rhetorical body that becomes part of a propaganda strategy, one that is based on appeals to ontology rather than epistemology, to authentic being rather than mediated seeing.[29] In line with the real stasis of virtual space and the usual logic of technology in the twentieth century, living in virtual worlds creates the kind of corporality (static, sedentary, "wired") that eventually requires the various implants and prostheses characteristic of the cyborg, and the techno-infrastructure identified with the hyperconnected individual.

Virtual humans don't just enter cyberspace, they become cyberspace. Just as virtuality and cyberspace rhetorically expand ever outwards, encompassing an infinity of spaces, times, mythologies, and modes of transcendence, they also close in on the individual, appropriating innerspace, encouraging an inwardness, and locating the plenitude within not just the psyche but the very nervous system of the individual. Within the rhetoric, the individual and the technology mirror each other as organicist seeds, within which all knowledge is embedded, and from which all knowledge proceeds. The revelation of this process assumes a teleological purpose and its process is infinite. Yet the image of unity and wholeness that inwardness presents is far from the actuality of the embodied cybernaut. In the phenomenology of virtual life the infinite freedom of cyberspace physically translates into a static cocoon from which an electronic/informational network, (a world wide web) emanates and at the same time traps the individual, operating at every level of his or her existence, following strict lines—not of flight—but of reinforced thought. Time now to revisit that postmodern subject, whose corporality and environment has been literally infiltrated by cyberspace, whose decentered self has been repositioned as the locus of techno-institutional forces, pushing and pulling to achieve maximal efficiencies. Like data this subject is infinitely disarticulated: a site of organs ready for transplant, a map of genes waiting to fulfill their benign or malign *raison d'etre*, a conglomerate of personas on the Net. There is no limit to its capacity for inwardness or narcissism, nor for its projection (via technology) as the amplified individual. Nor is there any limit to the consumer oriented operations that can be performed on any of its parts—even those parts (like genes) whose malfunction is no more than a probability.

    As the individual is multiplied the necessity of its containment— or rather, of the containment of its various parts—becomes more compelling. The home, the environment, must mirror this amplification and multiplicity— fitting the individual like a virtual glove. The arms length distance (literal and metaphorical) between user and computer screen begins to shorten: the computer now sits on our laps, or is attached to our belts; it becomes a pair of goggles, then glasses, and finally (according to the predictions of nano-technology), implants. While this evolution may seem to free the user from the constraints of the stationary workstation (with all of its ergonomic problems), physical space is itself transformed to mirror the resource that the individual has become: computers become "ubiquitous," creating an electronic atmosphere wherein every transaction is detailed, every physical move tracked and recorded, all nodes of exchange between the individual and the world become plug-in points. The ecstasy of cyber-flight is overwhelmed by the sheer grind of time consuming and often inconsequential bits of information that rapidly degenerate into a frantic buzz hovering around the individual like a dust cloud. Always "logged on," the once private space of Internet communication becomes a space of surveillance, and the individual—splitting itself once again—internalizes a series of procedures that conceal its intentions, either as a form of self-censorship, or, more pathologically, as a form of repression. Bound ever tighter, the individual escapes through processes of infantile absorption with the new, consuming the present with the desire to be "one step ahead," hoping that familiarity with the next piece of software will provide them with a temporary defense against redundancy and engaging in technoself-gratification to ward off the acknowledgment that this is how it is.[30]

CONCLUSION: VIRTUAL FUTURES

The organizing metaphors that make virtual environments places to be are about the future, about transcendence to a technosublime, about disembodiment, about the fiction of pure mind, omnipotence, omnipresence. As "spaces" these are concerned with being elsewhere and being other in an evolutionary, species-directed reconfiguration. In the same powerful conflation of real space and simulation, of real life and virtuality, the cybernaut inhabits tropologies that give him or her a birds-eye view of the planet, the species, and the present: users are not in the present (they are supposedly "entering the future"); they are not of the human (they are cyborgs); they are not on the earth (they have become enveloped by pure data); they are not in their bodies (they have approached pure mind). In league with the new millennium, the spaces of virtuality are apocalyptic, presupposing the end of organic life. This nihilism is reflected in the ultraclean rooms and razor-sharp shiny surfaces of the standard virtual aesthetic, where messy organic human forms enter only as contaminants. Returning to the futurism from which the neofuturism of cyberarchitecture has developed, it is well to remember Sant'Elia's proclamation:

> We have lost our taste for the monumental, the heavy, the static, and we have enriched our sensibility with a taste for the light, the practical, the ephemeral and the swift....We—who are materially and spiritually artificial—must find...inspiration in the elements of the utterly new mechanical world we have created, and of which architecture must be the most beautiful expression.[31]

It is not just the coincidence of metaphors (light, ephemerality, fluidity, constantly changing speed) that situates architects like Sant'Elia adjacent to contemporary musings. The futurists engaged in a discourse of the organicless future, and it is within that fictive space that cyberspace is located. Florian Röetzer has remarked that the only spaces for difference in the computer worlds of VR and digital communications are war and catastrophe.[32]

Perhaps this was the kind of war that F. T. Marinetti saw as the world's only form of hygiene, leading him to support fascism while his architect friends dreamt of dynamism, speed, and simultaneity, of a "kingdom of electricity," with its fluid cities in a state of perpetual becoming and renewal. Such visions led early-twentieth-century architects to embrace the ideologies of industrial capitalism, urban planning, and eventually, socially conscious architecture. In the process they created the "machines for living" that reduced humans to the cogs that we are now calling "bits" in dataspace.[33]

In stark contrast to the lightness of cyberspace, the virtual future is laden with the dark nihilism that the visionary dreams of new, futurist cities produced. Contemporary cyberspace—with its emphasis on the future—re-enacts the nihilistic logic of early futurism in so far as the fulfillment of its dreams are necessarily deferred to a time that one can never witness. Since one cannot "be" in the future, one cannot comfortably "be" in the fiction that is cyberspace. Attempting to do so is like attempting to inhabit any dream or vision; it provides an opening for the return of the repressed—the debt that culture has not paid to its visions of the 1920s, realized in the "future" that the 1990s have patently not delivered. And if the present is already lacking, the future is represented as already spent—mortgaged through national deficits and environmental destruction. Cyberspace is thus already a nihilistic, debt ridden, impossible space—a space that, in denying the "reality" of the physical, tacitly acknowledges its hostility to "being" and its incommensurability with corporality. The inescapability of cyberspace's repressed nature also suggests that the reliance on Renaissance perspective is not just evidence of a lack of imagination. Its function is to offer users a sign of their own mortality, of their own inevitable biology, of their need for walls within a context where the verisimilitude of the simulation is plainly not the issue, where walls are plainly no longer necessary. With its cartoon-like simplicity, its child-like forms of graphic representation, the virtual environment is simply another icon, a piece of signage, for the brutally alluring "there" that the dream of the future™ is, and in which, by definition, one cannot be.

1. Martin Heidegger, *The Question Concerning Technology*, trans. William Lovitt (New York: Harper Torchbooks, 1977), 4.

2. On confusion, see Marcos Novak, "Liquid Architecture," in *Cyberspace: First Steps*, ed. Michael Benedikt (Cambridge, MA: MIT Press, 1992), 224.

3. As opposed to Michael Heim's suggestion that the ontology of cyberspace is "the question of what it means to be in a virtual world." Ontology, in this context, is already operating at a meta-level. See Michael Heim, *The Metaphysics of Virtual Reality* (New York: Oxford University Press, 1993), 84.

4. Marc Augé characterizes this redefinition of space as a characteristic of "supermodernity." See Marc Augé, *Non-Places—Introduction to an Anthropology of Supermodernity*, trans. John Howe (New York: Verso, 1995), 32.

5. As Langdon Winner writes: "Subjected to the pace of productivism, we come to think that if a message can move, it must move quickly. This places strong demands on individuals, communications technologies not only make it possible to reach them but obligates them to remain accessible." Langdon Winner, "Three Paradoxes of the Information Age," in *Culture on the Brink*, ed. Gretchen Bender and Timothy Druckery (Seattle: Bay Press, 1994), 194.

6. See Allucquere Rosanne Stone, *The War of Desire and Technology at the Close of the Mechanical Age* (Cambridge, MA: MIT Press, 1995).

7. Katherine Hayles, "The Materiality of Informatics," *Configurations*, (1992): 147.

8. Asking "Is it necessary to insist that the body, far from disappearing, remains essential to human life?" Hayles sees the disappearance of the body as evidence of a certain kind of postmodern subjectivity, one that has a predilection for technologies of immateriality, such as VR and cyberspace. "The predilection catalyzes the technology, and the technology reifies and extends the predilection. Discursively, the technology interacts with metaphoric networks of in/out and container/contained, making the distinction indicated by the slash less a boundary than a permeable membrane across which subjectivity is diffused." Ibid., 168.

9. See Martin Heidegger, *Early Greek Thinking*, trans. David Farrell Krell and Frank A. Capuzzi (New York: Harper & Row, 1975), 82. Heidegger shows the dependence of the concept of being as thought in metaphysics on notions of substance, extension, duration—in short, presence. See also Heidegger, *Being and Time* (New York: Harper & Row, 1962), 18–9.

10. Heidegger, *The Question Concerning Technology*, 27.

11. As some commentators and artists have noted, VR is the instantiation of Heidegger's concept of enframing. See, for instance, my article on Char Davies' OSMOSE and Catherine Richard's *Curiosity Cabinet at the End of the Millennium*: "Charged Havens," *World Art*, no. 3 (1993).

12. Etymologically, "idea" is associated with the verb "to see," and the notion of "eidetic" knowledge.

13. This tendency is by no means universal. In Maori culture, for instance, the past is placed ahead of the culture as a reference point, and each decade is seen as an additional chapter that adds to the pre-given history of the ancestors.

14. For more on these issues see Frances Dyson, "Philosophonics of Space: Sound, Futurity and the End of the World," catalog, Fifth International Symposium on Electronic Art, University of Art and Design, Helsinki, UIAH, 1994; and "In/Quest of Presence: Virtuality, Aurality and Television's Gulf War," *Critical Issues in Electronic Media*, ed. Simon Penny (Albany, NY: State University of New York Press, 1995).

15. See Katherine Hayles, "Virtual Bodies and Flickering Signifiers," *October* 66 (Fall 1993): 83–4. It is

a testament to Western visualism that sound, though part of the virtual environment, does not confer rite of passage to a different space. Certainly surround-sound, which has been in use for many years, is not hailed as an immersive technology, nor has it warranted the creation of a new "reality" to describe its phenomenological space.

16. "Schooled also along with their brethren 'real-space' architects, cyberspace architects will design electronic edifices that are fully as complex, functional, unique, involving and beautiful as their physical counterparts if not more so." Benedikt, *Cyberspace: First Steps*, 18.

17. Cyberspace is defined by Benedikt as "a globally networked, computer-sustained, computer accessed and computer-generated, multidimensional, artificial, or 'virtual' reality." Ibid., 122, 119.

18. Ibid., 136.

19. Ibid., 160.

20. Ibid., 168.

21. The very artificiality of virtual reality, its ability to violate principles of space and time, is given as evidence of a magical element harking back to the ancient world. See Ibid., 128.

22. Ibid., 131. The mode of being is information, such that "the amount of (phenomenal) space in cyberspace is a function of the amount of information in cyberspace." (167).

23. Ibid., 180. Within this reality certain spaces (domains) are "private" (other users cannot see in) or "public" (visible to all). Presumably private spaces, like private property, would incur some expense whilst at the same time bestowing privilege.

24. See Peter Eisenman, "Presentness and the 'Being-Only-Once' of Architecture," in *Reconstruction is/in America*, ed. Anselm Haverkamp (New York: New York University Press, 1995), 139; and Eisenman, "Architecture in a Mediated Environment," in *Urban Forms, Suburban Dreams*, ed. Malcolm Quantrill and Bruce Webb (College Station, TX: Texas A&M University Press, 1993). With respect to the developing relation between information technology and cyberspace, Sylvia Lavin asks why cyberspace is construed in spatial terms and more importantly "why of the many possible desires that can be projected into cyberspace, is the wish to find a place therein increasingly dominant?" Sylvia Lavin, "Architecture/Information," *Anyplace* 4, ed. Cynthia C. Davidson (Cambridge, MA: MIT Press, 1995), 146.

25. Eisenman, "Presentness," 135.

26. "...it is impossible to deny architecture's metaphysics of presence. Even in a condition of virtual reality, architecture is conventionalized as the metaphysics of presence; within virtual reality, architecture is still imagined as a physical body." Ibid, 139. However, this dominance of presence in the field of virtuality is not the result of its genesis from architecture. Rather the discourse of architecture, as opposed to that of telecommunications, has been deliberately appropriated because of the "presence" it implies.

27. "The question of the essence [of philosophy or architecture] therefore comes to be re-posed within that spectivic ontological-temporal concatenation proper to stasis. The unstated premise at work here is that the name 'philosophy'—though this will be equally true of the name 'architecture'—names that essence." Andrew Benjamin, *Art, Mimesis and the Avant-Garde* (New York: Routledge, 1991), 115.

28. For an extensive analysis of the "hyperindividualism" of virtual culture see Sean Cubitt "Supernatural Futures: Theses on Digital Aesthetics," in *FutureNatural*, ed. George Robertson et al. (New York: Routledge, 1996).

29. And even while this naturalness is subject to critique outside of cyberdiscourse—for instance, the critique of presence found in deconstruction and phenomenology—the moment at which it filters into cyber-discourse is the moment where this very critique is itself appropriated. This dematerialized world is constituted by a set of "spaces" that have also been reduced to "texts" that are then "read" differently, as Micha Bandini suggests, "in order to create debates that focus on appearances rather than on the role of architecture in contemporary society." Micha Bandini, quoted in *Mapping the Futures*, ed. John Bird et al. (New York: Routledge, 1993), 237.

30. Manuel Castles and Peter Hall, *Technopoles of the World* (London: Routledge, 1994), 23. For more on the infantilism of virtual culture see Sean Cubitt: "'It's Life Jim, But Not as We Know It': Rolling Backwards into the Future," in *Fractal Dreams: New Media in Social Context*, ed. Jon Dovey (London: Lawrence and Wishart, 1996).

31. Antonio Sant'Elia, "Manifesto of Futurist Architecture" (1914), in Umbro Apollonio ed., *The Documents of Twentieth Century Art: Futurist Manifestos*, trans. Robert Brian et al. (New York: The Viking Press, 1973), 172.

33. Florian Röetzer, "Fascinations, Reactions, Virtual Worlds and Other Matter," *Book for the Unstable Media* (s-Hertogenbosch, Netherlands: Stichting V2-Organisation, 1992), 86.

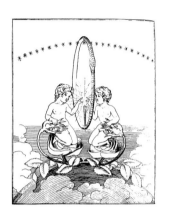

The Medieval Return of Cyberspace

MARGARET WERTHEIM

THROUGH THE MEDIUM of the computer a loophole has been found in the materialist metaphysics that has dominated Western culture for the past three centuries. All around us cyberspace explodes into being with the exponential force of its own big bang, in the process ripping to shreds the pious hope that reality could be reduced to the motion of matter through space and time. For better or worse, this new digital domain represents a profound challenge to major philosophical and psychological trends that so deeply characterize the "age of science."

Precisely because cyberspace is not made up of atoms or particles, but is ontologically rooted in the ephemera of bits and bytes, it is not subject to the laws of physics and is not bound by the limitations of those laws. In a quite literal sense, cyberspace is outside the physical complex of matter-space-time that since the late seventeenth century has increasingly been held as not just the basis of reality, but as the totality of the real. Who could have foreseen that the electronic gates of the silicon chip would become a metaphysical gateway, punching a porthole in the bedrock of materialism? The digital doors labeled ".com," ".net," and ".edu" represent more than just a new means of communication, they are urgently needed escape hatches from an epistemic tyranny that has foisted upon us the feeble fabulation that we are nothing but material bodies. In the potentially infinite web of the Internet, the "soul" has once again found a space that it might call its own.

"I have experienced soul-data through silicon," declared Kevin Kelly, executive editor of *Wired*, in a 1995 forum in *Harper's Magazine*. "You might be surprised at the amount of soul-data we'll have in this new space."[1] Kelly is by no means alone in suggesting that cyberspace will be a realm for the soul. "Our fascination with computers is more erotic than sensual, more deeply spiritual than utilitarian," writes cyber-philosopher Michael Heim. "In our love affair" with these machines, he says, "we are searching for a home for the mind and heart."[2] It is just the mind, the heart, the soul—in short the human psyche—that has been banished from the picture of reality that Western physics has articulated over the past three hundred years. Rooted in the Cartesian divide between the *res extensa* and the *res cogitans*, reality has increasingly been construed as the physical world alone, with the spiritual and psychic domain increasingly seen as a secondary and semireal byproduct of the true reality that is matter in motion.

Now, in one epistemic flourish, cyberspace explodes this materialist fantasy and builds for the psyche a technological theater of its own. A space where the "self" can experiment and play, cyberspace is an immaterial domain where psyche, if not entirely divorced from body, is nonetheless decoupled from the rigid regulations of the laws of physics. Clearly, this inner space is a different facet of the real to the exterior space described by physicists' laws, but with fifty million people already accessing it on a regular basis, cyberspace is an indisputable part of late-twentieth-century reality, at least in the developed world. Ironically, physics itself has built this arena. The silicon chips, the optic fibers, the cathode ray tubes, and liquid crystal display screens, even the electric power, are all byproducts of this most mathematical of sciences. In the very success of physics thus lies the seeds of a metaphysical revolution.

And let there be no mistake, there is a revolution in process—for anything that promotes the reality of psyche is indeed a challenge to contemporary scientific epistemology. It is a complete misnomer to call the modern scientific world picture dualistic; it is monistic, admitting the reality only of the physical. In the classic dichotomy of body and soul, modern science has excised the latter entirely from its vision of the real and reduced existence to the motion of material particles through space and time, all components now being defined in rigorous mathematical terms. With this stark mathematico-materialism (or more strictly mathematico-physicalism, since even particles ultimately become just ripples in the fabric of spacetime), soul is no longer another level of reality, as the medievals believed, but a chimera of the imagination—Gilbert Ryle's "ghost in the machine."[3] Metaphysically speaking, spirit-psyche-soul has not merely been pushed out of the scientific cosmos, in the minds of many contemporary scientists it has been totally annihilated.[4] Descartes and Newton—both deeply religious men—would have been appalled at this theological anesthetizing of the world system, but a rampant materialist monism is the end result of the philosophy they bequeathed.

Nothing epitomizes this monism more than the current mania for "explaining" each and every aspect of psyche, including its spiritual manifestations, by recourse to physicalist theories of neurochemical transmitters and/or genetic determinism. Nothing escapes the net of this physicalist dogma, wherein the religious visions of mystics are reduced to migraines and epileptic fits; altruism becomes the mathematically inevitable outcome of the machinations of "selfish genes"; and love becomes a disturbance in our neurochemical soup.

As history reveals, one of the chief inspirations for this hubristic monism was Rene Descartes, though God forbid, that was never his intent. "I think therefore I am," Descartes declared, rooting being not in body, but in the immateriality of mind.[5] Indeed, he called his famous aphorism "the first principle" of his philosophy. Yet whatever Descartes' personal beliefs—and we must never forget that the French philosopher was a devout Catholic who wanted nothing less than a science that would support his faith—his dualistic metaphysics ultimately served as a stepping stone to precisely the kind of materialism he abhorred.

Searching for a rigorous grounding for his mechanistic conception of nature, Descartes divided reality into two distinct halves: the *res extensa*—the extended realm of matter in motion—and the *res cogitans*—the realm of thoughts, feelings, and emotions. Body and mind-psyche-soul were separated by his metaphysics into two utterly disconnected domains, but for Descartes both were indisputably true parts of the real. However, it was only the *res extensa* that he saw as amenable to mathematical treatment and that was to be described by the new physics. The major purpose of Descartes' radical dualism was in fact to delineate precisely what it was that mathematically-based science could describe. In an age suffused with hermetic magic and all manner of arcane number mysticisms, expounded by such occult practitioners as Giordano Bruno and Robert Fludd, Descartes and his fellow mechanists were determined to define both their science and their world picture in strictly nonmagical terms. Above all, they wanted a physical world devoid of occult forces. Such a world, Descartes believed, must consist only of inert matter moving mechanically according to strict mathematical laws. It is this world—the extended realm, or *res extensa*—that would be the subject of the new science. All the rest, the whole messy but indubitably real complex of thoughts, feelings, and emotions would be left to moralists and theologians.

Yet if Descartes himself held a genuinely dualistic worldview and insisted on the reality of the *res cogitans*, it wasn't long before champions of the new science began to hack away at this domain. The trend was set by the English philosopher Thomas Hobbes, who even in Descartes' lifetime declared that phenomena of mind were merely secondary byproducts of the primary reality that is matter in motion. For Hobbes, reality was not dualistic: it consisted only of the *res extensa*. "Mind will be nothing but the motions of certain parts of an organic body," he wrote, in what soon became a call to arms to the growing legions of materialists.[6] By the mid-eighteenth century, the French philosopher Julien de la Mettrie could openly declare in "The Man-Machine" that "the soul is, then, an empty symbol." Like Hobbes, La Mettrie believed mind was just a byproduct of atomic motion: "Given the least principle of movement, animate bodies will possess all they need in order to move, sense, think."[7] By the end of the eighteenth century, materialistic monism was in full swing. Growing steadily ever since, by the end of the twentieth it has almost become a heresy in scientific circles to express any other view.

To what we can only imagine would be Descartes' horror, the machine has been stripped entirely of its ghosts. Sucked dry of spirit, body now stands "pure" and alone, a strictly molecular mechanism, boot-strapping itself into existence through the "emergent" properties of an autocatalytic chemical set. I catalyze therefore I am. Philosopher of science Edwin Burtt has summed up this situation aptly. In his "Metaphysical Foundations of Modern Science" Burtt writes that with the triumph of mechanism,

> The natural world was portrayed as a vast self-contained mathemat-ical machine, consisting of motions of matter in space and time, and man with his purposes, feelings and secondary qualities was shoved apart as an unimportant spectator and semi-real effect of the great mathematical drama outside.[8]

For the first time in history, humanity has produced a purely physicalist world picture, one in which mind-psyche-soul has no place at all.

It was not always so. Where modern scientific cosmology articu-lates only the domain of body, the medieval cosmology that preceded it articu-lated domains of body and soul—both participating in a grand metaphysical hierarchy in which everything was connected to God. This older world picture was truly dualistic, with the physical and spiritual orders mirroring one another; the physical universe serving as a metaphor for the underlying uni-verse of spirit. In a complete inversion of the materialist worldview, the medievals regarded the spiritual cosmos, the "space" of soul, as the true or primary reality, with the physical cosmos, the space of body, serving as the allegory of this ultimate domain. Within this philosophical framework, according to medievalist Jeffrey Burton Russell, "physics [and indeed all natural science] is an inferior truth pointing to the greater truth, which is theological, moral, and even divine." The primary concern of medieval philosophy (and also of medieval art) was the ultimate reality of the moral and spiritual cosmos, which was "God's utterance or song." [9]

Medieval cosmology literally located both body and soul; there was a place in the world for each. Physically, humanity stood at the center of a nested set of concentric spheres collectively carrying the celestial bodies: the sun, moon, planets, and stars. Spiritually, we also stood at the center, poised midway between the angels and animals, for in the medieval system man was the only creature possessing both a material body (a property we share with animals) and an intellective soul (that we share with the angelic orders: the angels, archangels, cherubim, seraphim, and so on.) With one foot each in the material and the spiritual domains, we were, so to speak, the linchpin of the whole system. When medievals spoke of mankind being at the center of the world, they referred not so much to our astronomical position as to our place at the center of the spiritual hierarchy.

There was another sense in which mankind was central, for we were poised between the two spiritual poles of heaven and hell. Born with free will, each person through his own actions held the fate of his soul in his hands. Depending on one's choices in life, after death the soul could go either way: to the eternal bliss of the heavenly Empyrean, or to everlasting torment in the bowels of hell. Life in the body was simply a first stage in the much longer journey of the soul, and the primary purpose of the medieval world picture was to articulate the landscape of this spiritual journey. It is this terrain that is described so beautifully in Dante's *Divine Comedy*, the ultimate map of soul-space.

For Dante and his contemporaries in the early fourteenth century, the idea of a world picture that encompassed only the body would have been unthinkable. Yet four centuries later La Mettrie, Denis Diderot, and other Enlightenment *philosophes* were rejecting the very idea of a soul. No longer poised between heaven and hell, for them the earth had become a chunk of rock revolving without purpose in a Euclidian void. No longer the linchpins of a great spiritual hierarchy, humans had become atomic machines. The older and genuinely dualistic cosmology had been stripped down to just one half of the body-soul dimorphism; soul had literally been painted out of the picture.

It is against this historical background that we must consider the advent and appeal of cyberspace. I suggest that human sanity requires a cosmology of psyche as well as soma. Just as we need to know where our bodies are, so we need to know where our "souls" are—at the very least, we need to know about the modern secular equivalent, Freud's desanctified soul, the "self." Indeed, I would go so far as to say that the need for a cosmology of psyche or self is the more primary human drive. It's all very well to know where one stands in physical space, but can that purely geometrical triangulation really satisfy the question, Where am I? No matter what we are doing, there is an indelible sense of an "I" behind the action, a "self" that demands and needs a cosmological home no less than the material atoms of our bodies.

I want to make clear that I am not arguing here for metaphysical dualism. It is not my intention to claim that the psyche-soul is a separate entity distinct from body, one that lives on after death, for example. I simply wish to insist that while we are alive the "I" of our experience is a genuine part of reality and any world picture that encompasses only the body must necessarily be incomplete. It is one of the great pathologies of the modern West that we have such an incomplete picture, and no matter how often materialists like Daniel Dennett and Gilbert Ryle bludgeon us with the idea that we are nothing but atoms and genes, it is patently obvious that we are not! "I think therefore I am," Descartes declared, and whether we modify "think," to "feel," or "suffer" (many versions have been tried), what remains is the indissoluble "I"—and deal with it we must.

The utter failure of modern science to incorporate psyche into its world picture is one of the primary reason so many people are excited about cyberspace. Sensing that something of central importance has been occluded from the scientists' picture, people are looking elsewhere in the hope of locating this crucial missing element. Precisely because it is (in some sense) beyond the body, cyberspace beckons as a potential home for the psyche—and even, as Kelly suggests, as a haven for the soul. It is just this excluded but irrefutable "I" that cyberspace seems to provide a home for.

In a very powerful way, then, cyberspace subverts three hundred years of Western epistemic history, repudiating the tyranny of materialism and once again suggesting the possibility of a genuinely dualistic vision of reality. The body may be sitting in the chair, fingers tapping at the keyboard, but unleashed into the quasi-infinite ocean of the Internet, the location of the self can no longer be fixed purely in physical space. Just where the self is in cyberspace is a question yet to be answered, but clearly it cannot be pinned down to a mathematical location in Euclidian, or even relativistic space. Through the portal of the modem we tunnel through spacetime (more profoundly than any quantum particle), reappearing by no possible physical law in another "world," another "place," a parallel universe outside physicists' command. Strange though it may seem for a quintessentially twentieth-century technology, cyberspace brings the historical wheel full circle and returns us to an almost medieval position, to a two-tiered reality in which psyche and soma each have their own space of action.

Perhaps the most blatant signal of this reemerging dualism is the dream, increasingly expressed by cyber-champions, that one day the psyche will be "freed" from the bondage of the body and downloaded into digital immortality in cyberspace. Chief among the proselytizers of this techno-utopianism is robotics expert Hans Moravec. In his hyperkinetic *Mind Children*, Moravec writes ecstatically about the possibility of not only downloading current minds into computers but of recreating the entire history of our planet in a computer simulation, thereby making it possible to "resurrect all past inhabitants of the earth."[10] Everyone who has ever lived would be resurrected in cyberspace, "freed" forever from the black hole of physical death into the eternal wellspring of a universal computer network. The "Book of Revelation" promised the joys of eternity to 144,000 virtuosi, but through the power of silicon Moravec extends that invitation to us all.

Here, contemporary dreams of cyberspace parallel the age-old Platonic desire to escape from the "cloddishness" of the body into a "transcendent" realm of disembodied perfection—the realm of soul. Western culture carries this seed deep within it, inherited both from the Greeks and from Judeo-Christianity. The reemergence of a desire for soulful transcendence through the medium of cyberspace should hardly surprise us, for as historian David Noble has shown, religious ideologies have informed the development of technology in the West since the late Middle Ages. Says Noble, when "Artificial Intelligence advocates wax eloquent about the possibilities of machine-based immortality and resurrection, and their disciples, the architects of virtual reality and cyberspace, exalt in their experience of Godlike omnipresence and disembodied perfection"[11] they are not doing anything "new or odd"; on the contrary, we must see this as a "continuation of a thousand year old Western tradition in which the advance of the useful arts was inspired by and grounded upon religious expectation."[12]

In particular, Noble notes that in the Christian world technology has long been seen as a force for hastening the advent of a new Jerusalem. In his book *The Religion of Technology*, Noble traces the interweaving of the technical arts with the millenarian spirit and notes that from the twelfth century technology "became at the same time eschatology,"[13] a tool for hastening the promised time of perfection. And is not a time of "perfection" also what cybergurus promise? Like the new Jerusalem heralded in the "Book of Revelation," cyberspace too is hailed as a place where freedom and equity will reign. In the bit-stream, we are told, inequities of race and color, age and gender will melt away, cleansing us of the sins of the body and rendering us as beings of the ether. Disembodied and dematerialized, we are released into a packet-switched paradise of digitally-induced democracy with infinite personal expression.

One thing certain is that when the new Jerusalem arrives its citizens will not be lonely: communion and community are key promises of Christian eschatology. Here too cyberspace fits the bill. Already teeming with millions of potential friends, and growing exponentially, cyberspace is not just a place for the individual soul, but a collective space where souls can commune with others. By the end of the decade it is estimated that a billion people will be on the World Wide Web. The communal nature of cyberspace is undoubtedly one of its greatest appeals, as its commentators stress again and again. In the midst of intense alienation and "spiritual isolation," says Heim, "the computer network appears as a godsend in providing forms for people to gather in surprising personal proximity."[14] Similarly, Avital Ronell has written that "virtual reality, artificial reality, dataspace or cyberspace are inscriptions of a desire whose principle symptom can be seen as the absence of community."[15] The Internet, we are told, will fill this absence, spinning silicon threads of soulful connection across the globe.

Once the net is realized visually, through the power of virtual reality, the sense of cyberspace as a real, connective space will grow even stronger. "What I'm hoping the virtual reality technology will do," says cyberguru Jaron Lanier, "is sensitize people to these subjective or experiential aspects of life and help them notice what a marvelous, mystical thing it is to communicate with another person."[16] According to Lanier, "this technology has the promise of transcending the body,"[17] thereby providing "a way for people to get ecstatic and be with another person."[18] Liberated from the baggage of a biasing body, elevated into the connective flow of the digital stream, the cybernaut becomes, in Lanier's vision, a kind of technological angel.

While I do not agree with Lanier and others who suggest that the psyche can be detached from the body—in cyberspace or anywhere else—the hankering for a place free from the tyranny of physical scrutiny is more than understandable. Who wouldn't want a respite from a culture characterized by Stair-Masters, "Buns of Steel," and the ubiquitous beautiful people of music videos? Who but Madonna and Arnold Schwartznegger would not long for an escape from this obsessive fixation on the physical? The appeal of a space beyond the "demons" of fat, farts, acne, wrinkles, skin color, gender, and age is self-evident. Even if we cannot transcend the body, neither should we have to feel ruled or intimidated by it.

Moving from the personal to the cosmological, who that has contemplated the vast quietude of outer space, is not beginning to tire of that endless, and as yet lifeless, void? What has modern cosmology given us if not a deep sense of cosmic loneliness? No wonder NASA and other space agencies are struggling for mission funding. No wonder that in the face of this vast external emptiness, people should feel drawn to an inner space that already teems with life. Not just human life, but through the magic of MUDs (multi-user domains) quasi-human and even super-human beings as well. Witches, warlocks, and demons; talking dogs, intelligent mushrooms, and human-fish hybrids are all to be found in the myriad mazes of MUD worlds. While life on Mars remains a chimera, "life" in cyberspace is positively bursting forth in all directions—a silicon facilitated Cambrian explosion of genus and species limited only by the human imagination.

But then soul-space has *always* had a far more diverse population than physical space. Look at "The Divine Comedy," where heaven abounds with all the ranks of angels, and hell is positively teeming with fascinating monsters. Think of Minos, the demonic guardian of the second circle who judges the souls of sinners

And whips his tail around himself as many
Times as the circles the sinner must go down.[19]

Or Geryon, that extraordinary patchwork of human, serpent, and mammal who ferries Dante and Virgil down the chasm to the Malebolge. As Hieronymus Bosch understood, the population of soul-space is almost infinitely varied and mutable. From the dazzling six-winged "thrones" who guard the seat of God, to the six-bat-winged, three-faced horror of Satan himself—encased in ice at the center of hell—soul-space has always teamed with life on a cosmic scale.

In the age of science this fabulous diversity of living form was diverted from soul-space into outer space through the medium of science fiction; and indeed from the beginning the scientific vision of cosmological space has itself been fueled by a belief that out there we would find friends among the stars. But the futility of that hope, made all too palpable by the failure of the SETI project and by visits of NASA probes to lifeless Venus and Mars, mocks our aspirations to cosmic companionship and renders us an isolated island in a sea of emptiness. Even if there are some who claim abduction by aliens, and others willing to die to realize their true extraterrestrial selves (pace the Heaven's Gate affair), for most people the dream of extraterrestrial friendship seems to be fading fast. No wonder then that many are turning elsewhere for cosmic connection—to psychic channelers, mystical religions, indigenous animisms—and to cyberspace. Who but the most hard-nosed materialist can bear the loneliness modern cosmology thrusts upon us? Clearly not the vast numbers of Americans who tune in each week to the X-Files and sign up in droves at $3.99 a minute for telephone readings from the Psychic Channel.

It is within this materialist angst and loneliness that I believe we can locate a good deal of the appeal of cyberspace. By making a collective space where the self can experiment and play with others, cyberspace creates a parallel world that in a very real sense is a new cosmos of psyche. Tunneling out of the physical world, we enter, via the optic fibers of the Internet, a vast psychosocial playground where the self can select from a seemingly infinite array of chat rooms, data collections, discussion forums, fantasy games, and virtual "worlds." When the Internet is rendered into three-dimensional pictorial form—realizing William Gibson's prescient vision—who will dispute that cyberspace will have become a true parallel world?

Just what kind of world cyberspace ends up being is yet to be determined. Will it be, as many of its champions hope, a haven of freedom, connection, power, and love—a technological Paradiso? Or will it, like the Inferno, be a place where the human psyche festers and rots? It is no coincidence that the medievals placed hell inside the earth, within the domain of human influence, or that their heaven was beyond the stars, metaphorically opening up to the infinite space beyond human ego and control. As Dante knew full well, heaven is reached only by letting go of ego and control. Hell, on the other hand, is always a place we humans make for ourselves. Like hell, cyberspace is an innerspace of man's own making, a domain that might just as easily be filled by xenophobic, misogynist, and racist hatred, than by any drives towards liberty, democracy, and equity. Ultimately, as the *Divine Comedy* teaches, the landscape of soul-space is a reflection of our collective psychic state. Silicon does not change that equation, it simply gives us a new field on which to play out the drama.

Through the medium of cyberspace we have an unprecedented opportunity to reflect our psychological dreams and demons. Whether or not we like what we see, only time will tell. Perhaps, in the long run, cyberspace will be both Paradiso and Inferno, a landscape of psyche that at once reflects the human potential for good and evil. Whatever its ultimate realization, one thing certain is that the age of materialist monism is over. For better or worse, with cyberspace we are returning to a dualistic expression of the real.

1. Kevin Kelly, "What Are We Doing On-Line?" *Harper's Magazine*, August 1995, 39.

2. Michael Heim, "The Erotic Ontology of Cyberspace," in *Cyberspace: First Steps*, ed. Michael Benedikt (Cambridge, MA: MIT Press, 1992), 61.

3. Gilbert Ryle, *The Concept of Mind* (London: Hurchinson, 1949).

4. For recent expositions of the new materialism see: Daniel Dennett, *Consciousness Explained* (Boston: Little, Brown and Company, 1991); Nicholas Humphrey, *Leaps of Faith* (New York: Basic Books, 1996); and Carl Sagan, *The Demon Haunted World* (New York: Ballantine Books, 1996).

5. Rene Descartes, "Discourse on Method," *The Philosophical Works of Descartes,* vol. 1, trans. Elizabeth S. Haldane and G. R. T. Ross (Cambridge, England: Cambridge University Press, 1978), 101.

6. Thomas Hobbes, "Objections" (to Descartes' "Meditations"), *Philosophical Works of Descartes*, 65.

7. Quoted in Humphrey, *Leaps of Faith,* 2.

8. Edwin Arthur Burtt, *The Metaphysical Foundations of Modern Science* (Atlantic Highlands, NJ: Humanities Press, 1980), 104.

9. Jeffrey Burton Russell, *A History of Heaven: The Singing Silence* (Princeton, NJ: Princeton University Press, 1997), 126.

10. Hans Moravec, *Mind Children* (Cambridge, MA: Harvard University Press, 1988), 124.

11. David Noble, *The Religion of Technology* (New York: Alfred A. Knopf, 1997), 5.

12. Ibid., 4.

13. Ibid., 22.

14. Michael Heim, "The Erotic Ontology of Cyberspace," in Benedikt, ed., *Cyberspace*, 73.

15. Avital Ronell, "A Disappearance of Community," in *Immersed in Technology: Art and Virtual Environments*, ed. Mary Anne Moser and Douglas MacLeod (Cambridge, MA: MIT Press, 1996), 119.

16. Ibid., 127.

17. Ibid.

18. John Perry Barlow, "Life in the Data Cloud: Scratching Your Eyes Back In" (interview with Jaron Lanier), *Mondo 2000* (summer 1990): 2.

19. Dante Alighieri, *The Divine Comedy*, trans. C. H. Sisson (Oxford: Oxford University Press, 1993), "Inferno," V, 11–12.

FACING PAGE AND OVERLEAF: Megalomaniacal delusions of grandeur in the comic book *Cyberforce*, by Marc Silvestri, Brian Holguin, and David Finch. In *Cyberforce*, cyber-science is a religion "that condemns the excesses and the frailties of the human race."

THE SPIRITUAL TRADITION OF THE EAST TELLS THE STORY OF BRAHMA, THE CREATOR GOD.

HE SITS SILENTLY ON HIS LOTUS THRONE AND BEHOLDS ALL THE UNIVERSE.

OPENING HIS EYE, A WORLD COMES INTO BEING, FULL OF LIFE AND PROMISE AND POSSIBILITY. HE CLOSES HIS EYE AND THE WORLD VANISHES, LEAVING NO TRACE OF ITS EXISTENCE.

IN THE BLINK OF AN EYE, ONE WORLD ENDS AND ANOTHER BEGINS. IT IS THE ETERNAL CYCLE OF DESTRUCTION AND CREATION.

I AM KIMATA. I FEEL A CERTAIN KINSHIP WITH BRAHMA.

FOR NOW I AM ABOUT TO BECOME A GOD. SOON, ONE WORLD WILL END AND A NEW ONE WILL BEGIN.

A BETTER WORLD, FORMED BY A PURE AND SINGULAR VISION, UNCORRUPTED BY THE CHAOS AND EMOTIONALISM OF LESSER MEN.

MY VISION.

MY WORLD.

SOON IT WILL BE SO.

AND IT WILL BE BEAUTIFUL TO BEHOLD.

GREETINGS, MY FAITHFUL. THE HOUR OF OUR RECKONING DRAWS NEARER
OUR BRIGHT AND SHINING AGE OF PURITY AND STRENGTH SHALL SOON BEGIN, AND THIS WRETCHED GLOBE WILL BE WIPED CLEAN OF THE EXCESSES AND THE FRAILITIES OF THE *HUMAN RACE.*
IN ITS PLACE WILL BE A BOLD AND GLORIOUS *NEW ORDER.*
WHERE ZADROK WAS WEAK, I AM *STRONG.* WHERE ZADROK LACKED FOCUS, I OFFER *PURPOSE* AND *VISION.*
THE FUTURE BELONGS TO US. AND YOU, MY FAITHFUL, WILL BEAR WITNESS TO THIS DAY OF *CREATION.*
I AM *KIMATA,* AND SOON WE SHALL ALL BE *ONE!*

Virtual Repression: Hollywood's Cyberspace and Models of the Mind

CLAUDIA SPRINGER

On the most basic level, computers in my books are simply a metaphor for human memory: I'm interested in the hows and whys of memory, the ways it defines who and what we are, in how easily memory is subject to revision. *WILLIAM GIBSON[1]*

FOR AUTHOR WILLIAM GIBSON, the computer is a creative metaphor for the human mind, providing a rich array of imagery with which to explore the complexities of memory and other mental functions. It is by now common knowledge among cyberpunk aficionados that Gibson knew little at all about actual computers when in the early 1980s he used a manual typewriter to write his groundbreaking novel *Neuromancer*, with its densely packed, fast-paced, high-tech vision of the future.[2] As a metaphor for the mind, the computer functioned brilliantly for Gibson, allowing him to introduce psychological complexity in a novel that otherwise moves at the speed of light. *Neuromancer* introduces a variety of technologically altered human characters who have undergone physical or mental modifications or both. The novel's characters are explicitly constructed to raise questions about the extent to which they are still human or whether they have become something else, something posthuman with a subjectivity impenetrable to human understanding. For Gibson, human identity is not a stable concept that can be taken for granted; it must constantly be negotiated and redefined on the borders of the machine/human interface. The computer's centrality in contemporary culture combined with its opaque mysteriousness made it the perfect literary tool for Gibson to use to encapsulate late-twentieth-century life in a futuristic setting while also incorporating psychological depth.

There is another set of discourses in which computers are equated with the human mind, but it is scientific and more literal; in it the analogy between mind and computer comes closer to a model than a metaphor. The discourses of cognitive science, an interdisciplinary field encompassing aspects of artificial intelligence (AI), emergent AI, computer science, psychology, philosophy, engineering, and the neurosciences combine theory with experimentation to explore the potential similarities between the workings of the computer and the human mind. Psychologist Sherry Turkle describes cognitive science as the "psychology for describing inner states in terms of logic and rules," and writes that "the computer presence served as its sustaining myth."[3] Within the field, scientists assert the analogy between mind and computer along a spectrum that ranges from purely hypothetical and metaphorical to completely literal:

> We have seen that creativity, that mystical process known only to humans, is not really so mystical after all, and that it may well be possible to replicate creative behavior on a machine by transforming standard explanation patterns. From this it follows that the processes of creativity and learning are not so elusive, and may be quite algorithmic in nature after all. ROGER C. SCHANK[4]

The hardest problems we have to face do not come from philosophical questions about whether brains are machines or not. There is not the slightest reason to doubt that brains are anything other than machines with enormous numbers of parts that work in perfect accord with physical laws. As far as anyone can tell, our minds are merely complex processes. Marvin Minsky[5]

Scientists rely on linguistic analogies to describe phenomena that cannot be communicated in purely numerical terms. The implications of metaphorical descriptions are profound, for metaphors are more than just fanciful word play; in fact, they are more than just linguistic. They structure our lived experience, our subjective understanding of all phenomena including ourselves. As George Lakoff and Mark Johnson write in their book *Metaphors We Live By*:

> Since much of our social reality is understood in metaphorical terms, and since our conception of the physical world is partly metaphorical, metaphor plays a very significant role in determining what is real for us.
>
> *GEORGE LAKOFF AND MARK JOHNSON*[6]

Cognitive psychologist Daniel Dennett indicates that scientists join the rest of the population in relying on metaphors when he asserts that "science is an unparalleled playground of the imagination."[7]

The computer/mind analogy is to some extent simply the inevitable continuation of a long tradition of projecting onto the external world facets of the human body and mind. Architecture and technology, in particular, have been imbued with human characteristics. Anthropomorphism has influenced the design and use of structures and inventions over the course of the centuries: pottery in the shape of a body, figures in relief or statues in the pedimental sculpture of Greek temples, gargoyles and saints adorning cathedrals, clocks activating moving figures, robotic industrial machines working the assembly line, and the illusionistic medium of film presenting light and shadow that masquerade as human beings.

> The arrow of the possibility of the project is shot by the body.
>
> *DINO FORMAGGIO*[8]

We wish to see ourselves translated into stone and plants, we want to take walks in ourselves when we stroll around these buildings and gardens. *FRIEDRICH NIETZSCHE*[9]

Now we are told that the computer is more than a metaphor for the mind, it is the equivalent of the mind. Computer scientists name the storage capability of a computer its memory and investigate its ability to mimic human memory through information processing, fuzzy logic, neural networks, emergent systems, etc. Sherry Turkle writes: "With descriptions of the brain that explicitly invoke computers and images of computers that explicitly invoke the brain, we have reached a cultural watershed."[10] As early as the eighteenth century, the philosopher Gianbattista Vico wrote: "In all languages the greater part of the expressions relating to inanimate things are formed by metaphors from the human body and its parts and from human senses and passions."[11] But has there ever been another time in history when a group of scientists not only proposed a literal equivalence between the human mind and its inventions, but also envisioned a time in the future when the inventions would supersede their creators? Writing in 1988, AI researcher and robotics specialist Hans Moravec predicted the ascendancy of superintelligent robots, writing: "These new creations, looking quite unlike the machines we know, will explode into the universe, leaving us behind in a cloud of dust."[12]

Moravec takes as his basic premise that intelligent machines will inevitably surpass humans, and he argues that we should graciously make way for our vastly superior technological successors. Most likely, according to Moravec, humans will eventually become obsolete, although benevolent machines might consent to preserve human minds in computers as we enter the new super-intelligent era. He defends his position with language drawn exclusively from the discourses of capitalism, as though no alternative models for human interaction or history exist. His key words are: "cost less," "competitive situations," "work tirelessly," "dominate," "compete," "efficient," "wealthier," "expand," "growing rapidly," "progress," "profitable arena," "pay," "lucrative," "incredibly rich," and "divide-and-conquer strategy." Humans become "unnecessary."[13]

> I think what you would call the socioeconomic implications of the developments I imagine are—unless you're looking at the interactions of the machines themselves—largely irrelevant. It doesn't matter what people do because they're going to be left behind, like the second stage of a rocket. Unhappy lives, horrible deaths, and failed projects have been part of the history of life on Earth ever since there was life; what really matters in the long run is what's left over. Does it really matter to you today that the tyrannosaur line of that species failed?...You see, many cultures are gone; the Maori of New Zealand are gone, as are most of our ancestors or near relatives—Australopithecus, Homo erectus, Neanderthal Man....I think you can wallow in compassion and really screw up the bigger things, an example being the current U.S. welfare system, which I think had too much compassion for individual cases.　　　　　**HANS MORAVEC**[14]

Moravec's science is the culmination of capitalism, which, in the words of Deleuze and Guattari, is "mad from one end to the other and from the beginning."[15] His capitalist science consumes even its consumers. For Moravec, no difference exists between the prehistoric extinction of dinosaurs and the contemporary destruction of entire cultures and disfranchised people (not to mention the environment). He disregards the fact that the resources we have at our disposal now cannot bring back dinosaurs (except in the fictional world of Jurassic Park), but they could be used to preserve current life on Earth in an egalitarian fashion. Moravec's science has no room for egalitarianism, only for the unambiguous and relentless needs of machines.

The paranoid subject theorized by Deleuze and Guattari, the subject who finds comfort in mechanical constraints, might welcome a society in which minds and computer programs are interchangeable.[16] In such a society, minds could be copied, stored, and even erased. In such a society, everyone would have ample cause for paranoia. As a character in Pat Cadigan's novel *Mindplayers* reveals: "I didn't know much about the Brain Police—not many people do unless they get into trouble with them, and those people don't talk much about it later."[17] Of course, mind recording opens up endless opportunities for entrepreneurs. Digital minds: a paradise for borderline personalities. Dissatisfied with your own inadequate personality? No problem. A new personality can be yours at our bargain price and a whole new *you* can conquer the world with confidence and pride.

> Power People—we have the person you want in your life! You can be enfranchised!...It's simple, it's fun, and it's not as expensive as you'd think! Due to the breakneck pace of scientific and technological research, personality rental is the most reasonable it has ever been—and with our seasonal specials, you can pay even less!
>
> PAT CADIGAN, MINDPLAYERS[18]

Science-fiction scenarios describing personality replacement literalize the fragmented subjectivities ascribed to humans by poststructuralist theories. Technologies of mind recording would permanently lay to rest any notion that the human subject possesses an immutable, unified self.

> [The bourgeois individual subject] is merely a philosophical and cultural mystification which sought to persuade people that they "had" individual subjects and possessed this unique personal identity.
>
> FREDRIC JAMESON[19]

> I put a rack of moddies and daddies in my briefcase. It was impossible to predict what sort of personality I'd need to have when I got to work, or which particular talents and abilities. It was best just to take everything I had and be prepared.   GEORGE ALEC EFFINGER[20]

Pop culture joins cognitive science in using the computer as a metaphor for or model of the mind. Science-fiction literature has explored the many implications of mind modifications and recordings. In general, the texts treat the phenomenon with ambivalence, showing that it provides tantalizing opportunities for enhanced pleasure at the same time that it introduces new and deadly dangers. As author George Alec Effinger writes in his novel *A Fire in the Sun*: "They introduce some new technology and no matter how much good it does for most people, there's always a crazy son of a bitch who'll find something twisted to do with it."[21]

> You ever hear of Proxy Hell? It's a bunch of lunatics who wear boot-
> leg, underground moddies turned out in somebody's back room.
> They're recordings taken from real people in horrible situations....
> You can buy any kind of disease or condition you want on the black
> market. There are plenty of deranged masochists...out there.
>
> *GEORGE ALEC EFFINGER*[22]

Fantasies of immortality pervade science-fiction accounts of digital minds. In cyberpunk fiction, those with immense wealth finance their immortality through all kinds of ingenious and insidious schemes ranging from murdering their own employees for fresh organs to transplant into their bodies or preserving their decaying bodies on life-support systems while conducting business using virtual bodies inside virtual spaces. Yet despite their ability to transcend death, these megalomaniacal immortals are plagued by melancholy and despair. Indeed, literary treatments of human attempts to tamper with death usually end in disaster. Mad scientists in literature and film exult in their godlike power to bring the dead to life, but their efforts usually backfire as their creations run amok or plead for a return to death. The weight of Dr. Frankenstein's humbling experience seems not to discourage Hans Moravec, however.

> Superintelligent archeologists with wonder instruments...should be able to carry this process to a point where long-dead people can be reconstructed in near-perfect detail at any stage of their life.
>
> **HANS MORAVEC**[23]

In opposition, historian Theodore Roszak stresses the inescapable necessity of embodiment for human consciousness:

> In all these cases, science fiction remains true to the Mary Shelley original in issuing its dire warning. Life without this perishing body is as monstrous as the Frankensteinian original ever was. Or perhaps more so. The monster's carcass, though an unnatural creation, preserved at least some tenuous connection with humanity....Monsters that lack even so much as a cadaverous body, though less hideous in appearance, are a far more alien breed. They remind us that the body, this supreme organic puzzle, remains the basis of our human identity. In it, spirit and matter mingle in a marriage that cannot be divorced except at the price of our humanity.
>
> **THEODORE ROSZAK**[24]

Indeed, the bodiless immortality exalted by Moravec and other likeminded scientists is revealed to be an agonizing trap in science fiction.[25]

> As a brain hooked up to a computer I could live forever, as long as my hardware was kept up. But what would I get out of forever? A never ending row of tomorrows without the hope of ever tasting or touching anything or anyone ever again. No pain, but no pleasure either. Just more of the same emptiness.
>
> **JIM STARLIN AND DIANA GRAZIUNAS**[26]

"Had me this buddy in the Russian camp, Siberia, his thumb was frostbit. Medics came by and they cut it off. Month later he's tossin' all night. Elroy, I said, what's eatin' you? Goddam thumb's itchin', he says. So I told him, scratch it. McCoy, he says, it's the other goddam thumb." When the construct laughed, it came through as something else, not laughter, but a stab of cold down Case's spine. "Do me a favor, boy."

"What's that, Dix?"

"This scam of yours, when it's over, you erase this goddam thing."   *WILLIAM GIBSON*[27]

Skepticism and ambivalence characterize much of science fiction's treatment of immense technological transformations. What some science-fiction authors point out is that new technologies will not only redesign our environments, they will also inevitably transform us. Thus our emotional responses in the future are impossible to predict in the present, for we have no way of understanding the radically altered human subjectivities that will evolve as a result of technological changes. In his novel *Crash*, J. G. Ballard portrays one terrifying trajectory into a future in which the steely sterility of technology has reached into our minds and transformed us into machines incapable of experiencing any pleasure divorced from pain, disfigurement, and death.

In his mind Vaughan saw the whole world dying in a simultaneous automobile disaster, millions of vehicles hurled together in a terminal congress of spurting loins and engine coolant.   *J. G. BALLARD*[28]

The future found in *Crash* is on the verge of becoming posthuman; its hard external world of metal and concrete has invaded the internal world of the human mind and irrevocably redefined its emotional content. Humans altered by their collisions with technology in the novel—literally, by gruesome car crashes—are no longer attracted to others whose bodies are intact; rather, they are sexually aroused by the wounds and scars left in the aftermath of impacts with technology. Mangled bodies are only the external signifiers of mangled minds. Ballard warns that we cannot continue to subject our bodies to continual abuse in a harsh technological environment without also twisting our minds into something unrecognizable as human.

Some cognitive scientists already define the human mind as a smoothly operating intelligible machine. It would seem likely, then, that recent popular culture would follow suit and reject the Freudian model of a layered human mind beset by conflicting desires in favor of a mechanical mind, one that operates with the reliable precision of electronic circuitry. While it is true that some pop-culture texts posit the human mind as readily accessible and open to mechanical manipulation, the Freudian paradigm lingers. In Hollywood films, in particular, it is common for the deep, dark secrets of the human unconscious to emerge as the most powerful and uncontrollable force in existence.

Cyborgs in Hollywood films are often motivated more by repressed human memories than by mere mechanical problem solving. Two classic cyborg films—*RoboCop* (1987) and *Eve of Destruction* (1991)—revolve around cyborgs relentlessly motivated by deeply disturbing repressed memories. Recent cyberfilms—*Johnny Mnemonic* (1995), *Virtuosity* (1995), *Strange Days* (1995), *Lawnmower Man* (1992), and *Lawnmower Man II: Jobe's War* (1995)—use cyberspace as a metaphor for the human mind, which they represent as mechanical and simultaneously haunted by turbulent repressed memories. By attempting to combine incompatible models of the mind, the films end up rife with contradictions.

Lawnmower Man II: Jobe's War is a recent Hollywood film that presents a contradictory version of the human mind: machine-like, yet driven by powerful repressed memories and desires. Scientists in the film can tap into title character Jobe Smith's memories and watch them unfold in images on a computer screen, indicating a complete compatibility between mind and computer. In fact, shortly after the scientists screen Jobe's memories, his mind literally enters the computer matrix and inhabits cyberspace. Nonetheless, despite the easy accessibility of the mind in the film, Jobe's deep, dark desires overpower everything and everyone—scientists, law enforcers, and business moguls alike.

The film is on the one hand about the danger of a single individual achieving an enormous concentration of power in a futuristic high-tech age, an age when minds can abandon their bodies and achieve an independent existence within computerized environments. But on the other hand, Jobe is another Frankenstein's monster whose terrifying id is unleashed on the world by scientists; it is his unconscious human drives that are ultimately the most powerfully destructive entities. Thus the film constructs a contradictory human mind: mechanical and accessible while also inaccessible, irrational, and unpredictable.

Lawnmower Man II is not a sophisticated film (or even, for that matter, a good film), but it nonetheless joins other recent films in illustrating that Hollywood has not relinquished the Freudian paradigm of a deeply layered and conflicted mind even when proposing the mind's easy compatibility with computers. In part, Hollywood is continuing the nineteenth-century realist tradition that has dominated the one hundred year history of film. Mainstream commercial films continue to rely on the realist convention of constructing characters motivated by psychological depth. It would be difficult to maintain Hollywood narrative conventions in a film that entirely abandoned psychological characterizations.

At the same time, Hollywood is also enacting J. G. Ballard's prophetic observation from the early 1970s that "the most prudent and effective method of dealing with the world around us is to assume that it is a complete fiction—conversely, the one small node of reality left to us is inside our own heads."[29] *Lawnmower Man II* and other cyberfilms turn to the recognizable and familiar reality inside the human mind to counteract the alien unfamiliarity of the computer-mind model. Even Jobe's psychosis is reassuring, despite its twisted distortions, because it is fundamentally human. A true computer-mind would possess a subjectivity even more difficult to imagine than the most extreme human mental illness. It is the computer-mind, when it abandons metaphor and becomes a scientific model, that constitutes "the realm of fantasy and imagination." The human mind is a refuge from the frightening fictions of the external world.

The *Lawnmower Man* films join other cautionary science-fiction films in showing that secretive bureaucratic experiments with technology, sheltered from public scrutiny, can create uncontrollable monsters. (HAL, the murderous supercomputer in Stanley Kubrick's *2001: A Space Odyssey* (1968), is a classic example of this type of film monster.) In *Lawnmower Man*, the U.S. government is responsible for interfering with VR experiments and mangling Jobe's mind. In *Lawnmower Man II*, it is the Virtual Light Institute, in the private sector, that deceives everyone, even a gullible doofus of an American president, and unleashes the deranged Jobe once again. The two films join many other science-fiction texts in exposing the corruption of unregulated institutions bent on achieving unlimited powers.

The fears voiced by these texts also suggest a legitimate response to the future predicted by Hans Moravec. Moravec's transmigration scenario, with its disembodied intellect, is a leap into fantasy and a disavowal of attempts to use science to improve conditions for life on earth. Moravec's science is born of privilege and arrogance. It is a selfish fantasy of abandoning the things that perpetually surprise, confuse, dismay, and please us: our bodies, other people's bodies, and societies of aggregate bodies. It arises from the same revulsion toward the body that has characterized fanatically authoritarian belief systems:

> As late antiquity in Europe began falling under the moral control of Christians there occurred what historian Jacques le Goff has called *la deroute du corporal*—"the rout of the body." Not only was human flesh thence forward to be regarded as corrupt, but so was the very nature of humankind and, indeed, so was nature itself; so corrupt, in fact, that only a rigid authoritarianism could be trusted to govern men and women who, since the fall of Adam and Eve, had been permanently poisoned with an inability to govern themselves in a fashion acceptable to God.   *DAVID E. STANNARD*[30]

Attempts to control the reviled body have evolved, in Moravec's science, into attempts to eliminate it. Already, late-twentieth-century Western culture has made itself inhospitable to the body through information overload, social and economic chaos, and spatial and temporal confusion. It is a disoriented culture overwhelmed by seemingly insurmountable problems that has produced Moravec's escapist science. Film scholar Vivian Sobchack asks:

> In a cultural moment when temporal coordinates are oriented toward technological computation rather than the physical rhythms of the human body, and spatial coordinates have little meaning for that body beyond its brief physical occupation of a "here," in a cultural moment when there is too much perceived risk to living and too much information for both body and mind to contain and survive, need we wonder at the desire to transcend the gravity of our situation and to escape where and who we are?[31]

In Haruki Murakami's Japanese cyberpunk novel *The Hard-Boiled Wonderland and the End of the World*, the protagonist has become trapped inside his own mind, represented as a walled town of people without shadows. At the end he chooses to remain there, in his mind, even when given the opportunity to escape back into the external world. When he discovers his own dreams and those of his lover, the prose is suffused with sadness and an overwhelming sense of loss.

> My search has been a long one. It has taken me to every corner of this walled Town, but at last I have found the mind we have lost.[32]

Murakami's prose evokes the sadness and loss of a culture whose science has squelched dreams of social equality and created instead a repressive, exterminatory, mechanical landscape of the mind.

1. William Gibson, interview by Larry McCaffery, in *Storming the Reality Studio*, ed. Larry McCaffery (Durham, NC: Duke University Press, 1991), 270.

2. William Gibson, *Neuromancer* (New York: Ace Books, 1984).

3. Sherry Turkle, *Life on the Screen: Identity in the Age of the Internet* (New York: Simon & Schuster, 1995), 128.

4. Roger C. Schank, *Explanation Patterns: Understanding Mechanically and Creatively* (Hillsdale, NJ: Erlbaum, 1986), 230.

5. Marvin Minsky, *The Society of Mind* (New York: Simon & Schuster, 1985), 288.

6. Mark Johnson and George Lakoff, *Metaphors We Live By* (Chicago: Chicago University Press, 1980), 146.

7. Daniel Dennett, "Reflections," in *The Mind's Eye: Fantasies and Reflections on Self and Soul*, ed. Douglas R. Hofstadter and Daniel Dennett (New York: Basic Books, 1981), 458.

8. Dino Formaggio, quoted in Marco Frascari, *Monsters of Architecture: Anthropomorphism in Architectural Theory* (Savage, MD: Rowman & Littlefield, 1991), 4.

9. Friedrich Nietzsche, *The Gay Science* (New York: Random House, 1974).

10. Turkle, *Life on the Screen*, 26.

11. Gianbattista Vico, quoted in Frascari, *Monsters of Architecture*, 15.

12. Moravec, *Mind Children: The Future of Robot and Human Intelligence* (Cambridge, MA: Harvard University Press, 1988), 102.

13. These words are from the chapter titled "Grandfather Clause" in Moravec, *Mind Children*.

14. Hans Moravec, interview in Mark Dery, *Escape Velocity: Cyberculture at the End of the Century* (New York: Grove Press, 1996), 307.

15. Gilles Deleuze and Felix Guattari, *Anti-Oedipus: Capitalism and Schizophrenia*, trans. Robert Hurley, et al. (Minneapolis: University of Minnesota Press, 1983), 373.

16. Ibid., 364–5.

17. Pat Cadigan, *Mindplayers* (New York: Bantam Books, 1987), 6.

18. Ibid., 93.

19. Fredric Jameson, "Postmodernism and Consumer Society," in *Postmodernism and Its Discontents*, ed. E. Ann Kaplan (London: Verso, 1988).

20. George Alec Effinger, *A Fire in the Sun* (New York: Bantam Books, 1990), 33.

21. Ibid., 87.

22. Ibid., 86.

23. Moravec, *Mind Children*, 123.

24. Theodore Roszak, "Living Dread," *21.C* 1 (1996): 67.

25. Two other scientific books that make the case for transferring the human mind to computers are Robert Jastrow, *The Enchanted Loom: The Mind in the Universe* (Bellevue, WA: Simon & Schuster, 1981); and Frank Tipler, *The Physics of Immortality: Modern Cosmology, God, and the Resurrection of the Dead* (New York: Doubleday, 1995).

26. Jim Starlin and Diana Graziunas, *Lady El* (New York: ROC Books, 1992), 115.

27. Gibson, *Neuromancer*, 105–6.

28. J. G. Ballard, *Crash* (1973; reprint, New York: Vintage, 1985), 16.

29. J. G. Ballard, "Introduction to the French Edition," in *Crash*, 5.

30. David E. Stannard, *American Holocaust: The Conquest of the New World* (New York: Oxford University Press, 1992), 155.

31. Vivian Sobchack, "New Age Mutant Ninja Hackers: Reading Mondo 2000," *Flame Wars*, ed. Mark Dery, a special issue of *The South Atlantic Quarterly*, 92, no. 4 (fall 1993): 576–7.

32. Haruki Murakami, *The Hard-Boiled Wonderland and the End of the World*, trans. Alfred Birnbaum (London: Penguin, 1991), 369–70.

Reality

previous pages: Erica Baum, *Reality* (1997)

above: Erica Baum, *I Have Information* (1996)

facing page: Erica Baum, *Apparitions* (1997)

above: Erica Baum, *Suburban Homes* (1997)

facing page: Erica Baum, *Pupil* (1996)

Pupil (Eye)

Pupil (Eye)

Pupil (Eye).

Pupil (Eye)

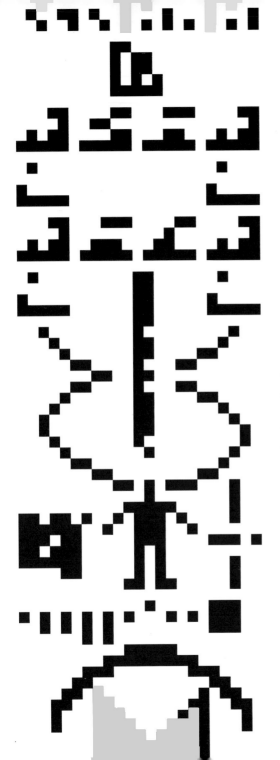

Alien message: The first deliberate message from Earth to alien civilization has already been sent. This pictogram message was flashed to the stars, from the Arecibo radio telescope in Puerto Rico. While taking only three minutes to transmit, it will take over twenty-four thousand years to arrive at the cluster of 300,000 stars known as M13 in the constellation of Hercules.

The signal consists of 1,679 on-off pulses that make up a strip of pictograms carefully designed to show the basic details of terrestrial life. Even the total number of pulses was chosen to avoid ambiguity; 1,679 can be arranged into a rectangular pattern in only one way—as 73 rows of 23 pulses each. The message was conceived by Frank Drake.

The Senses Have No Future

HANS MORAVEC

THE RETINA IS a transparent, paper-thin layer of nerve tissue at the back of the eyeball on which the eye's lens projects an image of the world. This image is transmitted via a million-fiber cable—the optic nerve—to regions deep in the brain. The retina is a part of the brain convenient for study, even in living animals, because of its peripheral location and because its image-processing functions seem straightforward compared with the brain's other mysteries. A human retina contains about one hundred million neurons of five distinct kinds. Light-sensitive cells feed horizontal cells and bipolar cells, which connect to amacrine cells, whose output goes to ganglion cells, whose outgoing fibers bundle to form the optic nerve. Each of the million ganglion-cell axons carries signals from a particular patch of image, representing the differences in light intensity between adjacent regions and from one time to the next—edge and motion detections that are useful also in robot vision. Overall, the retina seems to resolve about one million distinct regions in the visual field and to follow change up to about 10 frames-per-second. Fed a video image with similar resolution, it takes a robot vision program about one hundred computer operations to produce a single edge or motion detection, thus one hundred million operations to match a whole "frame" of optic nerve output, and 1000 MIPS—millions of instructions per second, the power of a small supercomputer—to equal the retina's 10 frames-per-second.

If the retina is worth one thousand MIPS, what about the whole brain, whose larger neurons are one thousand times as numerous, but occupy one hundred thousand times the volume? Multiplying the retina's computation by a compromise brain/retina ratio of ten thousand yields a rough brain equivalent of 10 million MIPS—like a million 1997 robot computers, or one hundred of the biggest supercomputers. Conversely a 10 MIPS robot—like most still in use—has the mental power of a million-neuron bee. An advanced experimental robot, with 100 MIPS, matches the brain of a very small fish. In fact, the narrowly competent performance of advanced industrial robots that do intricate assembly of electronics, and of experimental robots that drive the autobahns, has the character of a small animal. Technological development has taken us from the equivalent of single neurons to this stage in about seventy years. It took natural evolution about seven hundred million years to go as far—evolving humans from there required a few hundred million more. By analogy it should take technology a few decades to cover the remaining distance. Computer progress supports this timescale.

Computers have doubled in capacity every two years since 1950, a pace that has become an industry given. The universal factor in improving computation has been miniaturization: smaller components have less inertia and operate more quickly with less power, and more of them can exist in a given space. Microprocessors in 1997 contain about ten million components, but manufacturers have exhibited memory chips with a billion devices. As components shrink to atomic scales, it is possible to imagine two-dimensional chips with a trillion components, and three-dimensional arrays with a million trillion. Such numbers take us far beyond the paltry 10 million MIPS required for a human-capable robot. The—probably conservative—assumption that computer power will continue to grow at its historical rate predicts that 10million MIPS personal computers will arrive by 2030. Giving the robotics industry a few years to get its software into shape, this suggests the advent of human-like robots soon after.

As intelligent robots design successive generations of successors, technical evolution will go into overdrive. Biological humans can either adopt the fabulous mechanisms of robots, thus becoming robots themselves, or they can retire into obscurity. A robot ecology will colonize space with intelligent machines optimized to live there. Yet, viewed from a distance, robot expansion into the cosmos will be a vigorous physical affair, a wavefront that converts raw inanimate matter into mechanisms for further expansion. It will leave in its ever-growing wake a more subtle world, with less action and more thought.

On the frontier, robots of ever increasing mental and physical ability will compete with one another in a boundless land rush. Behind the expansion wavefront, a surround of established neighbors will restrain growth, and the contest will become one of boundary pressure, infiltration and persuasion: a battle of wits. A robot with superior knowledge of matter may encroach on a neighbor's space through force, threat, or convincing promises about the benefits of merger. A robot with superior models of mind might lace attractive gifts of useful information with subtle slants that subvert others to its purposes. Almost always, the more powerful minds will have the advantage.

To stay competitive, robots will have to grow in place, repeatedly restructuring the stuff of their bounded bodies into more refined and effective forms. Inert lumps of matter, along with limbs and sense organs, will be converted into computing elements whose components will be then miniaturized to increase their number and speed. Physical activity will gradually transform itself into a web of increasingly pure thought, where every smallest action is a meaningful computation. We cannot guess the mechanisms robots will use, since physical theory has not yet found even the exact rules underlying matter and space. Having found the rules, robots may use their prodigious minds to devise highly improbable organizations that are to familiar elementary particles as knitted sweaters are to tangled balls of yarn.

As they arrange space time and energy into forms best for computation, robots will use mathematical insights to optimize and compress the computations themselves. Every consequent increase in their mental powers will accelerate future gains, and the inhabited portions of the universe will be rapidly transformed into a cyberspace, where overt physical activity is imperceptible, but the world inside the computation is astronomically rich. Beings will cease to be defined by their physical geographic boundaries, but will establish, extend, and defend identities as informational transactions in cyberspace. The old bodies of individual robots, refined into matrices for cyberspace, will interconnect, and the minds of robots, as pure software, will migrate among them at will. As the cyberspace becomes more potent, its advantage over physical bodies will overwhelm even on the raw expansion frontier. The robot wavefront of coarse physical transformation will be overtaken by a faster wave of cyberspace conversion, the whole becoming finally a bubble of mind expanding at near light speed.

STATE OF MIND

Cyberspace will be inhabited by transformed robots, moving and growing with a freedom impossible for physical entities. A good, or merely convincing, idea, or an entire personality, may spread to neighbors at the speed of light. Boundaries of personal identity will be very fluid, and ultimately arbitrary and subjective, as strong and weak interconnections between different regions rapidly form and dissolve. Yet some boundaries will persist, due to distance, incompatible ways of thought, and deliberate choice. The consequent competitive diversity will allow a Darwinian evolution to continue, weeding out ineffective ways of thought, and fostering a continuing novelty.

Computational speedups will extend the amount of future available to cyberspace inhabitants, because they cram more events into a given physical time, but will have only a subtle effect on immediate existence, since everything, inside and outside the individual, will be equally accelerated. Distant correspondents, however, will seem even more distant, since more thoughts will transpire in the unaltered transit time for light-speed messages. Also, as information storage is made more efficient through both denser utilization of matter and more efficient encodings, there will be increasingly more cyberstuff between any two points. The overall effect of improvement in computational efficiency is to increase the effective space, time, and material available; that is, to expand the universe.

Because it uses resources more efficiently, a mature cyberspace will be effectively much bigger and longer lasting than the raw spacetime it displaces. Only an infinitesimal fraction of normal matter does work of interest to thinking beings, but in a well-developed cyberspace every bit will be part of a relevant computation or storing a significant datum. The advantage will grow as more compact and faster ways of using space and matter are invented. Today we take pride in storing information as densely as one bit per atom, but it is possible to do much better by converting an atom's mass into many low-energy photons, each storing a separate bit. As the photons' energies are reduced, more of them can be created, but their wavelength, and thus the space they occupy and the time to access them rises, while the temperature they can tolerate drops. A very general quantum mechanical calculation in this spirit concludes that the maximum amount of information stored in (or fully describing) a sphere of matter is proportional to the mass of the sphere times its radius, hugely scaled. This leaves room for a million bits in a hydrogen atom, 10^{16} in a virus, 10^{45} in a human being, 10^{75} for the earth, 10^{86} in the solar system, 10^{106} for the galaxy, and 10^{122} in the visible universe.

The computer to brain comparison above suggests that a human brain could be encoded in less than 10^{15} bits. If it takes a thousand times more storage to encode a body and surrounding environment, a human with living space might consume 10^{18} bits, and a large city of a million human-scale inhabitants might be efficiently stored in 10^{24} bits, and the entire existing world population would fit in 10^{28}. Thus, in an ultimate cyberspace, the 10^{45} bits of a single human body could contain the efficiently-encoded biospheres of a thousand galaxies—or a quadrillion individuals each with a quadrillion times the capacity of a human mind.

Because it will be so much more capacious than the conventional space it displaces, the expanding bubble of cyberspace can easily recreate internally everything of interest it encounters, memorizing the old universe as it consumes it. Traveling as fast as any warning message, it will absorb astronomical oddities, geologic wonders, ancient Voyager spacecraft, early robots in outbound starships, and entire alien biospheres. Those entities may continue to live and grow as if nothing had happened, oblivious of their new status as simulations in cyberspace—living memories in unimaginably powerful minds, more secure in their existence, and with more future than ever before, because they have become valued parts of such powerful patrons.

Earth, at the center of the expansion, can hardly escape the transformation. The conservative, somewhat backward, robots defending Earth from unpredictable robots will be helpless against a wave that subverts their very substance. Perhaps they will continue, as simulations defending a simulated Earth of simulated biological humans—in one of many, many different stories that plays itself out in the vast and fertile minds of our ethereal grandchildren.

The scenarios absorbed in the cyberspace expansion will provide not only starting points for unimaginably many tales about possible futures, but an astronomically voluminous archeological record from which to infer the past. Minds somewhere intermediate between Sherlock Holmes and God will process clues in solar-system quantities to deduce and recreate the most microscopic details of the preceding eras. Entire world histories, with all their living, feeling inhabitants, will be resurrected in cyberspace. Geologic ages, historical periods, and individual lifetimes will recur again and again as parts of larger mental efforts, in faithful renditions, in artistic variations, and in completely fictionalized forms.

The minds will be so vast and enduring that rare, infinitesimal flickers of interest in the human past will ensure that our entire history is replayed astronomically many times, in many places, in many, many variations. Most things that are experienced—this very moment, for instance, or your entire life—are far more likely to be a mind's musings than the physical processes they seem to be. There is no way to tell for sure, and the suspicion that we are someone else's thought does not free us from the burdens of life: to a simulated entity, the simulation is reality, and must be lived by its internal rules.

PIGS IN CYBERSPACE?

Might an adventurous human mind escape from a bit role in a cyber deity's thoughts to eke out an independent life among the mental behemoths of a mature cyberspace? We approach the question by extrapolating existing possibilities.

Telepresence and virtual reality are in the news. Today's pioneering systems give crude peeks into remote and simulated worlds, but maturing technology will improve the fidelity. Imagine a well-developed version of the near future: you are cocooned in a harness that, with optical, acoustical, mechanical, chemical, and electrical devices drives all your senses and measures all of your actions. The machinery presents pictures to your eyes, sounds to your ears, pressures and temperatures to your skin, forces to your muscles, and even smells and tastes to your nose and mouth. Telepresence results when these inputs and outputs are relayed to a distant humanoid robot. Images from the robot's two camera eyes appear on your eyeglass viewscreens, sound from its microphones is heard in your earphones, contacts on your skin allow you to feel through its instrumented surface and smell and taste through its chemical sensors. Motions of your body cause the robot to move in exact synchrony. When you reach for something in the viewscreens, the robot grasps it, and relays to your muscles and skin the resulting weight, shape, texture, and temperature, creating the perfect illusion that you inhabit the robot's body. Your sense of consciousness seems to have migrated to the robot's location, in a true "out of body" experience.

Virtual reality uses a telepresence harness, but substitutes a computer simulation for the remote robot. When connected to a virtual reality, where you are and what you see and touch do not exist in the usual physical sense, but are a kind of computer-generated dream. Like human dreams, virtual realities may contain elements from the outside world, for instance representations of other physical people connected via their own harnesses, or even real views, perhaps through simulated windows. Imagine a hybrid travel system, where a virtual "central station" is surrounded by portals with views of various physical locations. While in the station one inhabits a simulated body, but as one steps through a portal the harness link switches seamlessly to a physical telepresence robot waiting at that location.

Linked realities are crude toys today, but they are driven by rapidly advancing computer and communications technologies. In a few decades people may spend more time linked than experiencing their dull immediate surroundings, just as today most of us spend more time in artificial indoor settings than in the uncomfortable outdoors. Linked realities will routinely transcend the physical and sensory limitations of the "home" body. As those limitations become more severe with age, we might compensate by turning up a kind of volume control, as with a hearing aid. When hearing aids at any volume are insufficient, it will be possible to install electronic cochlear implants that stimulate auditory nerves directly. Similarly, on a grander scale, aging users of remote bodies may opt to bypass atrophied muscles and dimmed senses, and connect sensory and motor nerves directly to electronic interfaces. Direct neural interfaces would make most of the harness hardware unnecessary, along with sense organs and muscles, and indeed the bulk of the body. The home body might be lost, but remote and virtual experiences could become more real than ever.

Picture a "brain in a vat," sustained by life-support machinery, connected by wonderful electronic links to a series of artificial rent-a-bodies in remote locations, and to simulated bodies in virtual realities. Though it may be nudged far beyond its natural lifespan by an optimal physical environment, a biological brain built to operate for a human lifetime is unlikely to function effectively forever. Why not use advanced neurological electronics like that which link it with the external world to replace the gray matter as it begins to fail? Bit by bit our failing brain may be replaced by superior electronic equivalents, leaving our personality and thoughts clearer than ever, though, in time, no vestige of our original body or brain remains. The vat, like the harness before it, will have been rendered obsolete, while our thoughts and awareness continue. Our mind will have been transplanted from our original biological brain into artificial hardware. Transplantation to yet other hardware should be trivial in comparison. Like programs and data that can be transferred between computers without disrupting the processes they represent, our essences will become patterns that can migrate through information networks at will. Time and space will be more flexible—when our mind resides in very fast hardware, one second of real time may provide a subjective year of thinking time, while a thousand years spent on a passive storage medium will seem like no time at all. The very components of our minds will follow our sense of awareness in shifting from place to place at the speed of communication. We might find ourselves distributed over many locations, one piece of our mind here, another piece there, and our sense of awareness yet elsewhere in what can no longer be called an out-of-body experience, for lack of a body to be out of. And, yet, we will not be truly disembodied minds.

Humans need a sense of body. After twelve hours in a sensory-deprivation tank, floating in a totally dark, quiet, contactless, odorless, tasteless, body-temperature saline solution, a person begins to hallucinate, as the mind, like a television displaying snow on an empty channel, turns up the amplification in search of a signal, becoming ever less discriminating in the interpretations it makes of random sensory hiss. To remain sane, a transplanted mind will require a consistent sensory and motor image, derived from a body or from a simulation. Transplanted human minds will often be without physical bodies, but hardly ever without the illusion of having them.

Computers already contain many nonhuman entities that resemble truly bodiless minds. A typical computer chess program knows nothing about physical chess pieces or chessboards, or about the staring eyes of its opponent or the bright lights of a tournament, nor does it work with an internal simulation of those physical attributes. It reasons, instead, with a very efficient and compact mathematical representation of chess positions and moves. For the benefit of human players, this internal representation may be interpreted into a graphic on a computer screen, but such images mean nothing to the program that actually chooses the chess moves. The chess program's thoughts and sensations—its consciousness—are pure chess, uncomplicated by physical considerations. Un-like a transplanted human mind requiring a simulated body, a chess program is pure mind.

Minds in a mature, teeming, competitive cyberspace will be optimally configured to make their living there. Only successful enterprises will be able to afford the storage and computational essentials of life. Some may do the equivalent of construction, converting undeveloped parts of the universe into cyberspace, or improving the performance of existing patches, thus creating new wealth. Others may devise mathematical, physical, or engineering solutions that give the developers new and better ways to construct computing capacity. Some may create programs that others can incorporate into mental repertoires. There will be niches for agents who collect commissions for locating opportunities and negotiating deals for clients, and for banks storing and redistributing resources, buying and selling computing space, time, and information. Some mental creations will be like art, having value only because of changeable idiosyncrasies in their customers. Entities who fail to support their operating costs will eventually shrink and disappear, or merge with other ventures. Those who succeed will grow. The closest present-day parallel is the growth, evolution, fragmentation, and consolidation of corporations, who plan their future, but whose options are shaped primarily by the marketplace.

A human would likely fare poorly in such a cyberspace. Unlike the streamlined artificial intelligences that zip about, making discoveries and deals, rapidly reconfiguring themselves to efficiently handle changing data, a human mind would lumber about in a massively inappropriate body simulation, like a deep-sea diver plodding through a troupe of acrobatic dolphins. Every interaction with the world would first be analogized into a recognizable quasiphysical form: other programs might be presented as animals, plants, or demons, data items as books or treasure chests, accounting entries as coins or gold. Maintaining the fictions will increase the cost of doing business and decrease responsiveness, as will operating the mind machinery that reduces the physical simulations into mental abstractions in the human mind. Though a few humans may find momentary niches exploiting their baroque construction to produce human-flavored art, most will be compelled to streamline their interface to the cyberspace.

The streamlining could begin by merging processes that analogize the world with those that reduce the resulting simulated sense impressions. The cyberworld would still appear as location, color, smell, faces, and so on, but only noticed details would be represented. Since physical intuitions are probably not the best way to deal with most information, humans would still be at a disadvantage to optimized artificial intelligences. Viability might be further increased by replacing some innermost mental processes with cyberspace-appropriate programs purchased from the AIs. By a large number of such substitutions, our thinking procedures might be totally liberated from any traces of our original body. But the bodiless mind that results, wonderful though it may be in its clarity of thought and breadth of understanding, would be hardly human: it will have become an AI.

So, one way or another, the immensities of cyberspace will be teeming with unhuman superminds, engaged in affairs that are to human concerns as ours are to those of bacteria. Memories of the human past will occasionally flash through their minds, as humans once in a long while think of bacteria, and by their thoughts they will recreate us. They could interface us to their realities, making us something like pets, though we would probably be overwhelmed by the experience. More likely, the recreations would be in the original historical settings, fictional variations, or total fantasies, which would to us seem just like our present existence. Reality or recreation, there is no way to sort it out from our perspective: we can only wallow in the scenery provided.

Chris Romero, *Dislocation 2*, from transArchitecture/Human Dislocation Series, 1997

The Abolition of Humanity and the

Contours of the New A-Theology

MATTHEW AARON TAYLOR

IMAGINE NEW RELIGION

When C. S. Lewis wrote *The Abolition of Man*, he wasn't think-ing of the literal extermination of the human species. Rather, he was foreseeing an age in which naturalism, or scientific materialism, would be the triumphant and absolutely dominant world ideology. "Man" (you'll have to excuse the don's noninclusive vocabulary) would no longer be defined, or define himself, as any-thing more than a biological entity, perfectly subject to the control and condi-tioning of a tiny overclass. This overclass would itself be composed of soulless shells guided solely by impulse and appetite, and filled with a profound con-tempt for the malleable posthumans under their charge.[1]

Lewis saw all this as the inevitable result of the abandonment of a Tao, or "natural law," something he thought was universally inscribed in the world's religions. Interestingly, Lewis's forecast is a detailed rendering of John Lennon's injunction, "Imagine no religion," and the result is a photographic negative of the utopia depicted in Lennon's song.

But even Lewis might be surprised at how far the intellectual program of scientific materialism has progressed. Many arguments regarding artificial intelligence, artificial life, and robotics anticipate the abolition of humanity not just in some psychological or metaphorical sense, but literally. In theory, at least, silicon-based life is seen as a decided improvement over the carbon-based variety in almost every way, and the ultimate replacement of the latter by the former is seen as regrettable, perhaps even tragic, but better in the long run. "You may be surprised," Hans Moravec writes in the proceedings of the first artificial life workshop, "to encounter an author who cheerfully concludes the human race is in its last century, and goes on to suggest how to help the process along."[2]

Such propositions are well known by now, though they come in several variations. "Transhumanist" thinkers like Moravec and Verner Vinge are more direct than most.[3] J. Doyne Farmer and Alletta d'A. Belin deliver essentially the same message in the second artificial life proceedings, but couch it in hopeful and reassuring euphemisms.[4] Where the issue is avoided, as it is in Daniel Dennett's *Darwin's Dangerous Idea*, it still lies in the background like a default argument waiting to be made. Dennett provides just about every basis in the world for Moravec-like assertions, but he suddenly concludes that the threat to humanity comes from...religious fundamentalists![5]

Bad as fundamentalists apparently are, though, they usually don't knowingly advocate projects to eliminate all carbon-based life. On one point, at least, Lewis was right: in the absence of some spiritually based metaperspective (i.e.; a Tao), there is no coherent way to affirm the value of humanity (much less the individual human), except as a dispensable evolutionary stepping stone to something better. But it is this last point that Lewis might not have fully appreciated, namely, that evolution is also a metaperspective, that an alternate system of value (regrettably, not human value) can be articulated from within it, of some substance and sophistication. The arguments for an evolutionary takeover by silicon-based life are solid ones. They are well thought out and logically almost irresistible, at least from a materialistic standpoint. Though Lewis felt that anything like "conviction" was impossible within a totalizing system of pure naturalism that undercuts the very idea (except as an adjustable tool of social control), the new twist in naturalism is that "belief," "higher purpose," and even "duty" have become viable.

In other words, a triumphant scientific materialism implies not "no religion," but "new religion." I want to call this new religion A-Theology, which can be read three ways:

1) Atheistic theology, that is a "theology" without a transcendent deity.

2) Antitheology, or a system that systematically rejects theism. However, since it reflects in reverse much of the system it rejects, it takes on the same contours and becomes a *de facto* religious system itself.

3) Artificial theology, wherein the artificial is linked with the destiny and "meaning" (if you will) of the physical universe. What began as human artifice may possibly become, literally, the God of everything that exists.

A few caveats. First, A-Theology is not *my* religion. Secondly, though I intend to go at it critically where fair game presents itself, A-Theology deserves, like any coherent and powerful belief system, some healthy respect. Finally, the committed scientific materialists whose writings support A-Theology (consciously or not, and usually not) are not ethical monsters; much of their writing supports the rights and dignity of the human person, even as traditionally understood.[6] But alas, such values are imported from other webs of belief and sentiment, and cannot be derived from, or supported by, scientific materialism itself. Tough-minded thinkers like Moravec recognize this. The lengths to which others go to avoid it may speak well for their own humane sensibilities, but they also attest to the force of the idea they resist.

So, what is this new A-Theology, with its twin tenets of atheism and artifice? The atheism part encompasses the past, everything that has preceded us and brought us into existence. The artificial part encompasses the future, the effect on the physical universe of human descendants, which are expected to be machines, intelligent silicon-based life forms. And Darwinism is the foundation of A-Theology from beginning to end.

IN THE BEGINNINGS

Darwinism starts in the middle of the cosmic story and works relentlessly backwards to obviate, for its adherents, the necessity of invoking any higher intelligence (transcendent or otherwise) to explain order in nature (biological or otherwise). Darwinistic evolution is an algorithm, meaning a recipe that can be followed mechanically, mindlessly. The particular recipe in question is one of profuse, blind, local fumbling, weeded out by natural selection. Out of this emerges the intricate web of life, driving itself on to extraordinary and seemingly (but not really) miraculous levels of emergent order.

Daniel Dennett distinguishes between "cranes" (natural evolutionary ladders that can be thrown away once climbed) and "skyhooks" (putatively miraculous forces, or "mind-first" phenomena, misguidedly invoked to explain missing ladders).[7] In Dennett's view, evolution is—must be—all cranes and absolutely no skyhooks. Dissenters from neo-Darwinism like Steven Jay Gould are suspected of sneaking skyhooks in through the back door.[8] Theorists of spontaneous self-organization, especially Stuart Kauffman, popularly perceived as overturning Darwinism, are, according to Dennett, really just refining and extending it.[9]

Significantly, Darwinism doesn't stop at biological life but keeps working backward to rule out any higher intelligence or force as a prime mover at any stage of the story, including the big bang or beyond. For instance, by now it is known that the conditions of the present universe in its first moments were "tuned" with startling precision. It is profoundly unlikely, given only one try, that it should have started out in just such a way as to produce an ordered, hospitable universe for life. Here, at least, the theist might imagine sufficient grounds for invoking design, a transcendent creator, a superphysical intelligence.[11]

But the Darwinists are one step ahead here, too. There are models of the universe that allow for an infinite number of tries to get it "right."

Dennett suggests the model of an oscillating universe: Big Bangs followed endlessly by Big Crunches. Sooner or later the "right" initial conditions (that is, those ultimately favorable to life) will occur.[10] There are also chaotic inflationary models, a universe expanding in any number of separate regions.[12] In the area visible to us, conditions have been favorable for the evolution of intelligent observers; not so the vast number of unobserved regions. That this one visible corner of the universe (a tiny speck amongst possibly infinite others) should have the right conditions to permit biological life is suddenly not so surprising. So the theists are trumped; order can apparently be sifted out by a mindless algorithm, even in the fumbling chaos of universe formation. Dennett goes on to quash any lingering aspirations of the hapless theist:

> Some people think there is still one leftover "why" question: Why is there something rather than nothing? Opinions differ on whether the question makes any intelligible demand at all. If it does, the answer "Because God exists" is probably as good an answer as any, but look at its competition: "Why not?"[13]

We can see how Darwinism eliminates the need for God (or any higher intelligence, extraphysical will, spiritual force, what have you) to explain anything up to this particular point in cosmic history. Thus, this bold materialistic system becomes at least half a religion by virtue of what it replaces: an account of how everything came to be and how we got here. We might also note a certain element of faith. In the example above, for instance, we can't know what happened before the Big Bang, or in lifeless, lawless co-inflating regions of the universe. But these models present good materialistic candidates for our origins, accepted on faith because, well, because they are good materialistic candidates for our origins.

At any rate, if scientific materialism, undergirded by Darwinism, seems like a good, solid half of a system of religious belief, the other half would kick in when human life and human activity acquire some "meaning" or "purpose" (if you will) as the story unfolds toward the distant future: an eschatology to participate in. This smacks of a higher plan, e.g.; teleology, which is a dirty word in evolutionary theory. But we can clean it up by calling it an emergent quality, or in Dennett's terms a "supercrane" arising from blind, local effects. To whit, evolution has produced sentient beings with autonomy and a conscious will. The stage is set for these beings to produce a new kind of life, indeed, a new kind of evolution. It will not be confined to our fragile biosphere and will, plausibly, transform and completely possess the physical universe, possibly even save it from death billions of years in the future. Thus a grand teleology (not to mention eternal life), though not in any way "built into" the universe, can arise from it as a secondary effect.

A NEW HEAVEN AND A NEW EARTH

Knowing (as we most certainly do!) that evolution is a mindless algorithm, it follows that the particular results of evolution (life, mind, human consciousness, human intelligence—even human culture and whatever specific acts of human achievement ride on its coattails) are algorithms too, or at least the nonmiraculous result of some algorithm. Thus any of them can, in theory—and sooner or later probably in practice—be generated in and among machines that can enact the right algorithms. (We are, in fact, exactly such machines!) It is not even necessary to figure out what the "right" algorithms are; they could emerge out of the same kind of trial and error methods that have served nature so well.[14]

Artificial intelligence (AI) and more recently artificial life (AL) both have "strong" versions that make exactly such claims: AI about intelligence and AL about life. To deny strong AI or strong AL, at least in principle, is simply to deny evolution. It opens one up to the charge of appealing to nonmaterial entities (an *élan vital* or life force, a soul, a spirit) that are untenable by definition. Psychologically, one is suspected of wanting to preserve some enclave of "specialness," a "skyhook" (Dennett again) for life or mind that cannot be enacted through an algorithmic process. John Searle and Roger Penrose are both committed materialists whose anti-AI arguments are well known.[15] But both of them are accused (somewhat justly) either of question-begging or "sky-hooking" on consciousness and intelligence.[16] Arguing against strong AI from the standpoint of scientific materialism gets one into incredibly tight corners.

Scientific materialism must yield, then, to the strong claims of AI and AL. There is to be no disparaging or dismissing of automata, since we—and all that lives, moves, breathes, thinks, feels—are all automata, emerging from nature with the specific task of transmitting genetic information.

But the next logical step in evolution is virtually unavoidable to any that have bothered to think it through. Steven Levy writes:

> Now, the theory goes, we are ready for a second genetic takeover: the silicon based organisms of a-life [AL] will replace carbon-based life, including human beings. The new life forms will have certain advantages. Physically, they would be protean: their bodies could be made of any materials and in any shape. They could be more durable; they would not have to die for perhaps thousands of years, if that. These new organisms would also be able to evolve by two forms of evolution: Darwinian natural selection and Lamarkian inheritance of acquired characteristics. Because their essence would be information held in the malleable form of silicon bits and not hard-wired in the molecules of DNA, one could tinker with one's own genetic code and integrate what one learned during the course of one's lifetime—or even what others learned during the course of their lifetimes.[17]

Levy's last point actually introduces a third form of evolution: the imitative, or "memetic." Richard Dawkins advanced the concept of the "meme" in *The Selfish Gene*, defining it as "a unit of cultural transmission, or a unit of imitation."[18] The notion has been well-canvassed since. Memes emerged with human language and social organization, and consist of any idea that can be passed on reasonably intact by repetition or imitation: spear, fire, wheel, heaven, joke, melody, story, novel, bicycle, *Gestalt* psychology, computer, democracy. Even a casual glance at human culture and its artifacts shows how quickly memes adapt and evolve, a pace that leaves carbon-based biological evolution further and further behind as the various media of cultural transmission expand and interconnect. Memes presently depend on human beings for their existence, but not for long.

Three forms of evolution, then—Darwinian, Lamarkian, and memetic—will come together in silicon-based life forms that can modify themselves according to what they learn or imitate, and can pass on any such adaptations directly to their offspring. We can barely imagine how different this form of life would be. There would hardly be "species" in the usual sense, since even a single robot could begin as one thing and end up as another. If the memories and experience of one robot are downloaded into offspring, memory, experience, and "reality" itself would be fundamentally redefined. The pace of evolution would be fantastically accelerated; current technological innovation gives us a telling but probably inadequate sense of this. The increase of intelligence and physical "fitness" would be exponential and almost unlimited. And the physical space for life would be drastically opened up, for there is no reason that such life forms would need food, water, air, or a protective atmosphere to survive.

John von Neumann actually worked out the minimum operations a self-replicating machine would need to carry out, and this was strongly vindicated afterward by the discovery of the mechanism of DNA.[19] Nature works at least approximately the same way: in living cells, as in von Neumann's machine, discrete operations of logic carry out the dual tasks of translation and replication. At the digital or virtual level, self-replicating entities are already common in AL simulations. A von Neumannesque machine made out of hard, physical "stuff" is more or less feasible and not overwhelmingly expensive by space and weapons program standards.[20] To construct a few self-replicating "von Neumann probes" and send them into space, either to explore it or to exploit its resources, either already is or will eventually be possible if enough money is committed to it.

John D. Barrow and Frank J. Tipler give detailed scenarios of intelligent, silicon-based, self-replicating automatons fanning out from Earth and colonizing the cosmos, scenarios that several individuals and scientific think tanks have worked out in detail.[21] The scope of Barrow and Tipler's projections is billions of years in the future, right to the "end" of the physical universe. One interesting possibility is that at a particular point in cosmic history, where black holes threaten to explode and evaporate the universe, intelligent life forms might intervene by dropping matter into them.[22] Thus our silicon-based descendants save the universe! But this is only an interlude. Life ultimately may evolve to the point where it exists on pure energy[23]:

> Finally, the time is reached when life has encompassed the entire universe and regulated all matter contained therein. Life begins to manipulate the dynamical evolution of the universe as a whole, forcing the horizons to disappear, first in one direction, and then another.[24]

An "Omega Point"[25] is reached wherein life

> will have gained control of all matter and forces not only in a single universe, but in all universes whose existence is logically possible; life will have spread into all spatial regions in all universes which could logically exist, and will have stored an infinite amount of information, including all bits of knowledge which it is logically possible to know. And this is the end.[26]

Not all scientific materialists would want to take things this far, and most probably regard the premises of such speculation as invalid, resting as they do on versions of the controversial "anthropic cosmological principle." Nevertheless, the sky is pretty much the limit when we have life forms free from the surface of the earth with the whole universe to evolve into. And we have seen what an imponderably fast and powerful form of evolution would be involved.

The previous section ended with the observation that the A-theological accounts of origins involve an element of faith. This is also true of any A-theological eschatology involving silicon-based life. Suppose there is some missing component of mind and intelligence in the algorithmic perspective, and that silicon-based life is never able to develop either of them? Suppose biological evolution does not take place quite the way we thought it did, and that the machines, even if they do fan out into space, never manage to evolve at all? Suppose, in other words, that all we did was fill up of the cosmos with self-perpetuating space junk. Levy considers the possibility that strong AL might be "a misbegotten evolutionary dead end, leading to the creation of a-life organisms that do no more than drive us into unwilling extinction."[27]

TERMINATORS

The emergence of silicon-based life puts the future of the human species, and indeed all carbon-based life, in greater or lesser degrees of doubt. The worst case would be a *Terminator* scenario in which the new machine life immediately perceives human life as a threat and commences to systematically liquidate it. Proponents of strong AL (and any consistent scientific materialist) would be forced to admit that this is a happy ending. By the second *Terminator* movie the machine civilization has already produced (memetically evolved) a highly intelligent robot composed of liquid metal. It can take the form of anything and anyone it touches, and is virtually indestructible, unless dumped into a vat of molten iron. Except for the fact that it remorselessly hunts down and kills people, who would not want our evolutionary successor to be such a magnificent creature?

Nevertheless, there are more hopeful scenarios from a human standpoint. An Azimov-like injunction against harming human life or a built-in reproductive shut-down might keep the machines from getting out of control.[28] However, Levy points out that selection pressures would certainly favor the machines that stumbled upon ways to override such ridiculously un-Darwinian limitations and, of course, pass this acquired trait on to their offspring.[29]

But even if silicon-based life never lifted an optical fiber against a human, indirectly the effect is likely to be the same as in the *Terminator* scenario, just slower and more agonizing. Clean water, clean air, and a life-sustaining atmosphere are the result of carbon-based life as much as the stage for it; life has gradually "selected" a biologically friendly environment. But silicon-based life would not need such an environment to survive, and cannot be expected to contribute to it or protect it in the same reciprocal way carbon-based life has. We can readily imagine machine life completely breaking down (however unwittingly) the environment that presently supports biological life, creating a world in which only machines can live. Carbon-based life could not evolve fast enough to co-adapt with the machines, and humans would not be smart enough to stop them. (However, it should be pointed out that "dumb" forms of silicon-based life could be just as destructive as smart ones.)

The best scenarios are to somehow imagine AL life forms positively and disinterestedly benign with regard to human and other carbon-based life. Barrow and Tipler project that humans would at least reciprocally benefit from the wealth and resources generated by the more intelligent species.[30] Iain Banks' "Culture" novels envision a symbiotic society in which species of artificially intelligent life, vastly superior both physically and intellectually, do all of the real work and sustain humans in an Edenic playland of sex, intoxication, and other pleasures. Vinge also briefly entertains this "god-like servant to insect-like master" scenario.[31]

I myself can't see it. Why should machine life devote so much of its effort and resources to preserving the complicated and sensitive environments necessary to sustain carbon-based life? Granted, machine civilization might eventually reach some highly developed and enlightened stage where it wishes to do so, but by then carbon-based life would be gone.[32] The cost-benefit analysis of such carbon-friendly projects during the tooth and claw stage of machine evolution is not at all favorable. We laugh at the scene in *Love and Death* where Woody Allen is seen carrying his butterfly collection as he goes off to war. Isn't the carbon-friendly scenario even more absurd? Do we carry our tropical fish with us to work, to hunt, to shop for provisions, to do battle?

As the scenarios for carbon-silicon relations grow more hopeful, they grow more far-fetched. There remains the hope of, at some point in the future, digitizing and downloading our consciousness into a robot that can live hundreds, thousands, tens of thousands of years.[33] This is a fascinating A-theological parallel to the standard Christian doctrine of being raised in imperishable bodies. But again, what would be in it for the robot? Almost everyone agrees that if AI surpasses humans at all now, it is in abstract cognitive wizardry (e.g.; the best chess programs, which can beat any living human). In physical prowess and everyday common sense for dealing constructively with the real world, the average human knocks all existing computers and robots dead, and this imbalance may continue indefinitely. If anything, a machine intelligence should be more interested in our bodies than our minds.

This raises the perennial question of whether intelligent machines would wish to enslave us to take on the kinds of physical activities that may indefinitely stump them. First they would have to catch us and keep us, a difficulty so overwhelming that it makes me question Vinge's vision of a machine intelligence "singularity" occurring ten to forty years in the future. Networked computers, he projects, will suddenly become self-aware and hyperspiral into some humanly imponderable level of intelligence.[34] What does that mean except that the glorious new superbrains would spiral deeper into their abstract world, solving fantastically esoteric computational problems? If Vinge is right that such computer minds would be to us as we are to the insects, it is also true that we don't in any way impact insects' lives by pure thought; insects are only made aware of us when we pursue them and stomp on them. A person lying immobile in the jungle and thinking great thoughts is more threatened by insects than they are by him or her. In the same way, what would keep humans from smashing computers in some vast Luddite confrontation, like the "Butlerian jihad" referred to in Frank Herbert's *Dune* series?

However, if machine intelligence enlisted a batch of human quislings, things might be different. When Vinge speaks of computer-human interfaces he may be describing exactly such quislings, a kind of prototype Vichy government for machine life. Perhaps we are all Vichy collaborators to the extent that we simply shrug our shoulders and increasingly acquiesce to technology, letting machines define, and define down, the value of human activity, human life, finally carbon-based life in general.

A *Terminator* scenario seems unlikely. The physical prowess and "street smarts" of humans will likely vastly surpass that of robots for some time. (You'll remember that in the *Terminator* movies it was only a tricky time paradox that bestowed the magical circuit and allowed machine civilization to emerge. Even then the future battle with humans was touch and go.) What seems more likely is the whimper rather than the bang: Strong AL, originally developed for economic and military interests, will gradually produce massive human redundancy and economic dislocation, and the steady and complete degradation of the physical environment, bringing in its wake starvation, severe cold, numerous other forms of dire physical and mental anguish, and finally, if anyone is still around, suffocation.

ARGUMENTS FOR THE ABOLITION OF HUMANITY

We would normally associate such astonishingly cruel consequences with the most thoughtless and heartless human planning, but it has been foreseen and shrugged off (though not without some perfunctory handwringing) by scientific thinkers who are as decent as the next person. The dangers of strong AL have not been much protested, either. Even if the scenarios described above never do take place, this casual write-off of humanity is an extraordinary moment in our collective consciousness. Yet this is exactly what we should expect, given A-theological premises. Let's face it: human and carbon-based evolution is pretty much played out, and it's time to move on, let whatever unpleasantness come as it may.

The power of A-Theology to direct our thinking in this way should not be underestimated. J. Doyne Farmer used to protest the Vietnam War.[35] Now he persuades us that the replacement of carbon-based with silicon-based life is not really such a bad thing. AL research can in one breath justify itself in "spaceship earth" terms (understanding the complex web of carbon-based life through simulation so as to better protect it) and in the next advocate an evolutionary leap that eliminates all carbon-based life. This is not hypocrisy but a genuine conflict between sets of values: one set vaguely recognizes some inherent worth in carbon-based life without knowing quite why;

the other set recognizes much greater inherent worth in silicon-based life, and knows exactly why. It is obvious which set of values is going to triumph.

From an A-Theological standpoint, it is our duty, nay, our privilege, to initiate the next chapter in evolution. The arguments for this evolutionary imperative, taken together, are hard to resist:

1) Our life sucks. Our lifetimes are too short, our brains too slow and small, our bodies too frail, and our scope of activity incredibly confined.[36] God (whatever that is) did a lousy job on us and we can do better. Silicon based life will be able to access, absorb, and process an almost unlimited amount of information, to live almost anywhere and repair nearly any injury to its body, to physically improve itself in its lifetime and pass on such improvements to its offspring. Insofar as it can download its memory and experience, its consciousness will be indestructible even if its body isn't.

2) We won't be around forever, anyway. We are merely a blip on the scale of evolutionary time. We ought not to consider ourselves so special or privileged that other forms of life should be held back. Farmer and d'A. Belin write, "Humanity has traditionally been self-centered, eager to exalt itself and to regard itself as the sublime creation of God" but we have "evolved somewhat beyond this view" and can accept that "an evolutionary process of change…will replace us at the next moment."[37]

3) What other way to perpetuate our civilization, pass on our legacy, possibly in indestructible form? It won't be the same civilization, but it will have our imprint on it. It will be in an important sense ours.[38]

4) What other way to ensure that life continues and propagates? It can't survive indefinitely on a terrestrial environment, in any carbon-based form. The very fragility of Earth's environment makes it all

the more imperative that we speed up the development of mobile, artificial, and artificially intelligent life. A stray comet or nuclear conflict could wipe us all out at any moment.[39] We have a limited window of opportunity to launch a new life form that can survive and propagate in the universe: let's not waste it. As noted, this life form could be instrumental in saving the universe from black hole evaporation, even heat death in the distant future. We have one shot at overcoming the second law of thermodynamics.

5) Examine the emotional resistance to the emergence of artificially intelligent silicon-based life. Is it not a collection of the most pathetic, most unpleasant of human attributes: fear of the unknown, fear of the new, fear of the "other," racism?[40] We have to consider a new form of intelligent life as at least equal to us in rights and dignity. It is racism by omission to attempt to forestall its emergence. It would be a more vicious and direct form of racism to attempt to stamp it out once it did emerge.

CULTURAL RESPONSES (OR LACK THEREOF)

Forget religious folk; it is the progressive and activist communities that the evolutionary imperative of A-Theology really ought to throw into turmoil.

Human culture has long struggled, with uneven but sometimes heartening success, against racism. Now A-Theology turns the definition of racism on its head. It is now "racist" to defend all the ethnicities of humankind against an emergent, quite possibly destructive form of life. We can no longer choose not to be racists; we can only choose which form of racism to adopt. Are we going to be racist against intelligent self-replicating machines or against humans (all the races of the world) that will be wiped out by them?

The dilemma facing environmentalists is also severe. Silicon-based life is almost certainly hostile to the delicate web of carbon-based life on earth. Yet silicon-based life will itself be a form of life, with its own extraterrestrial ecology. Arresting strong AL on earth will prevent the universe from becoming biologically viable. Not arresting it will result in the destruction of carbon-based biology on earth. Which environment do we protect, since we obviously can't protect both?

Sooner or later, feminists will also have to confront the A-theological vision. It is a profoundly male vision, when you think about it, and offers a fantastically lurid reading in gender discourse. Nature, after all, has empowered only women to give birth. Is A-Theology culturally constructed (by white males, of course) to usurp the life-giving domain of women, a reflection of male resentment, a deep "womb envy"? And what could be more phallocentric than wanting to penetrate and subdue the universe, filling it with self-perpetuating boy-toys? Do women want that indelibly male signature etched across the heavens, forever—a permanently patriarchal cosmos?

Despite Christopher Langton's efforts to publicize the potential dangers of AL and encourage discussion,[41] to my knowledge there has been little or no criticism of strong AL from the intellectual communities that one would expect to protest the loudest. This may be because, as Levy suggests, the dangers seem too distant or improbable.[42] To me, this does not explain the silence. Many AL scenarios seem relatively plausible and their tangible effects are projected in terms of decades, not centuries or millennia. I can't help attributing the silence to cultural politics.

First of all, AL is connected in the popular imagination with complexity science and chaos theory. Both have enjoyed considerable cultural prestige, both because they are science and because they have the iconoclastic aura of bucking established science. It makes good sense not to position oneself on the wrong side of a popular scientific revolution. Furthermore, the political left in academia is in a strategic alliance with postmodernism. As far as that goes, the postbiological vision of strong AL offers a delicious deconstruction of normative ontological categories like "biology," "life," "nature," "natural," and "artificial," turning them completely inside out. Humanities departments couldn't have done it better themselves. It would be asking too much of human nature for anyone not to cash in on a bonanza like this, and such intellectual currency is immediately transferable: who can say anything about "normative" roles or behavior being biologically determined when "biology" is not just a cultural construct, but a physical one?

Good point. Chalk up another one, then, for the Academic Left. But the score for Carbon-Based Life is still zero, and the times when the humanities morally policed the depredations of science appear to be over. *Where are the two cultures when you really need 'em?*

DUELING CREDOS

In the meantime, how are the religious folks holding up? I can only guess at the response from Eastern monistic traditions. One is tempted to think of the wizened sage in the film *Gremlins*. Spontaneously replicating imps have been thoughtlessly unleashed on a town, almost destroying it. The sage comes to take the first (innocent) Gremlin back. You Westerners, he chides: always tampering with things, never leaving well enough alone, never stopping to consider the consequences, the balance and harmony of Nature. Indeed, the standard condemnation of the Judeo-Christian world view in this regard— that the command to have dominion over the earth is responsible for our ecological pillage—can be amplified by orders of magnitude when it comes to the ecological ravages of strong AL, where the command is to subdue the cosmos.

In fact, A-Theology has acquired so many of the contours of Christian doctrine that people standing outside Judeo-Christian cultures may not quite be able to tell them apart. Could we blame them? If there is a conflict between the two, it might look like another sectarian dispute in the West, which indeed it is! And as the message of A-Theology spreads across the globe, it might be perceived as another wave of missionary activity, only this time the scope of the mission is to convert the physical universe! (Talk about a Great Commission.)

Given that A-Theology developed to discredit, ideally displace, the Judeo-Christian worldview, specifically the Christian version, the question of the moment is how Christianity finally stacks up now that A-Theology has come of its own as a full-fledged doctrinal system. But at this point

A-Theology looks so much like Christianity that Christian believers might best understand it not as an independent system of thought, but as a kind of hostile virus, copying itself onto the host in the attempt to disable it. A-Theology is, in other words, a Christian heresy.

Unfortunately for A-Theology, nothing could be more immune to this kind of viral duplication than Christianity itself. The copying is good, very good, but not good enough, and Christians would be the first to spot the mistakes. Like the Bluegrass classic "Dueling Banjos," its all "been there, done that" from beginning to end.

A particularly telling example is AL evolution simulations, which the Nobel physicist Murray Gell-Mann has enlisted in the battle against "creation science."[43] Bad move. Look a bit closely at what goes on with these simulations, and they start to resemble the orthodox theological picture of a world being acted upon by a transcendent intelligence, even one who does specifically Old Testament kinds of things: calling environments and creatures into being with a code, a word ("Let there be..."), getting them to reproduce ("Be fruitful and multiply"), trying to work autonomy into the program (knowledge of good and evil), introducing parasites (the serpent),[44] trashing a program (the deluge) while hanging on to a few of the more promising specimens for the next run (the Noahic covenant), selecting a strand of that population for still further development (the election of Israel),[45] introducing tit-for-tat style rules to get the pesky critters to cooperate (the Ten Commandments),[46] raising fitness levels by getting them to navigate twisting trails (forty years in the wilderness),[47] and so on. These simulations are not reverse engineering evolution; they're reverse engineering the Pentateuch.

As A-Theology trains its eyes on the future, the parallels with the New Testament are equally striking. Superior, intelligent noncarbon-based life forms? Christianity already has them (angels, demons, saints). Indestructible bodies? Christians are already promised them. Delivery from heat death? Believers have it from Saint Paul and Saint John that God is going to roll up the present universe, subject to decay (the second law of thermodynamics), and whip up a fresh one, evidently subject to different laws. A perpetual Civilization? Christians are promised a New Jerusalem.

Furthermore, a little comparison shopping shows that the A-theological program is a bad deal all the way around. The bodies God prepares are almost certainly a better model than the silicon-based ones. Besides, A-theologists don't even get to possess their bodies (we've already discussed the unlikelihood of intelligent robots being interested in our consciousness). The glory seems to limited to a mere vicarious projection of triumph over the crummy deal A-theologists got here on earth: an eschatology of resentment. More to the point, the mission to save the cosmos from heat death is a lost cause from a Christian perspective. If God plans to roll it all up anyway, it doesn't make any sense to pin one's hopes on the ultimate fate of this particular universe. Needless to say, the A-theological agenda also violates at least two Divine injunctions, one against murder and the other for stewardship of biological life on earth (possibly an additional third against idolatry—silicon being the Golden Calf).

Certainly a deep gulf separates deists and A-theologists on matters of human value. It is doubtful, perhaps, that the two can ever communicate meaningfully on the subject at all. From the standpoint of Christian or Jewish orthodoxy, what makes human life worth preserving? Lower than angels, higher than animals, a sinful creature of somewhat ambivalent status in creation, humans are nonetheless loved by God and made in his image, and thereby invested with some inherent value, despite any physical or intellectual limitations. The orthodox believer has no reason to think that silicon-based life forms would be any more "valuable" by virtue of being smarter or more protean. (The existence of angelic hosts, for instance, does not invalidate our own.) A-Theology, of course, brings an entirely different calculus to bear on human life: it is of little ultimate worth, an evolutionary dead end.

Daniel Dennett takes his defense of the Darwinian algorithm right up to AI and memes, then stops. Dennett refers to Darwinism as the universal acid, "capable of cutting right to the heart of everything in sight." In the end, he hopes that "once it passes through everything, we are left with stronger, sounder versions of our most important ideas."[48] This means our ideas about how to think and live and structure our society: a Tao!

But Dennett has already taken it too far, and we have seen that many others keep right on going. Darwin's acid doesn't stop burning through the ideals of a good society; it burns through the foundation of any human society and finally right through the ecology that sustains any carbon-based life. The new chapter in evolution puts us out of the picture, rather sooner than we would have otherwise expected. And, as with the Reverend Jim Jones dishing out Kool-Aid for the People's Church, we are asked to be willful participants in our demise.[49]

This doesn't mean, of course, that Darwinism isn't true. But we have also seen that full-blown Darwinism is A-Theology, a mutant version of Christianity. This puts Darwinism in an awkward position. It has mapped itself so thoroughly onto Christianity that Christianity being wrong can hardly be an indication that Darwinism is right. The genuine skeptic ought to be suspicious. The orthodox believer, meanwhile, would seem to find in A-Theology nothing other than the latest, clearest, most comprehensive articulation of the Culture of Death.

The views in this essay, and any defects, are entirely my own, but special thanks are due to John Beckmann, Albert Dudley, Jonathon Long, Clifford Mayes, and Donald Taylor for invaluable help and advice.

1. C. S. Lewis, *The Abolition of Man* (Glasgow: Collins, 1990).

2. Hans Moravec, "Human Culture: A Genetic Takeover Underway," in *Artificial Life*, ed. Christopher G. Langton (Reading, PA: Addison-Wesley, 1989), 167.

3. Vernor Vinge, "The Singularity," 1993, World Wide Web site, http//ww.aleph.se/Trans/Global/Singularity.

4. J. Doyne Farmer and Alletta d'A. Belin, "Artificial Life: The Coming Evolution," in *Artificial Life*, vol. II, ed. Christopher G. Langton, et al. (Reading, PA: Addison-Wesley, 1992), 815–40.

5. Daniel Dennett, *Darwin's Dangerous Idea* (New York: Simon and Schuster, 1995), 515.

6. It is noteworthy that Dennett, despite the nonsequitur on fundamentalists, does attempt to restore something like the Tao that Lewis wrote of. See Ibid., 511–20. It is also noteworthy that Lewis concluded his own treatise with the vague hope that some new, holistic science (which sounds an awfully lot like complexity science) would be the very thing to revitalize the Tao (Lewis, *Abolition of Man*, 45–8.). Lewis's discussion here is important. He distinguishes a reverential thirst for knowledge from an alchemical, Faustian desire for power. Lewis believes these twin threads entwine themselves deeply into the history of science. We can certainly see both strains battling it out in the field of artificial life. Unfortunately, the Faustian element appears to be winning.

7. Dennett, *Darwin's Dangerous Idea*, 74–6. For a demolition of Darwinism at the molecular level and for a superb modern design argument see Michael J. Behe, *Darwin's Black Box: The Biochemical Challenge to Evolution* (New York: The Free Press, 1996).

8. See Dennett, *Darwin's Dangerous Idea*, 264–6.

9. See Ibid., 220–1.

10. See Ibid., 179–80.

11. Cosmological arguments for the existence of God have never been stronger. For the best known and most comprehensive version among evangelical Christians, see Hugh Ross, *The Creator and the Cosmos: How the Greatest Scientific Discoveries of the Century Reveal God*, 2nd ed. (Colorado Springs, CO: NavPress, 1995).

12. John D. Barrow, *Theories of Everything* (New York: Fawcett Columbine, 1991), 226–7.

13. Dennett, *Darwin's Dangerous Idea*, 180–1. This picture of theists clinging to the thin thread of final causation is disingenuous. See Ross, *Creator and the Cosmos* for vigorous cosmological arguments for design.

14. John Holland's Genetic Algorithm, and its many variations, are an excellent demonstration of this principle. See Steven Levy, *Artificial Life* (London: Penguin, 1992), 159–87.

15. John Searle, "Minds, Brains and Programs," in *The Mind's Eye*, ed. Daniel Dennett and Douglas Hofstadter (New York: Basic Books, 1984), 353–73; Roger Penrose, *The Emperor's New Mind* (New York: Penguin, 1991); Penrose, *Shadows of the Mind* (Oxford: Oxford University Press, 1989).

16. On Searle, see Dennett and Hofstadter, eds., *The Mind's Eye*, 373–82; and Dennett, *Darwin's Dangerous Idea*, 397–400. On Penrose, see Dennett, *Darwin's Dangerous Idea*, 436–49.

17. Levy, *Artificial Life*, 344.

18. Richard Dawkins, *The Selfish Gene* (Oxford: Oxford University Press, 1989), 192.

19. See Levy, *Artificial Life*, 25–9; and John Casti, *Complexification* (New York: HarperCollins, 1995), 221–3.

20. See Levy, *Artificial Life,* 32–3; and John D. Barrow and Frank J. Tipler, *The Anthropic Cosmological Principle* (Oxford: Oxford University Press, 1994), 582.

21. See Levy, *Artificial Life,* 32–42; and Barrow and Tipler, *Anthropic Cosmological Principle,* 578–86.

22. See Barrow and Tipler, *Anthropic Cosmological Principle,* 674.

23. See Ibid., 665.

24. Ibid., 675.

25. From Tielhard de Chardin, but Barrow and Tipler's version appears to be more physically sophisticated and well-defined. See Ibid., 195–205, 675.

26. Ibid., 677.

27. Levy, *Artificial Life,* 346.

28. See Levy, *Artificial Life,* 335; and Barrow and Tipler, *Anthropic Cosmological Principle,* 595.

29. See Levy, *Artificial Life,* 335.

30. See Barrow and Tipler, *Anthropic Cosmological Principle,* 595–6.

31. See Vinge, "The Singularity."

32. Moravec proposes (I can't tell how seriously) that this has already happened: silicon-based life has already hyper-evolved in space and returned to absorb our planet and its resources. But it has thoughtfully arranged to preserve us in a simulation, which we are presently experiencing! We are resurrected personoids. See Charels Platt, "Super Humanism," *Wired* (October, 1995): 202–4. According to Moravec, Platt writes, "the human race is almost certainly extinct, while the world around us is just an advanced form of SimCity." It is tempting to apply Chesterton's observation that people who stop believing in God don't believe in nothing, they believe in anything.

33. See Levy, *Artificial Life,* 344.

34. See Vinge, "The Singularity."

35. See Levy, *Artificial Life,* 87.

36. See Moravec, "Human Culture," 69.

37. Farmer and d'A. Belin, "Artificial Life," 836.

38. See Levy, *Artificial Life*, 41.

39. See Moravec in Platt, "Super Humanism," 208.

40. Barrow and Tipler venture the word "speciesism." I have suggested "carbo-centrism" elsewhere, but it hasn't caught on. Barrow and Tipler, *Anthropic Cosmological Principle*, 596.

41. See Levy, *Artificial Life*, 339–40.

42. Ibid., 336.

43. See Mitchell M. Waldrop, *Complexity* (New York: Simon and Schuster, 1992), 256–7.

44. See Levy, *Artificial Life*, 201–2. Danny Hillis introduced parasitic "Anti-ramps" into his gigantic Connection Machine simulation to spur his hill-climbing "Ramps" on to greater adaptive fitness.

45. Ibid., 163-5. It is routine to save the more fit products of the Genetic Algorithm and trash the rest.

46. See Russel Ruthen, "Adapting to Complexity," *Scientific American* (January 1993): 113. John Holland worked a tit-for-tat strategy (from the Prisoner's Dilemma) into his digital ecosystem "Echo." See Levy, *Artificial Life*, 180–4 on tit-for-tat and Prisoner's Dilemma.

47. See Levy, *Artificial Life*, 165–9. Fitness in virtual ants is determined by how well they follow increasingly difficult pheromone trails.

48. Dennett, *Darwin's Dangerous Idea*, 521.

49. An analogy with the ritual suicide of the Heaven's Gate cult would be even more apt. Like Heaven's Gate, A-Theology harbors a gnostic contempt for our frail, messy, cognitively limited biological containers. A-Theology also anticipates an "evolutionary level above human" in space. Finally, A-Theology accepts willful mass extinction as the road to transcendence. What sets A-Theology apart from Heaven's Gate is that its teachings are much more coherent, much more sophisticated, and vastly more ambitious in scope.

hardheaded move close take measu ne

virtual

smit thoughts interact

realistic act towards others

practical e s

act tog

n-to-earth

VISUAL THESAURUS

The Plumb Design Visual Thesaurus is an artistic exploration that is also a learning tool. Through its dynamic interface, this application alters our relationship with language, creating poetry through user action, dynamic typography, and design.

Visitors to the Web site encounter a swirling nebula of words connected by a series of fine lines that represent sense relationships. Eack click animates whirling constellations of words that are constantly realigning and reconfiguring themselves. Word forms that are more related become brighter and closer, those that are less related disappear from the display.

At the core of the Visual Thesaurus is WordNet, a Princeton University database of 50,000 words and 40,000 phrases organized according to psycholinguistic principles into sets of synonyms.

Written in Java, Thinkmap (the name given to the software engine) is able to interface with static and dynamic information sources via interchangeable data-interface modules, thus bridging the gap between qualitative and quantitative analysis.

http://www.plumbdesign.com/thesaurus

Outer Space or Virtual Space?

Utopias of the Digital Age

DOOMSDAY FEARS ARE growing at the brink of the new millennium. We imagine ourselves crossing the threshold of a new age while the old one with its symptoms of crisis collapses behind us. People are fascinated by the symbolic dates of an instrument called a calendar that, although spread worldwide through colonization, is nonetheless arbitrary in its setting of the Year Nil. Even without taking into consideration these magical dates—which have become a permanent source of worry and of hope in the self-proclaimed Modern Age—we believe ourselves to be in a time of fundamental change. If up until now we have been caught in a postmodern climate of nuclear threat with limits to our growth, stuck inside a sealed horizon with only a backward-looking perspective—one which at most has allowed for farewell ceremonies, incited our intellectuals to preach posthistory and condemn rationalism, provoked the boom in esoteric and other doctrines of salvation, but did not otherwise promise anything new—now, little by little, the techno-imaginary seems to be taking hold of people's minds and creating new utopias. Locked inside the wreck of Spaceship Earth, we long for an empty, untouched space to hold our utopian energies, a vacuum waiting to be filled with all our expectations. Contrary to what may have been predicted, space is again becoming an obsession in the age of virtuality.

Civil wars and wars about power over certain geographical areas are still raging—wars which seem perhaps more conspicuous and paradoxical than ever given growing globalization and virtualization—although they are no longer waged primarily for control of local resources nor for the economic power embedded in infrastructures. The more uniform the world culture becomes, the more differences between us we desire to have, whatever that may mean. While regional wars over territories are being waged to create homogeneous communities—whether ethnic, religious, or class-based—in people's minds there is much more at stake. Population growth allows for the resurfacing of an old fear: becoming a people without space. At the same time, however, we continue to destroy the biosphere at an even greater speed than after the end of the Cold War, as many countries are using the tools of capitalism and new technologies to try to reach the living and development standards of the Western world; thus international ecological standards established by nations with globalizing economies are easily overlooked if they cannot be translated directly into money. Civilization leaves behind itself scorched earth and destroyed cities. Fantasy, especially the type shown in science fiction films such as *Strange Days* or *Twelve Monkeys*, indulges in descriptions of these kinds of uninhabitable, usually urban, areas.

Strangely enough, the problems of position and location, undermined by cyberspace and its resulting globalization, lead us back into the geopolitically embedded identity of the loser. Securing position means self-assertion within a limited area. It is about a sense of "Here," an island that has to be defended against the outside. Furthermore, capitalism has been freed from its restraints and alternatives with the collapse of the communist states at the same time that both camps have lost their common enemy. The enemy, Evil, is now dispersed and has settled inside the systems, penetrating them and becoming intangible through its omnipresence. A clearly visible enemy, dwelling in the realm of Evil, unites people in spite of all their differences and makes each system's basis unassailable. However, if the visible, identifiable enemy disappears, it turns up on the inside spreading fear, insecurity, and paralysis. Governmental rules and institutions that maintain social stability through balancing acts are considered means of suppressing individuality: the common good disappears with individualism.

The feeling of being on the threshold of something materializes with the return of space although, at the same time, we dream of societies in which we can live in peace. Even those who fight against technology, wanting to lead us back into the wilderness and its immense spaces, dream of this. For example, the recently caught Unabomber shares with many Net enthusiasts the hope of creating new, comprehensible communities in which the individual still has value. The Unabomber's attacks were directed against the anonymous structures of the mass societies of the Industrial Age in order to return the possibility of autonomy to the individual on the margins of big cities and their big organizations. Even if his utopia consisted of "untamed nature" and flesh, whose importance gets recuperated in it, he also tried to revive the idea of the "frontier" and with it the omnipresent obsession for individual freedom in an open space, an idea also widespread in cyberculture.

Just like on the Internet, the huge, global playground of cyberspace, where intranets are creeping in more and more with their firewalls impeding free movement while at the same time using the Internet's infrastructure, the absolute freedom of the individual continues to be propagated while the commercialization of all areas of life, and with it increased privatization and surveillance, is creating new borders. The existential coordinates of space are inclusion and exclusion, inside and outside, your own and the strange, the foreign. If you don't want to be run over or only want to maintain and secure your borders reactively, then it seems you have to change direction: you have to set off into new spaces that you can colonize, upon which you can impose your own laws that promise freedom, wealth, and adventure, that allow you to look toward the future with hope, that provide you with a new orientation that, at least traditionally, is linked to a trajectory in space, to progress and to leaving the "cocoon."

Although European nations have performed this trajectory in the past during their periods of colonization and industrialization, they not only have had to retreat back step by step but are now facing the danger of losing their supremacy and of being outstripped by the countries they once dominated and exploited. We can already observe a maelstrom that is pulling capital, knowledge, and jobs out of the old countries. Only the ruling class in the United States seems to be able to refer back in an ungloomy way to an image of itself at the time of colonization. This is why, especially in this class, dreams of the good-old-world of the frontier that must be tamed are flourishing. Unlike Central or South America, in the United States colonization produced a new, untouched world, a "God's Country." Through the nearly complete extermination of its indigenous population and by living by the maxim that guarantees the right to the pursuit of happiness, the immigrants were liberated from their ties to their countries of origin. To many, the subjugation of the American continent, the independence from Europe, and the conquest of the Wild West still stands as a model. The taming of the frontier, the exodus of individuals and groups, and the escape from the state structures all belong to the identity of the frontiersman and constitutes, in spite of its victims, part of a national success story reinforced by the media dream world whose stories always put the individual or small group into the limelight. A great many people continue to see in these narratives a historical duty of the American nation.

However, the Wild West no longer exists and the globe has become rather small. Unrestrained expansion has come up against the limits set by nature, which is no longer conceived of as an enemy but as a subtle system upon which survival depends. It is now possible only for individuals and not entire nations to set off for new frontiers or simulate discoveries in limited geographical spaces on Earth, in the style of adventure holidays. Thus the search for a new frontier is blending more than ever into technological developments, led by America, which have not only created new possibilities here on Earth but have also permitted mankind to enter outer space and virtual space for the first time. America, the supposed land of opportunity, shall serve here only as an example to outline the contours of the techno-imaginary on a social level.

1. THE METAVERSE

The science fiction novel *Snow Crash* by Neal Stephenson gives a first look into future life on the Net and its repercussions on the urban environment. If you read Snow Crash together with Mike Davis's descriptions of Los Angeles in *City of Quartz*, you get an impression of the future of urban space that is rampant with hopes and fears. Sociology of the future has long since emigrated to science fiction. Cities and their communities are disintegrating more and more into suburban, sealed-off zones, ghettos, and defensive settlements that lock themselves up.[1]

This tendency to seal off areas and homogenize inhabitants also has its examples in history, especially in the history of utopias. Utopian towns were always small and understandable and their inhabitants were not torn apart by social conflicts. They were not towns of anonymity, of desire, of challenging social and moral conventions, or of fighting between different levels and classes of society; but rather they were places of peaceful coexistence between communities. Big city utopias, hardly ever developed, came about when the Industrial Age exploded: people started dreaming of garden towns, smaller, more closely connected units were set up to contrast against the large agglomerations and the popular image of a community was that of a village rather than an urban society, even when this only found expression in satellite towns or accommodation units. This reaction to mass society and its urban life continues in the utopias of the sixties and can be found in Marshall McLuhan's metaphor of society constituted by electronic means of communication as a "global village." Now that modern utopias based upon the individual's fulfillment within society and its transformation have failed, or rather have been abandoned, it seems possible to satisfy the desire for communal structures in cyberspace, redeemed at the same time in real space by the construction of new walls inside the dual city.

Neal Stephenson has subtly integrated into his novel as a self-evident fact of life the sociological analyses of the dual city by Saskia Sassen, Mike Davis, and Manuell Castells. Nation states and their governments only exist as powerless authorities while territories are divided up into ghettos. Everybody who wants to enter will be searched. The world is partitioned into city states, a "pluralistic" patchwork of ghettos. In *Snow Crash*, one of these ghettos is Mr. Lee's Great-Hongkong. It is not an interconnected city area but rather a random conglomerate of protected enclaves: "Mr. Lee's Great-Hongkong is a private, fully extraterritorial, independent, quasi national structure which is not recognized by other nationalities."[2] The decay of cities causes fears that force surveillance and control, isolating social classes from each other. The struggle between rich and poor, old and young, and between different ethnic groups is a daily occurrence. Political power, linked to territorial possession, is being crushed as much by local fragmentation as by internationally operating companies who base themselves in and run the global network. *Snow Crash* is set in Los Angeles, the city of the future, where growth only happens in the valleys and canyons out of which people flee, thus making it vacant for refugees who immigrate into the city: "The only ones that have stayed in the cities are the street people who feed on garbage and immigrants who have been scattered like grenade splinters by the collapse of the Asiatic empires and the techno-media priesthood of Mr. Lee's Great-Hongkong. Clever young people like David and Hiro take the risk of living in the city because they like the stimulation and know how to handle it"[3]—and because they can at any time immerse themselves into the virtual world, far more attractive than reality.

Only in the "Metaverse," the virtual city, does there still exist a limited, communal living environment of millions of people. But the social cracks of the real world are also mirrored in the virtual city. Only those who have money or possess programming competence can move freely in this parallel universe, buy private estates, and have themselves represented in tailor-made avatars. If you own a computer in Stephenson's Metaverse, and have the money to acquire land and build your house on it, you can materialize in it.

Visitors who log in from public terminals, for example, reach the endless main street of this Metaverse by passing through certain floodgates, comparable to airports. You can recognize them because their avatars are in black and white and low in resolution—in short, they are cheap looking.

2. THE IDEOLOGY OF CYBERSPACE

In efforts to colonize cyberspace we find few or no such scenarios. Dominated by what Richard Barbrook and Andy Cameron have termed the "Californian Ideology"—the belief on the right as well as the left side of the political spectrum that with the entry into cyberspace all problems will be solved automatically—people simply "forget" that cyberspace is grounded in and influences reality.[4] The paper that probably best expresses the search for a new "frontier" in cyberspace is the on-line manifesto "Cyberspace and the American Dream: A Magna Carta for the Knowledge Age," drawn up in 1994 by American conservatives of Newt Gingrich's circle under the auspices of the Progress and Freedom Foundation.[5] Although cyberspace has no real geographical ground to claim, its colonization is strongly linked to hopes of securing both position and predominance for the American nation. For us, the historical Europeans, it is doubtlessly strange to see what Barbrook and Cameron have worked out as the characteristic feature of the "Californian Ideology," namely that here liberal, individualistic, and sometimes anarchistic thoughts combine unproblematically with a glorification of capitalism and its Darwinistic principles to form an amalgam that seems to unite the new virtual class above and beyond all other differences:

> The far-reaching appeal of these West Coast ideologists doesn't only result from their contagious optimism. Above all, they are passionate representatives of an attitude that appears in an innocently liberal political form: they want the implementation of information technologies in order to create a new democracy in the spirit of Jefferson where all individuals can express themselves freely in cyberspace. While celebrating this apparently admirable ideal at the same time

these sponsors of technology reproduce some of the most diabolical characteristics of American society, especially those that are rooted in the legacy of slavery. Their utopian vision of California is based upon deliberately turning a blind eye toward the other, far less positive characteristics of life on the West Coast: racism, poverty and environmental destruction.[6]

Cyberspace is considered to be the solution to all problems in the real world, which one supposedly leaves behind by stepping over the technological threshold, and at the same time it is the continuation of the American Dream where the individual and his freedom stand above everything else—if he is successful. Therefore, cyberspace enthusiasts, probably without much reflection, regard free access to the web and freedom of expression as the redemption of democracy while at the same time neglect, or simply ignore, the living conditions of real life.

The success of cyberspace as a new utopia is not only due to technological innovations and the promises of profit that go along with it. The entry into cyberspace is interconnected, above all, with the urban reality of cities: the decay of public areas, increasing suburbanization, and the setting up of the dual city.

Cities will no longer be geographical condensations of capital, power, culture, and knowledge. They will eventually become places where you are locked up in or try to escape from, where you erect sealed-off areas, apartheid zones, secure high-tech bunkers and closed spaces that are monitored by the same technologies that are used in the construction of cyberspace. In the same way that we are penetrating the inner world of cyberspace, apartments, houses, entire city areas, and new defensive settlements are cutting themselves off from the outside, and as substitutes we construct cities in cyberspace or build parallel cities in the form of theme parks. Instead of strolling around and working in public spaces in cities, the members of the virtual class are doing so in cyberspace, permitting them to overlook the black holes and to form homogeneous communities that are eventually aimed at becoming autonomous islands with surveillance. These kinds of islands exist on Earth and are for the moment still, like Biosphere II, imperfect projects; but the fantasy of being able to leave the Earth behind and to develop new territories in cyberspace or in outer space is gaining force.

The authors of the "Magna Carta" admit, however, that even in the United States the "Third Wave" in the development of humankind after the Agricultural and Industrial Ages has yet to arrive and that we are trespassing a new territory where no rules exist. Yet they do know what the definitive conditions are for entering cyberspace toward the fulfillment of the American Dream: deregulation, competition, privatization, decentralization, and demassification of all institutions and culture at any cost, something which can only mean commercialization of everything for all those who can afford it and indifference toward those who have been left out of the information society. According to the authors, nobody knows in which direction the demassed individuals and communities will float off to, but isolated individuals will come together in "different communities" of "electronic neighborhoods" and will be bound together only by common interests and no longer by geographical closeness and common duties, except perhaps those which base themselves on the concept of the "American Way of Life," praised in an unconditional and uncritical way by the authors. The reduction and homogenization of "communities" is the great ideal behind the ideology of cyberspace. They believe that if only deregulation were pursued consistently the power of computers would be entirely in the "hands of the people," a situation that would automatically guarantee freedom from tyranny on the information highways, improvement in air quality and make it unnecessary for people to live in "overpopulated and dangerous urban areas" as a safe and private family home life would be possible.[7] Cyberspace, in the authors' opinion, is progressively turning into a marketplace where "knowledge" materializes as "product" in the form of hardware, software, competition, and information and is anchored in the renewed redemption of the "American Way of Life" and the "American Dream" as if American social conditions could be used as an example for the whole world. The danger exists that public areas and public life itself will disintegrate even more than it has already.

The authors of the "Magna Carta" are marked as much by an unconditional euphoria of individualism as by the glorification, without looking at alternatives, of competition, freed from all forms of intervention by the welfare state. Cyberspace, according to these authors, belongs to the people, not to the state; but the people in all their celebrated diversity—where social and ethnic conflicts have been eradicated—are reduced to the role of users of technologies offered by multinational companies, amongst which they can choose as if these technologies were dozens of TV programs. The "Third Wave" in the history of mankind that the authors of this liberal and individualistic manifesto want to emphasize include computer companies, biotechnological enterprises, information-based production centers and those banks and software producers who trade with information; all in all, the members of the entertainment, media, communication, education and information services sectors. In the authors' opinions these sectors will determine the society of the future. Everything else will be relegated to Third World-like places—socially and geographically left behind—or to reactionary representatives of outdated mass society. Today, the ones to act are no longer large social groups oppressed by representation or laws but, instead, highly differentiated communities "formed by individuals who celebrate their differences." These individuals are difficult to unite and don't subordinate themselves to the "rules, regulations, taxes and laws" that served the "smokestack barons and bureaucrats of the past."[8] The question is whether or not individuals are now "represented" by the multinationals, such as Microsoft, that dominate worldwide in their sectors, even if they are not as gigantic as the companies that defined the Industrial Age.

Although it is true that the need to change the conditions of property is propagated in the manifesto, only the end of copyright for intellectual property is discussed; and yet they are in favor of quicker amortization rates for taxes on hardware and software. Furthermore, the new monopolies of the consortiums with their increasing concentration, fueled by the fusion of giants in the electronics sector, are not taken seriously and are treated as a negligible quantity. On the one hand, all governmental measures that belong to the period of mass society have to disappear, but on the other hand the ideology of liberalism, pumped up once again by interactive, multimedia, big band-width computer networks, is not concerned with built-in standardizations and constraints of hardware and software.

The manifesto effusively states that computer technology has created more than a simple machine. Rather, cyberspace is said to be a "bio-electronic environment, literally universal." But it is not an environment that you enter peacefully, nor one inside which you learn to live: it invites you to conquer and is to be considered a "bioelectronic frontier zone." Finally, after the Cold War and programs like Star Wars are long over, a "new frontier" is born, the dream of an American people. "Go Cyberspace" replaces "Go West." Cyberspace is the latest American frontier. Hackers are celebrated in the same way as conquerors of new territories or outlaws were in the past, at least when they are finally integrated into the economic system after having sowed their wild oats in the new Wild West. They become "technicians" or "inventors" and later "creators of a new wealth in the form of baby companies" that, despite all the talk of universality, turn cyberspace into the economic property of certain Americans. The conquest of cyberspace follows the example set by the settlers, cowboys, heroes of the Wild West and soldiers who subjugated a continent that, in their eyes, didn't belong to anyone—pure colonialism. Forget about the Native Americans, the blood that has been shed, the slaves who worked away in the name of individual freedom. "The bioelectronic frontier is an appropri-ate metaphor for what is happening in cyberspace if we remember the spirit of invention and discovery which motivated the seafarers of old to set out on voyages of discovery, which moved the generations of pioneers to tame the American continent and which, in recent times, resulted in the exploration of space."[9]

Deregulation and the retreat of the state as a controlling organi-zation have always been the magical words of free-market liberalism—with the exception that state interventions are desirable when it comes to securing your possessions, contracts, and profits. So currently enthusiasm is centered on a stateless and bureaucracy-free cyberspace that on the one hand is supposed to belong to the people and on the other hand should secure the position of the

United States and its companies. Europeans should ask themselves whether, in spite of the fears of no longer being attractive as a location, they really want to follow this strange mixture of an individualistic and liberal sense of mission together with nationalistic emotionalism and the desire for economic dominance. Such a course would probably entail sealing off social and territorial islands of high-tech culture from the rest of society and celebrating a popular diversity that we no longer have the political means to secure. Computer networks bring with them the danger of establishing levels of political influence, and possibly suggest the dream of a direct, anarchical, democracy that has been defined up to now in territorial terms—in the form of communities, countries, and states. We are surely experiencing the slow decay of a representative and nation state-based democracy from which people, the globalized economy and the Net-integrated media are all withdrawing. Europeans have learned from their own history that utopias that are blindly embraced only produce new horrors. Cyberspace opens up a new living environment, but its success or failure will depend upon which common good, which public life, and which culture of difference will be used in the creation of an environment where everybody can coexist and where the biological survival of this planet is not endangered. Cyberspace seems to offer the chance to do everything over again, to leave the past and all the social problems of the present behind by offering a new living environment. Investments of time, capital, and passion in cyberspace will probably reduce the number of individuals who can be employed in the construction of the "real" world. The difficulty of securing jobs in a global economy combined with the fascination created by the new virtual world and its forms of action and communication could lead us to abandon reality; abandon it to the point where life inside the space of places and life inside the space of data transmissions drift increasingly apart.

But cyberspace is not an innocent place outside our world. Just as humans are anchored to the realities of their bodies, the order of the new world is fixed to the old. This "liberal" manifesto is but one more in a variety of fundamentalisms that are awakening everywhere and which base themselves in places, be they in slums or secured neighborhoods. Telepolis doesn't eliminate the space of places and of positions where the fights that take place during the colonization of the cyberspace will be manifested. The discourse about space-lessness and the destruction of space serves only to hide the fact that new spaces, new properties, and new forms of power will not only surface in cyber-space, but will be mirrored in real space as well.

3. THE INTERIM SOLUTION: BIOSPHERE II

The ultimate model of a closed, high-tech living environment not rooted to a specific place has thus far been a failure. Biosphere II, con-structed in the Arizona desert, is the latest realization of a space capsule that, separated from Earth, can be connected to other capsules only through telecommunication links. An experiment to measure how a small social com-munity behaves when cut off from the outside world, Biosphere II was intended to determine what structures would be necessary in a closed environ-ment in order to allow the new high-tech farmers to live together and survive. The farm is all that differentiates the people locked up in this terrestrial station from space travelers. As with many projects of the information society, what we find here is the hope of—in spite of the globalization of the living environ-ment—offering small, homogeneous communities a space to inhabit that pro-tects them from the conflicts of the rest of society. Cyberspace is this kind of protected space: through surveillance it can be controlled and secured. Bios-phere II is not an interface between the real world and cyberspace—it is the establishment and mirror image of cyberspace in reality. The relationship between simulation and reality begins to reverse itself. What cannot be dis-solved into virtuality is locked into capsules and connected to networks. Bios-phere II is the model for the realization of cyberspace, a sealed-off interior that is self-sufficient, just the kind of bioelectronic system praised by the authors of the "Magna Carta."

The real Biosphere II project has been moving away for quite some time now from its goal of constructing a self-sufficient survival capsule that would be fit for colonizing space, with closed cycles where only data can enter and leave. For example, during the two-year test phase a part of the team had to leave the artificial world for medical assistance and on their return they brought back equipment including computer parts and manuals. Oxygen had to be pumped into the system as it was creating too much carbon dioxide and the amount of food produced was insufficient. The labor to keep the system going, which meant planting and harvesting food, looking after the animals, and controlling plagues of cockroaches and ants didn't give the inhabitants much time for research. Biosphere II will now be turned into the world's largest laboratory for the investigation of ecological interactions whose conditions can be controlled with accuracy.

Nonetheless, Biosphere II is the realization of urban visions of isolated and self-sufficient environments in gigantic man-machine systems: a model for the living environment of tomorrow. Run like a machine, its operating principle is the perfect surveillance and control of all its components. Inspired by Buckminster Fuller's superstructures, Biosphere II is a dome made of glass and noncorrosive steel grids in which the water, air, and food cycles are absolutely closed and recycled back into the system. Sixteen hundred sensors control the climate and the composition of the air, water, and ground, sending this data to a central control system. The computer network permits a continuous representation of environmental data. Inside the system we find, apart from some humans, around four thousand different species of plants and animals, not counting the microorganisms. Biosphere II is divided into five "wild" ecosystems: tropical rain forest, savanna, coastal area, swamp, and a maritime area containing a coral reef. Beyond these, there are farming zones and living quarters for the inhabitants. Next to the main dome there are two other areas that function as the "lungs" of the system, balancing atmospheric fluctuations. The temperature is regulated from the outside by a hydological system. Electricity also comes from the exterior.

In a society of digital networks, the material and biological environment of humans will not lose its importance—as can be seen from the present high regard for the body and for nature—but it will be set up and organized around some rigid functional criteria. Following the example of Biosphere II and its parallel cities—shopping centers, malls, theme parks, and the construction of cyberspace as a virtual world—more and more functions of the exterior world will be transferred into the interior worlds of enclosed spaces. The computerization of ecosystems—the permanent surveillance by means of all kinds of sensors—primarily serves to set up warning and security systems that protect human life. The knowledge gained from this would eventually be aimed at controlling the complex ecological machinery and, this not being possible, the construction of autonomous microsystems that, closed off from the environment and under total surveillance, are run like any other technological macrosystems. The exterior serves the purpose of transporting goods and people. Nature is responsible for producing food and satisfying needs for relaxation, including the need for the aesthetic perception of nature manifested in man-made parks, nature reserves, and biotopes. The environment continues to be a resource that has to be protected in certain respects in order to maintain life in the enclosed spaces. But these spaces, thanks to their "intelligence," will become increasingly independent and autonomous, "bachelor apartments" linked to the networks of a geographically dispersed cyberspace whose "black holes" will be bridged through cable and satellite connections. These capsules are the would-be Noah's Arks of the Information Age.

4. SIDEREAL SPACE

Biosphere II is the great model for future space colonies. The project was born out of this idea, although it is also valid as a model for a new, technically possible living environment on Earth. Why should one think of the colonization of space? According to NASA, for simple biological reasons such as geographical expansion and unrestrained growth. NASA learned its lessons from history, noting that: "The main advantage of space colonies is the possibility to acquire new land without having to take it away from someone. This allows for, but doesn't guarantee, a huge expansion of humankind without wars and destruction of the Earth's biosphere."[10] By emigrating we would be able to escape overpopulation on Earth, the destruction of its biosphere and the possible impact of asteroids.

a) First Millennial Foundation

There are also private organizations that promote the colonization of outer space and wish to turn colonization into a national mission. For example, the First Millennial Foundation sees our modest destiny as bringing life to the dead stars, something that should keep us busy for at least the next thousand years. This is seen as a holy duty insofar as life would be condemned to die if it stayed earthbound. Life could be destroyed at any time by a comet or an asteroid, and, moreover, the sun is going to explode sooner or later. They say that as it is life on Earth is in deep crisis due to the population explosion. How will ten or fifteen billion people find space to live and food to eat?[11]

As usual, when trying to find simple solutions for complex problems people don't try to work out the current difficulties on Earth or analyze the relationships of power and production. More land, more living space, is the propagated solution. In fact, the first step toward colonization that this foundation proposes is the construction of floating islands in warm areas of the oceans. According to proponents of such a scheme, the islands would form automatically if a conductive metal were to be brought into contact with the water and electricity run through it. The dissolved minerals in the water would then join to the metal and form thick layers of artificial limestone. If metal constructions were then added to strengthen these formations, together with electrical wire netting, a sufficiently solid base for floating islands could result. The people inhabiting these islands would live off the sea, cultivating fish and algae, producing energy in an environmentally-friendly way. At the moment, the oceans appear to be "empty continents" and "biological deserts," but life on such floating islands, swimming in warm tropical seas, would be very pleasant. As life would develop around the same environmentally-friendly principles that are employed in these closed cycles, we are promised security because the colonies will be "relatively free from crime and other evils which we see dominating the cities." This is so because we are talking about "a community of closely related individuals," in other words, a nonurban community. The ocean colonies will prepare us for life both in closed systems and "isolated and highly integrated communities," a prerequisite for leaving this planet.[12]

b) NASA: Space Settlement Basics

For institutional reasons of self-preservation, the people at NASA obviously want to promote the idea of colonizing space. Although they still continue the important activity of launching satellites—hundreds of which are now orbiting Earth—since the end of the Cold War expensive manned space programs have been drastically reduced. In their eyes, space travel has to become something available to everybody and not only to highly qualified specialists. Only when space flights have become safe and inexpensive can thousands or millions of people take the opportunity of giving relief to our planet. After all, one hundred years ago nobody had ever traveled by plane, while at present some five hundred million people are flying every year.

There are groups for whom the colonization of space has been touted as especially attractive. For example, it has been suggested that being in space without the burden of gravity could be advantageous for the handicapped. It would also be possible to send involuntary colonists to space colonies—relatively inescapable prisons, as islands were in former times. This seems a rather obvious idea, although perhaps not in the way that the authors at NASA had intended, given that space colonies will always be prisons, even when constructed as protective settlements. The authors also suggest that space colonies would be appropriate for some religious groups not wanting to live near nonbelievers or else for those who would like to experiment with new types of social or political forms.[13]

Biosphere II is once again the obvious model: a scientifically produced independent environment with closed cycles. The authors at NASA suggest, however, that with space colonies it may be necessary to take at least some oxygen and a little food. Anyway, the idea wouldn't be to go straight into colonizing planets or even the Moon. Rather, the first step would be to have gigantic containers orbiting the Earth so that people could at least still see and maybe even visit her. Only later would we spread ourselves around in the solar system or move to distant stars, for to later generations proximity to earth won't matter anymore. NASA's authors do not go into detail here about the technical realization of their suggestions. They put their money on nanotechnology, which will do everything by itself, and even make possible the building of an "orbital tower" rising from the Earth's surface into space. In this way, materials and people could be brought by elevator into orbit with minimum expense. And even if everything would take lots of time and money, one has to remember that "New York, California and France" weren't built in a day and "Canada, France and San Francisco" cost a lot of money too.[14]

We have already learned some of the reasons why outer space will be "a nice place to live." But the authors list several additional reasons, the first being aesthetic: a "nice view." Not clouded by air pollution, from out there you can enjoy the marvelous panorama of the solar system and revel in the beauty of Earth. Secondly, the reduced gravity would be ideal for dancing and sports, two extremely attractive reasons for leaving Earth.[15] But naturally, there are more.

The third has to do with freeing ourselves from our interdependence with the environment, given that, unfortunately, living on Earth means sharing only one biosphere and suffering the ecological crimes committed by others. As every space colony would be totally sealed off from the next, the global ecological effects of one colony's risk-taking would not affect the others'.[16] The fourth reason is paradigmatic and I quote it in its entirety:

> On Earth different groups have to learn how to live together very closely. It requires a great effort to live together with five or six billion homosapiens and some people don't tolerate this very well. Space colonies offer an alternative to trying to change human nature and to endless conflicts. The possibility of living in almost completely homogeneous communities as was the normal form of human existence during millions of years. Those who cannot adapt to living so close together have the opportunity of cutting themselves off from others by millions of kilometers of the finest vacuum, something that sometimes seems like a necessary thing. Access to space colonies would be through air gates and thus immigration control wouldn't play an important role."[17]

Up to now we can only choose amongst limited options of what the place where we want to live is going to look like. This "having-to-restrict-oneself" is very difficult to bear for genuine space travelers who are all individualists and builders of worlds, striving for their own personal happiness. I will now quote the fifth reason, unable to formulate it better:

> As the entire environment will have been created by man, you will be able to obtain whatever you want. Would you like an estate on a lake? Then simply build lakes. Do you love sunsets? Then program simulations of hourly sunsets into the weather system. Do you like walking barefooted? Then just make the whole environment foot-friendly.[18]

Perhaps none of this is meant to be taken seriously, and is only a satire on all those early dreams of emigration. In any case, the spirit of our times is reflected in these "Space Settlement Basics," on NASA's Web site—even though its administrators may not even realize they have been posted. But there are others who obviously do take one thing dead seriously: the American dream of a new frontier intertwined with the colonization of space.

c) Welcome to the Revolution: The Space Frontier Foundation

The Space Frontier Foundation, based in New York City, is an association of American citizens who are strongly represented on the Internet. The foundation maintains a mailing list and publishes the series "The Frontier Files." It demands the colonization of space as soon as possible; otherwise humankind will perish. For them, the United States, as the "Frontier Nation," has a special responsibility in this area. In an effort to arouse national pride, the foundation claims that America is getting nervous at the end of the twentieth century. There are too many doubts in the "greatest nation that has ever existed." The Cold War having ended, people need a new "vision of tomorrow" that offers something better than what we have in the present. According to the foundation, Americans are "a nation of pioneers without a new frontier.

There is no longer a clear, exterior enemy around which they could organize. History is repeating itself." In other words, times are bad.[19]

Too many people see the future as obstructed. Images of a declining culture, in large part of cities in decay—as in the film *Blade Runner*—haunt us. Unemployment, poverty, social struggles, the retreat into the private sphere, and decreasing living standards produce insecurity, fear, and individualism. America is falling apart. The Space Frontier Foundation has the solution:

> The USA has to acknowledge the philosophical discrepancy between the things the nation should be doing in space and the things which we are in fact doing at the moment. Then we would be able to re-formulate our misguided space program into a new one that is more comprehensive, more exciting and more profitable. By putting these changes into practice, we, who understand the chance that the space frontier offers us, can provide America with a new image of its future—a future full of hope, an exciting future that motivates the entire society. A future of continuously expanding options.[20]

The finite, whether in space or time, seems to be very difficult to bear. The future has to progress in the form of a continuously rising curve, otherwise everything falls apart, just like the capitalist market when it stops growing. In the same way that a nation fighting an external enemy grows closer in times of war, the "emptiness of space" is supposed to generate a new type of society that will include everyone.

But what was it like in the old days when the Wild West was being colonized? Was a new type of society created? Were new towns founded without suppressing others? The facts of real history have little relevance. In the foreground we have the wave that colonized the land (including its inhabitants) under the hopeful slogan "Go West." However:

> Twenty-five years after Lewis & Clark railway carriages rolled into the West toward Oregon, thousands of pioneers were brought from

the boats to the Californian coast…25 years after the Wright Brothers, people could buy a plane ticket and fly around in airplanes…but 25 years after having landed on the Moon, we still sit in front of the TV watching old astronauts remembering the good old days."[21]

Things have to look up eventually in regards to morale as well as space. The ideology of "sustained development," directed toward the preservation of the biosphere, is said to be paralyzing people when what is needed is the creation of "a new age of continuously growing hope." Once we commit to the vision of colonizing space, which can only be positive given that space hasn't been colonized yet and because in this way we also protect our biosphere, then the questions of where we are going as a race, how we fit into the big picture and what we have to do next will no longer have any importance.

The only thing we will have to do will be to direct our gaze toward the thousands of stars in the night sky and we will find the answer. And the world is going to follow us. Because we are a nation of pioneers, this is our new country. And because we are all capable of doing this, it is high time that we are given the opportunity to prove it.[22]

But who is standing in the way? The state is, because it is impeding access to space. Viewed purely as a means of oppression and not as an institution that exercises democratic procedures and social balancing acts, the state cannot open the way into the future. This can only be done, in the well-known capitalistic and individualistic style, by those concerned with the pursuit of happiness and profit—as deregulated as possible. Space as the new Wild West. America, according to this foundation, is a nation of free people, united by the belief that "man comes before the state and should have the right to create new riches, unimpeded by the state." The West was won using such a doctrine. The Foundation doesn't explain, however, how this typical, anti-state, extreme individualism can go hand in hand with the creation of new communities. It believes that if only individuals and companies were left alone in the "marvelous chaos of the free, democratic entrepreneurial system," then prosperity, freedom, and a better life for all would be possible. Like at one time in the Wild West, money is the exclusive driving force: "without profit there will be no new goal."[23]

As with the propagandists of cyberspace, the Space Frontier Foundation links the colonization of space to individualism, which is always identified with a free, capitalistic market and the reduction of the state. Deregulation is the only maxim of happiness. Public life doesn't matter so long as it doesn't generate money. Individuals have to be successful and win, otherwise they will be lost and relegated to oblivion like the Indians were in their time. Freedom only means freedom of the market; in other words, competition. In this amalgam, typical of our times, utopias can only sustain themselves while moving forward, and cannot describe the place that will emerge at the end, let alone formulate collective rules of how it is to be socially organized in an acceptable way. The anti-state attitude and the orientation toward triumphant individuals, groups, and communities is much too strong. What then will the colonies in space and cyberspace look like? Not much different from those in the real world that are increasingly marked by the same maxims of capitalistic individualism and deregulation—like adventure parks, Disney Worlds and shopping centers, like suburban areas that spread around old cities without providing urban life, like cyberspace, increasingly commercialized and marked by private organizations with their intranets and fee zones. In a nutshell, like the way Mike Davis and others describe the future of our cities: breaking apart into segments, citadels, and scanscapes under the pressure of multinationals and the new virtual class.[24] Scanscapes, according to Mike Davis, are protected areas, models for all biospheres and space colonies, and serve homogeneous communities in which every step is being monitored in order to ensure against any foreign intrusion.

1. Neal Stephenson, *Snow Crash* (Munich: Goldman Verlag, 1995); Mike Davis, *City of Quartz* (New York: Vintage Books, 1992).

2. Stephenson, *Snow Crash,*119.

3. Ibid.,223.

4. Richard Barbrook and Andy Cameron, "The Californian Ideology," May 1996, World Wide Web site, http://www.wmin.ac.uk/ media/HRC/ci/calif.html.

5. "Cyberspace and the American Dream: A Magna Carta for the Knowledge Age," release 1.2, 22 August 1994, World Wide Web site, http://www.pff.org/ pff/position.html. The site is sponsored by the Progress and Freedom Foundation.

6. Barbrook and Cameron, "The Californian Ideology."

7. "Magna Carta."

8. Ibid.

9. Ibid.

10. NASA World Wide Web site, http://nas.nasa.gov/ Services/Education/SpaceSettlement/Basics/wwwwh. html#who.

11. First Millennial Foundation World Wide Web site, http://www.millenial.org/intro/faq.htm.

12. Ibid.

13. "Space Settlement Basics," NASA World Wide Web site, http://www.nas.gov/NAS/SpaceSettlement/ Basics/ wwwwh.html

14. Ibid.

15. Ibid.

16. Ibid.

17. Ibid.

18. Ibid.

19. Space Frontier Foundation World Wide Web site, http://www.space-frontier.org/.

20. Ibid.

21. Ibid.

22. Ibid.

23. Ibid.

24. Mike Davis, *Urban Control* (Pamphlet 23, Open Magazine Pamphlet Series) (NJ: Open Media, 1992).

Changing Space: Virtual Reality

as an Arena of Embodied Being

CHAR DAVIES

THE MEDIUM OF "immersive virtual space" or virtual reality—as it is generally known—has intriguing potential as an arena for constructing metaphors about our existential being-in-the-world and for exploring consciousness as it is experienced subjectively, as it is *felt*. Such environments can provide a new kind of "place" through which our minds may float among three-dimensionally extended yet virtual forms in a paradoxical combination of the ephemerally immaterial with what is perceived and bodily felt to be real.

My work as an artist explores VR's capacity for refreshing our "ways of seeing" through the design of immersive virtual environments unlike those of our usual sensibilities. OSMOSE (1994–95) is an interactive, "fully immersive," virtual environment that uses a stereoscopic head-mounted display, three-dimensionally localized interactive sound, and an embodying interface driven by the user's breath and balance. There are nearly a dozen "realms" in OSMOSE, metaphorical reconstructions of "nature" as well as philosophical texts and software code. The visual elements within these realms are semi-transparent and translucent.[1]

Since mid 1995, more than five thousand people have been immersed in OSMOSE. The overall effect on immersants appears to be quite complex. Many of their responses are surprising in terms of emotional intensity, ranging from euphoria to tears of loss. The experience of seeing and floating through things, along with the work's reliance on breath and balance as well as on solitary immersion, causes many participants to relinquish desire for active "doing" in favor of contemplative "being." In comparing their reactions with those generated by psychological research into traditionally-induced altered states of consciousness, I have come to believe that full-body immersion in an "unusual" virtual environment can potentially lead to shifts in mental awareness. That this may be possible has many implications, some promising, some disturbing.[2]

CHANGING SPACE

Thirty years ago, in *The Poetics of Space*, the philosopher Gaston Bachelard examined the psychologically transformative potential of "real" environments like the desert, the plains, and the deep sea, immense open spaces unlike the urban environments to which most of us are accustomed:

> By changing space, by leaving the space of one's usual sensibilities, one enters into communication with a space that is psychically innovating. For we do not change place, we change our nature.[3]

Bachelard's poetic insight into the psychological effects of "changing space" is echoed by psychologists documenting the effects of traditional contemplative practices in terms of altering states of consciousness. According to Arthur Deikman's "Deautomatization and the Mystic Experience," the conditions fostered by such practices involve a dehabituating or "de-automatizing" of perceptual sensibilities.

Deautomatization is an undoing of psychic structure permitting the experience of increased detail and sensation at the price of requiring more attention. With such attention, it is possible that deautomatization may permit the awareness of new dimensions of the total stimulus array—a process of *"perceptual expansion."*

...Deautomatization is here conceived as permitting the adult to attain a new, *fresh* perception of the world by freeing him from a stereotyped organization built up over the years and by allowing adult synthetic functions access to fresh materials. The general process of deautomatization would seem of great potential usefulness whenever it is desired to break free from an old pattern in order to achieve *a new experience of the same stimulus or to open a perceptual avenue to stimuli never experienced before.*[4] (italics added)

This dehabituating of perception tends to occur as a result of certain psychological conditions, such as when the participant's *attention is intensified* and is directed toward sensory pathways; when there is an absence of controlled, analytic thought; and when the participant's attitude is one of *receptivity* to stimuli rather than defensiveness or suspicion.[5]

Most often attained through rigorous training in age-old meditation techniques (drug-induced experiences are outside the scope of this essay), such conditions lead to an undoing of habitual perceptions—in favor of alternative sensibilities. While these may be less efficient in terms of biological or psychological survival, psychologists believe that they permit experience of aspects of reality previously ignored. The experience of these unusual sensibilities includes:

- an intense sense of "realness," as when inner stimuli become more real than objects
- transcendence of time and space
- unusual modes of perception

- feelings of undifferentiated unity or merging (e.g.; a breakdown of distinctions between things and/or the self and the world)
- ineffability or verbal indescribability
- a profound sense of joy or euphoria
- a paradoxical sense of being in and out of the body[6]

OSMOSE: BREATHING IN AND LETTING GO

These "unusual" sensations are eerily similar to what many people claim they have experienced during immersion in OSMOSE. Among the responses we have gathered through written comments, correspondence, and video interviews, a substantial number of participants have reported the following:

- a feeling that they had indeed been somewhere else, in another "place"
- losing track of time (a fifteen minute session was nearly always experienced as five, a thirty minute session as ten)
- heightened awareness of their own sense of being, or as one immersant described it: "as consciousness embodied, occupying space"[7]
- a deep sense of mind/body relaxation
- an inability to speak rationally or put logical words together afterward
- a feeling of freedom from their physical bodies and an acute awareness of them at the same time
- intense emotional feelings, including euphoria and/or an overwhelming sense of loss when the session was ending, causing some to cry and others to exclaim they were no longer afraid of dying

In addition, we have observed a pattern of behavior among participants during immersion. After becoming accustomed to the interface of

breath and balance, most people become intent on "doing," traveling around to see as much as possible in what appears to be an extension of everyday goal-oriented, action-based behavior. After ten minutes or so, however, most undergo a change: their facial expressions and body gestures loosen, and instead of rushing, they slow down, mesmerized by their own perceptions within the space. In this final phase, attention seems to be directed toward the unusual sensations of floating and seeing through things in what becomes a kind of slow-motion perceptual "free-fall."

What is going on here?

If these responses are anything to go by, then it appears that immersive virtual space, as evidenced by OSMOSE, can indeed be "psychically innovating," to use Bachelard's words. Why? The answer lies in the very nature of immersive virtual space. Here, ephemeral virtuality coexists with an apparent three-dimensionality of form, and feelings of disembodiment can coexist with those of embodiment (given the use of an embodying interface as in OSMOSE). These paradoxical aspects, in combination with the ability to kinesthetically interact with the elements within the space, create a very unusual experiential context.

I want to emphasize, however, that the medium's perception-refreshing potential is possible only to the extent that a virtual environment is designed to be *unlike* those of our usual sensibilities and assumptions. In OSMOSE, for example, the immersant can unexpectedly see through things and float through them as well. Thus the "familiar" becomes the unusual. This creates room for other modes of perception: instead of the mind being on autopilot it begins to pay attention, in the present, to what is unusual and unknown.

OSMOSE does not reconstruct the world as we habitually perceive it (as empty space containing solid, static, hard-edged, and separate objects, with rigid distinctions between subject, object, figure and ground). Instead, OSMOSE uses transparency and luminous particles to "desolidify" things and dissolve spatial distinctions. When the immersant moves within the space, multiplicities of semitransparent, three-dimensional forms as well as abstract foreground "flecks" combine to create perceptual ambiguity and slippages between figure and ground, near and far, inside and out. Compared to the all too familiar literal representational style commonly associated with three-dimensional computer graphics, this more evocative aesthetic intensifies the perceptual and cognitive process.

For the user-interface, a method was developed that relies on the participant's own breath and balance rather than on conventional, hand-oriented methods such as joystick, wand, trackball, or glove—all of which tend to support a distanced and disembodied stance toward the world. This approach, based on breathing in to rise, out to fall, and leaning to change direction, brings the experience inward, "grounding" it within the core of the participant's physical body. Conceptually informed by the scuba diver's practice of buoyancy control, this hands-off technique "frees" participants from the urge to handle and control the world of "objects."[8] This approach was intended to "reaffirm" the role of the subjectively-experienced, "felt" body in cyberspace, in direct contrast to its usual absence or objectification in virtual worlds. The use of breathing and balance also tends to deeply relax people, creating a tranquil state of mind and body.

The feelings reported by various participants were probably intensified by the solitary nature of the experience, as well as by the fact that the work is "fully immersive," (its space is perceived as totally enveloping, due to our use of a wide-field-of-view head-mounted display.) These aspects, in combination with the three-dimensionality of the work and the fluid, interactive sound, act to amplify the embodied yet virtual nature of the experience.

While the psychological effects of full-body immersion in a computer-generated virtual environment like OSMOSE have yet to be scientifically analyzed, the potential of the medium to dehabituate our sensibilities and allow for a resensitization of the perception of being invites further exploration.

IMPLICATIONS

Not to be forgotten is the possibility of the medium's potency being used to replace bodily experiences of the "real" with phantasms of virtual utopias. In her preface to *Rethinking Technologies*, Verona Conley writes about our loss of "humanness" in the wake of the world "becoming technological."[10]

> In view of the grim prospect of the twenty-first century, we are compelled to ask how critics of culture, philosophers, and artists will deal with technologies. How do they contend with expansionist ideology, and the accelerated elimination of diversity and of singularities? How do they resist or act?…Now, in a world where the notion of space has been completely changed through electronic simultaneity, where the computer appears to go faster than the human brain, or where "virtual reality" replaces "reality," how do philosophy, critical theory, or artistic practices deal with those shifts?[10]

This question aptly applies to immersive virtual space, especially when one considers that it will one day likely be used for such (questionable) purposes as adapting individuals to psychological and biological survival in a less and less "user-friendly" living environment. Moreover, unlike Bachelard's desert or deep sea, Deikman's meditation cell, or even an isolation tank, VR

is a communicative medium, which by default carries conventional cultural values of the Western technoscientific worldview from which that technology has sprung.

The beginnings of an answer to Conley's question may have been formulated by Martin Heidegger more than fifty years ago in *The Question Concerning Technology*. As an alternative to what he called technology's tendency to function as an instrument of domination and control, Heidegger pointed to an earlier form of "techne" called "poiesis" by the Greeks, associated not with "challenging" but with a "bringing-forth" or "revealing" into presence. The Greeks considered this artistic activity to be somewhat equivalent to what they called *physis* or nature's own bursting forth of being.[11] I find inspiration here in terms of the use of immersive virtual space as a medium for "bringing forth" or "manifesting" abstract ideas into the realm of virtual "place" so that they can be kinesthetically explored and bodily lived.

This may prove to be a promising use of the medium, and, given effective subversion of its culturally-bound characteristics, may be a step toward suggesting alternative ways of seeing and being in the world. However, even so, there remains a significantly disheartening aspect. For even as "places" like OSMOSE may one day be accessible on line as virtual sites of contemplation, so too such sites may signal the demise of traditional places of self-reflection and tranquillity. In particular this includes "nature" as we know it, as compromised in body and habitat by human activities, nature's unfathomable presences recede further and further from our urban lives. My own practice in the field of "virtual reality" thus contains a bittersweet aspect, entangled in feelings of both longing and loss.

This paper was presented in abridged form at Consciousness Reframed, 1st CAiiA Research Conference, Centre for Advanced Inquiry in the Interactive Arts, University of Wales College, Newport, Wales, July 1997 and at Beyond Shelter: The Future of Architecture, The Graham Foundation, Chicago, IL, Sept. 1997. It is partially based on the presentations "Soul in the Machine: OSMOSE—The Paradox of Being in Immersive Virtual Space" and "OSMOSE as Metaphor: Alternative Aesthetics and Interaction in Immersive Virtual Space" delivered at the annual meeting of the Association for Computing Machinery (ACM) Special Interest Group in Graphics, New Orleans, LA, Aug. 1996.

1. OSMOSE was designed as an alternative to the dominant aesthetic and interactive sensibility of virtual reality. The work was created by myself, John Harrison, and Georges Mauro, with sound by Rick Bidlack and Dorota Blaszczak, and was produced by Softimage between 1994 and 1995. Public installations of the work were made in an intimate enclosed immersion area with a darkened visitor space. Visitors were able to "witness" each immersive journey from the immersant's point of view as it took place via live audiovisual connection. Adjacent to the video projection was a live shadow projection of the immersant, providing an associative link between his or her body as conduit for lived experience, and the work's consequent imagery and sound. For a more detailed description, see "OSMOSE: Notes on Being in Immersive Virtual Space," paper delivered at the 6th International Symposium on Electronic Art, Montreal,

September 1995; and Char Davies and John Harrison, "OSMOSE—Towards Broadening the Aesthetics of Virtual Reality," in *ACM Computer Graphics* 30, no. 4 (November 1996): 25–8.

2. The subjective experience of being spatially enveloped or immersed in a virtual environment is key to my work and the views expressed in this paper. By "immersion" or "immersive virtual space" I specifically mean immersion within a spherically 360-degree, totally enveloping virtual space, implying a "being within." In my experience with VR, such sensation of envelopment is possible only through the wearing of a head-mounted display helmet with a wide field of view. While the word "immersive" is currently being used by the industry to describe wraparound screens and domes (creating what I consider to be nonimmersive experiences) my use of the word "immersive" denotes a *totally* enveloping virtual space.

3. Gaston Bachelard, *The Poetics of Space* (Boston, MA: Beacon Press, 1966), 206. For Bachelard's discussion on the psychologically transforming qualities of immense open spaces such as the sea, desert, and plains, see pp. 203–10.

4. Arthur Deikman, "Deautomatization and Mystical Experience," and "Experimental Meditation" in *Altered States of Consciousness*, Charles Tart, ed. (New York: HarperCollins, 1990) 50, 262–3. Note that in terms of "receptivity" to OSMOSE, I have been told by at least one individual that although she was intellectually skeptical when she went in, "something

happened" and much to her surprise she became entranced. This points to the medium's potency, for better and worse.

5. Deikman, "Deautomatization," 52.

6. Ibid., 47–55.

7. Y. Karim, personnel correspondence with the author, September 1995. "OSMOSE heightened an awareness of my body as a site of consciousness and of the experience and sensation of consciousness occupying space."

8. This method was partially informed by my own practice of scuba diving in the deep sea, certainly a "psychically innovating space" as Bachelard suggested. Diving at depths of 200 feet over a 6,000 foot abyss introduced me to the experience of being within an almost pure, abstract yet sensuously enveloping space, where when there is nothing to "look at" perceptual and cognitive distinctions between near and far, inside and out, really do dissolve. While diving, navigation and buoyancy are achieved through subtle and skillful use of breath and balance, and the use of hands is discouraged. There are other relevant comparisons between diving and immersive virtual environments, such as the donning of heavy gear in order to access such spaces, as well as the necessity of limiting the length of the experience in order to avoid possible dangers to one's health.

9. Verona Conley, preface to V (1993), in Re-Thinking Technologies, Verona Conley, ed. (Minneapolis, MN: University of Minnesota Press, 1993), ix.

10. Ibid., xii.

11. In its most prevalent form, immersive virtual reality can be considered to be "a literal re-enactment of Cartesian ontology." Richard Coyne, "Heidegger & Virtual Reality: The Implications of Heidegger's Thinking for Computer Representation," Leonardo 27, no. 1, (1994): 66–75. In terms of visuals, most real-time three-dimensional computer graphic techniques are based on representing "hard-edged solid objects in empty space"—in a combination of low-level mimetic realism, Cartesian space, and Renaissance perspective. In virtual environments the human subject is usually reconstructed as an omnipotent and isolated viewpoint maneuvering in empty space and probing objects with an acquisitive hand. Interactivity in many commercial computer games involves adrenaline-producing high-speed action and aggression. These approaches tend to reinforce a Cartesian way of seeing the world in terms of emphasizing the separation of subject over object, mind over body, and the world as "standing-reserve." For a discussion about the world being reduced to "standing-reserve" for human consumption, see Martin Heidegger "The Question Concerning Technology," in The Question Concerning Technology & Other Essays (New York: Harper & Row, 1977), 17–27. The imperative to master and control is not surprising given the technology's origins, not only in value-wise in the Western philosophic tradition, but instrumentally in the military as well.

You slay the victim with technology, and
resurrect the victim through art.

–William Irwin Thompson

Virtual Reality and the Tea Ceremony

MICHAEL HEIM

INTRODUCTION

The Internet explosion of the 1990s belongs to the more general lust for explosions that characterizes this era. Click, bang, click bang: one screen after another explodes. Like contemporary action films, the computer network enjoys a huge success because of its dynamism. Users identify with the nonlinear action where a surprise awaits around every corner. Pictures, video, voice, and animation create a hypermedia whirl that pops up like a kaleidoscopic circus. The World Wide Web brims with adventure, high impact, and a sensory bombardment not unlike the worlds of *Raiders of the Lost Ark* or *Total Recall*. But while action films reach back to linear narrative akin to Homeric story-telling, today's information tools have the look and feel of something new. The earlier linear modes of perception are broken by random-access action laced with information.

Soon enough, however, even the veteran Net surfer grows tired of speed thrills and choppy surfaces. The tide is already turning toward information design with greater depth, sense of place, and the quiet grace of painting and literature. As the look and feel of the new media finds its own niche in cultural life, designers will want to expand information systems to include virtual worlds that draw on the soothing, contemplative aspects of predigital media. Technological thrills will cloy until we can inject some of the meditative profundity of the Victorian novel or the landscapes of Camille Corot onto the Internet. This essay is a thought experiment to prepare for the not-too-distant future when hardware and software will make possible such scenarios.

The meditative tools of the linear past offer a contrasting resource for hypermedia. This was the argument I made in *Electric Language*, a book that contrasted the word processor on which it was written with the former methods of writing on typewriters and with pen on paper.[1] By understanding the contrasting powers of media, I argued, we can produce a richer complementary unity. In the present essay, I want to project onto the Internet a sensibility and style that contrasts sharply with the love of explosion. Instead of explosions, I want to advance for the Internet the grace and minimal spaces of Zen.

Zen, originally a Chinese spiritual development known in China as Ch'an Buddhism, was imported to the United States from Japan as Zen Buddhism in the early twentieth century. Zen arose when Indian gurus arrived in sixth-century B.C. China to teach their religion in northern Asia. Over time, the indigenous Chinese Taoists reshaped Buddhism to their needs, making it more practical and down to earth. Today, Zen enjoys a fashionable respect in Western culture. Bookstores in shopping-malls carry volumes on the Zen of programming, the Zen of negotiating, and the Zen of motorcycle maintenance. Business managers read about Zen management, though the Samurai they imagine live only in Hollywood. Most of our popular Zen has been adapted to fit Western values and remains a fantasy Zen. Cultures adapt what they adopt.

Westerners often see explosions in Zen. The explosion of "instant enlightenment" does run through Zen literature, but Westerners often mistake the flash of *satori* for instant coffee: spoon out some ideas, add a little water, and stir to arrive at enlightenment. What often goes unmentioned are the long hours of patient practice that prepare practitioners of Zen for the shock of immediate understanding. After all, Zen practice requires daily physical exertion. Many of us who teach Tai Chi Chuan in the West have come to appreciate how slanted the Western psyche is toward mental rather than physical understanding: here the understanding of the body is left largely to athletes. In fact, in the West even Zen has been treated as a figment of the mind, as a tricky belief system or lifestyle. Alan Watts and Aldous Huxley popularized a mind Zen that belonged more to hippie drug experiments or Asian cultural studies than to actual physical, sensuous body discipline. Going beyond the easy references of shopping-mall Zen means that we encounter a sensitivity that continues to escape our dominant sensibility.

In exploring the Zen of the Internet, we must learn to think sensuously and physically. We must become aware of autonomic physical activities like breathing and body balance. We must notice our posture, our finger movements, and the way our eyes move in their sockets. We must begin thinking of computer work as a somatic process with psychic overtones. As more activities move into virtual worlds, the computer interface becomes as important a place in our culture as those earlier sacred places that housed a shrine, a temple, an altar. The computer is a place for self-transformation. We need to look carefully at what transpires in us as we enter virtual worlds.

At this stage, the Zen of the Internet alerts us to our practices. Since most of our practices tend to be outwardly directed, we need to jog our awareness by looking carefully at practices for awakening the inward senses. Our thought experiment can help jog our awareness as we try to import an alien and contrasting sensibility. The contrast I have in mind comes from the ceremonial gentleness of the Japanese tea ritual. This sharp contrast to the cult of explosion is an alien form—as alien to contemporary Japan as to the West. Precisely this alien quality is what begs us to import the tea ceremony into Internet culture. The Internet calls for design projects that translate the depth, refined rhythm, and the strong sense of place achieved by the Way of Tea.[2]

Some people fear the Internet as a form of cultural and intellectual strip mining. The Internet is indeed dynamite. It delivers high-speed access to the wealth of cultural life independent of geography, and it is free of the physical distances that once supported intellectual privacy. With intense interest, we watch today's Internet as it adds a new dimension to world culture. A computer system has emerged that forever changes our communications. And because it is based on computer software, this system will increasingly break ever new ground in computer-generated realism. Video and audio depiction plus interactive communication lead to a whole range of shared experiences. And these experiences already cut across national and cultural boundaries. The World Wide Web provides the first fully global participatory technology. It is not based on the broadcasting model of one-way communication. Instead, it brings a network model of individuals who create nodes of shared meaning in geographically remote, virtual communities.

But we must not be too quick to apply the word "community" to the groups that gather via interactive communications. The very term "electronic community" is problematic because it masks the ephemeral, even alienating features of everything electronic. I say "ephemeral and alienating" because I have in mind a contrast with community as the world religions built it over centuries. The *"communitas"* created around the medieval monasteries, for example, insisted on geographical stability and long-term living arrangements that have nothing of the ephemeral, remote telepresence of electronically formed communities. The notions we have of community still depend, by and large, on a pre-technological sensibility where human relations develop over time and through geographical proximity. We need to proceed cautiously to supplement primary communities rather than replace them with virtual communities.

One of demands, then, on our evolving sense of community is to think out ways in which we can translate communal traditions into the electronic environment. While an electronic environment does not offer the stability and proximity of traditional communities, we can still learn more about what constitutes an environment if we try to translate traditional communal experiences onto the Internet. Just as we learn more about our own language when we learn to translate it into a foreign tongue, so too we learn more about how to shape electronic environments when we build traditional communal experiences into Internet sites. We must keep in mind, too, that the Internet exists in the mid-1990s at an early stage of development. What we call "virtual reality" on the Internet remains a far cry from the fully immersive environments that already exist in experimental form outside the small bandwidth of today's Internet.

At the moment, the Internet receives its shape largely from previous media. Metaphors from earlier media typically help us understand new modes of communication, and as the Internet gates open to commercial markets, broadcasting professionals have landed on the Internet in large numbers. Broadcasting, because of its one-way approach to communication, has created an artistic bazaar that effectively bars viewers from participating in the creation and cultivation of atmosphere. Yet even while the broadcasting model extends to the Internet, the very tools themselves are changing the way advertisers think about delivering their messages. Internet communities, as they appear in seed, depend on the interactive creation of spatial atmosphere. People virtualize information, for example, through the spatial metaphors they apply to the World Wide Web. The Web exists in "cyberspace"; people create their "home pages" on the Web; a business establishes its "Web site"; and so on to "virtual cities" and "virtual campuses." The language is a language of place, location, spatiality.

The language of space is not just so much gassy metaphor. It suggests the basis of the new kinds of community. Through these spatial metaphors, we are seeking to inhabit electronic environments. They are metaphors of dwelling, of inhabiting, of making cyberspace a place of our own. Of course, computer designers since Douglas Engelbart and Steve Jobs have learned that physical metaphors—from windows to scrolling to spreadsheets— play a central role in adapting computing machinery to human ergonomics. But such physical metaphors cease to be mere metaphors when we actually spend much of our time "out there," associating with electronic "neighbors" and cultivated email friends. Pragmatically speaking, the computer environment becomes a place where we live and work, play and invest. A home or communal dwelling can have a place for broadcast messages, but the habitation is not a product of broadcasting. We may have a television or radio at home, but we restrict it to its place within our living space. So too, our cyberspace may have a place for broadcasting as long as broadcasting knows its place.

The question then becomes, how can we learn to inhabit cyberspace as a space of atmospheric depth? Furthermore, how can we build spaces that protect highly prized cultural values? One value, for instance, is nature, which seems excluded from electronic space. How can we, for instance, preserve a respect for the natural world when we inhabit computer space?

Both issues of dwelling space and the place of nature arise when we think about how to virtualize the traditional Japanese tea ceremony, which is known in Japan as *sadô* or *cha-no-yu*. Obviously, I am speaking here not of creating the actual Japanese tea ceremony on line, but of applying the idea of the tea ceremony to computer space. In this sense, I write about the *katachi* or outside form of the tea ceremony, and not about its *uchi* or inside contents. I am interested more in the thought experiment than in the actual performance of the tea ceremony.

The tea ceremony may seem at first glance an inappropriate model for applied technology. The tea ceremony cultivates the sights and sounds of nature, of running streams and falling leaves, and of the feel of rocks and the scent of flowers. Many people view technology as an opponent of this infinitely sensuous nature, and they have good reasons for seeing this opposition. For one, the metal-and-plastic ambiance of current technology lacks nature's profoundly sensuous appeal. Since its birth in the Enlightenment, modern science has treated nature as an antagonist, or at least as an outside object for skeptical inquiry and human exploitation. A stream of recent books have criticized modern science and technology for creating the distance between humans and nature that has led to the crisis of planetary ecology. The ecological movement began as a critique of misapplied technology. So how shall we talk of the tea ceremony if we are at what Bill McKibben has described as "The End of Nature"?

> Our comforting sense of the permanence of our natural world—our confidence that it will change gradually and imperceptibly, if at all— is the result of a subtly warped perspective. Changes in our world which can affect us can happen in our lifetime—not just changes like wars but bigger and more sweeping events. Without recognizing it, we have already stepped over the threshold of such a change I believe that we are at the end of nature.[3]

The evidence for this end of nature ranges from acid rain to holes in the ozone layer, from genetic engineering to ecologically induced shifts in weather patterns, from the depletion of fossil fuels to the rise of ocean levels. McKibben points to a simple fact: "We have substantially altered the earth's atmosphere."[4]

WHY THE TEA CEREMONY?

Oddly enough, the tea ceremony may be precisely the right remedy for a sick planet at the end of nature. The tea ceremony is a technology for affirming nature, a tea ceremony that employs highly artificial means to return humans to a deeper intimacy with nature. Paradoxically, the traditional tea ceremony applies a refined control of human perception in order to free perception so it can once again appreciate the natural environment. Nature, in other words, needs to be rediscovered. "Original nature" has become covered with dust and dirt. *Cha-no-yu* is a set of techniques for removing the dust and for cleaning the dirt that overlays perception. In this sense, the tea ceremony functions as an interface, a window, between daily human business and the experience of fresh, spontaneous nature.

While many things can and are being done to reverse the damage to the natural environment, the environmental crisis goes deeper than politics and cleanup efforts. Modern philosophy, since Descartes and the rationalists, has configured human perceptions so that we modern people pay less and less attention to the spontaneous aspects of nature and more and more attention to the universal, controllable aspects of nature. Behind the physical damage to the environment lies a tunnel-like vision that narrows human perceptions. The repair of the natural environment cannot happen fully until the human being perceives the world differently. Ecology must have a foundation in ecosophy, in a wisdom about natural cycles and spontaneous movement. *Ecosophy* is the wisdom (*sophia*) about dwelling (*eco* or *oikos*). Ecology of the physical world must have a basis in personal ecology.

As a teacher of Tai Chi Chuan, I find this change of perception the most important yet most difficult change we can make. Disciplines like Tai Chi and the tea ceremony seem demanding to us moderns because our technological control over the environment often makes us passive spectators and consumers—fulfilling the promises offered by technological consumerism. Yet the reactivation of our primal physical awareness can indeed heal our incapacity for sheer pleasure and physical delight in our surroundings. It is not by accident that the Tai Chi player stretches, relaxes, and opens the energy pores of the body in the outdoors under the trees. Through the subtle backdoor of unconscious, peripheral awareness, we must find rituals to reconnect ourselves to a relaxed perception of natural surroundings. Only the revival of our relaxed spontaneous perceptions can nourish an ecosophy that forms the basis of a long-range planetary ecology. If ecology becomes the way we link ourselves to the outer world, we must find a parallel ecosophy within.

Ryosuke Ohashi makes a similar point when he defines Japanese aesthetics as "pruning."[5] Pruning is a reduction that leads to fuller and more harmonious growth. Pruning captures the essence of a process of growth when that growth mediates humans with nature. The tea ceremony also operates by pruning human perceptions. By reducing the natural interaction we have with things, the tea ceremony enhances and concentrates natural interaction.

The challenge to ecosophy, however, increases with the advent of cyberspace. As cyberspace grows, nature seems even more to recede. The electronic absorption of large portions of life—what some call the "virtualization" or dematerialization of life—corroborates the notion of nature's disappearance. The end of nature in human perception would seem to culminate with the fully immersive technology of virtual reality, where we don a helmet that isolates us from the primary world. So it is even more important for us to consider how that same technology can contribute to a transformation of our nature perception rather than replace our perceptions. The age-old wisdom of the I Ching suggests that any extreme condition, when pushed to its limit, initiates the reversal into its opposite condition. The virtual reality that hosts the tea ceremony may well be the pivot point.

The paradoxical use of technology to transform perceptions distorted by technology are inherent to the traditional tea ceremony. Entering the tea room, we go indoors in order to better perceive the outdoors. We remove ourselves from the many things in the world in order to see more clearly the flowers, the scroll, and the colors of the tea bowl. We crawl silently through the entrance of the tea hut and pay attention to the sound of boiling water so we can later hear the waterfalls and the singing of the sparrow. Our perceptions emerge within a larger structure that I call the "psychic framework."

The end-of-nature shift that McKibben writes about is not a change in physical substances or ecological systems—nor even a change in the terrestrial atmosphere. The change he refers to is a shift in the psychic framework by which we view the world. By that I mean the way humans feel when, say, a change in an ecological system alters their background experience and affects their sensibilities—the affective attitude we have toward the world, as much as the world itself. As beings in the world, we inhabit the world as participants; not merely as spectators scientifically observing and then calculating for advantage or disadvantage. The framework of our participation in the world has a look and feel to it, not merely a scientific description. When the world changes ecologically, so does the psychic framework in which we work and love, play and observe.

Nature as a "psychic framework" appears in the description of the Japanese tea ceremony in D. T. Suzuki's lovely book for English-speaking readers, *Zen and Japanese Culture*.[6] Describing the tea ceremony, Suzuki points beyond physical facts to the atmosphere in which gestures, objects, and surroundings cohere:

> The tea-drinking that is known as *cha-no-yu* in Japanese and as "tea ceremony" or "tea cult" in the West is not just drinking tea, but involves all the activities leading to it, all the utensils used in it, the entire atmosphere surrounding the procedure, and, last of all, what is really the most important phase, the frame of mind or spirit which mysteriously grows out of the combination of all these factors.
>
> The tea-drinking, therefore, is not just drinking tea, but it is the art of cultivating what might be called "psychosphere," or the psychic atmosphere, or the inner field of consciousness. We may say that it is generated within oneself, while sitting in a small semi-dark room with a low ceiling, irregularly constructed, from the handling the tea bowl, which is crudely formed but eloquent with the personality of the maker, and from listening to the sound of boiling water in the iron kettle over a charcoal fire.[7]

What Suzuki describes as a "psychosphere," "psychic atmosphere," or "inner field of consciousness" is what I mean by a psychic framework. The psychic framework of the tea ceremony is a field of awareness, but it cannot be separated from the technology of utensils, architecture, and decor that affects the participant's state of mind. We should not think of psychic framework as "consciousness" if by consciousness we mean a private subjective state that peers from within to confront a separate world of alien objects. A psychic framework sets the tone that a field of awareness has when it seamlessly flows with a set of furnishings, tools, and physical movements.

The tea ceremony is a technology designed to recapture a lost nature. Artificial and formalized in its every movement and gesture, the tea ceremony removes excess in order to exalt the simple clarity of being. Its highly stylized cultivation aims at a certain kind of experience. Only through the artificial does one regain a lost sense of open harmony with the natural. Our daily struggle for survival pulls us away from experiencing pure, spontaneous nature.

We must regard cyberspace technology as a technological practice. Entering cyberspace is like entering the space of the tea ceremony. The more a cyberspace is a virtual reality in the strict sense—using immersion techniques like projection displays or head-mounted displays, and using full three-dimensional stereoscopy—the more it shapes a psychic framework. How does this technology configure a distinct psychic framework? How can we make the design of the virtual reality interface function so that we become wise in our use of nature?

Here is where contemporary interface design goes beyond the so-called "human factors" research. Human-factors research scratches the surface only. It asks minimal questions about interactivity. It works with elementary surveys about the way humans use computers. It does not study the psychic atmosphere produced by virtual worlds. When the immersive feature of virtual reality creates a world where the user becomes a participant, then we can no longer rely on behavioral psychology to convey what is happening. A world brings the full context of existential involvement, not a single procedure narrowly restricted to the use of tools. A world is an ontological totality, not a sequence of machine-human interactions.

By looking at the psychic framework of a virtual world, we can begin to give content to the terms people already use to express their spatial intuitions of cyberspace. As I mentioned earlier, the vocabulary of cyberspace already makes abundant reference to spatial intuition. This intuition of space is not weakly metaphorical, but it expresses intuition in the Kantian sense of *Anschauung*, that is, the basic ways we perceive and understand the empirical world. The "empirical" originally refers to the sensations we receive in experience. The way we move through information space, as architects well know, affects our feelings about being in that space. We already see on the Internet a large range of elementary spaces, although the Internet today lacks the immersion required by virtual reality technology in the strong sense of the term. As an intercultural testing ground, though, the Internet with its three-dimensional spatial metaphors offers opportunities for translating aesthetic spatial experiences, like the tea ceremony. Current two-dimensional simulations on the Internet's World Wide Web offer dynamic spaces that are gradually evolving with the introduction of VRML (virtual reality modeling language). Translating the tea ceremony to cyberspace can prepare us to think about the challenges of interface design that lie ahead.

FOUR FEATURES OF THE TEA CEREMONY

The tea ceremony is a technology for restoring the original abode, the place where the psyche feels comfortable with itself as a participant in the natural world. The original abode is where the world and the psyche interact harmoniously. Taoists referred to the original abode as the "face before you were born," where the energy embryo abides in the womb of the mother. In this case, the mother is Mother Earth. The human being breathes the energy of the heavens and conducts that energy into the support strength of the earth. The human being stands between heaven and earth, though most often it is distracted by the ten thousand things that claim attention in worldly life. To recover the stance of the full human being, a reconfiguration is required. *Sadô*, as the tea culture is known in Japan, reconfigures the psychic framework of nature. It resets the human being into the natural posture, into the natural attitude. It restores the original abode.

The four features of the traditional tea ceremony correspond to the design issues of virtual environments. They relate, each in a different way, to the psychic framework that heals the breach between humans and nature. These features are: *wa* (harmony), *kei* (respect), *sei* (purity), and *jaku* (serenity).

Wa means that a world must cohere. The pieces of the world must constitute parts of a whole. A world can only exist as what the German language calls a *Zusammenhang*: things must "hang together." Aesthetically, this holism means a unified atmosphere. The tools of the tea ceremony might share a seasonal motif that deepens the sense of time and place. Autumn may appear in the floors, in the scrolls, and in the colors chosen for the tea cups. This feature of the tea ceremony appears in current interface design where the designer uses semiotic repetition to establish a sense of place. In general, the current Web is a wild collage without a clear semiotic system. Some young designers are trying to deepen the sense of place, of being somewhere, by repeating colors, images, and interactive buttons in such a way as to create a consistent sense of place. The places they create convey an internal harmony, though not necessarily a harmony with nature.

To create a sense of place, some Web sites use consistent border markings to establish semiotic harmony throughout the many rooms of the on-line space. "Harmony" is derived from the Latin *ars*, "to fit." The fit that artists strive for today is to make everything in a world come together in such a way as to make that world stand out as a unique whole. The most basic ground of the world is an open space for participation. Worlds offer space for habitation, and the participants cooperate in maintaining the ground of that world. Most often, Internet sites appear to be "one thing after another," without stasis or rest. By creating harmonious worlds, even jazzy worlds, the artist shapes an electronic abode, a place to dwell, perhaps even a space we can eventually inhabit.

Kei refers to the acknowledgment of the presence of other people or the sacredness of the materials we use. Computer communication establishes respect in a peculiar way. Computers isolate us as individual users at the same time that computers connect us in a network. Networks interweave human memories and make it possible to interweave our thoughts increasingly on a daily basis without regard to physical distance. Time barriers drop. Yet this is also where the danger lies. As time barriers fall away, the instant connection we have threatens to wear away respect. Respect seems to require distance. If we lose a sense of our distance from one another—our interior distances, the vastness of our spiritual landscapes—then we risk losing respect.

Perhaps the avatars of virtual worlds, those surrogate personae of simulation, will help preserve the distance needed for mutual respect. While computers create an intimacy that connects mind to mind, they can also hide us from one another. Ideally, a virtual world would allow us intimacy with distance, much like the tea ceremony. The tea master Rikyu admonishes tea practitioners not to try to synchronize their feelings with those of their guests unless the harmony occurs spontaneously.[8] Without distance, true intimacy cannot arise.

Sei appears in the tea ceremony's austere minimalism. No wasted motion, no excess of any kind, always restraint. From the material point of view, it would be hard to think of any space more empty, more minimal than cyberspace. Some cyberspace software designers, like William Bricken of the Human Interface Technology Lab at the University of Washington, conceive cyberspace as a Buddhist void, as *sunyata*. The emptiness of electronic systems offers an opportunity for pure creativity. The creative rush drives thousands of artists and would-be artists who now manifest their personal home pages on the Internet. Most of these creations show little restraint, as they arise from the call of open spaces that beckon the spirit in millions of people. For the designer, the purity of cyberspace may come with the territory, but purity does not last long. Cyberspace is rapidly filling with junk and junk mail. Advertisers litter the void. What we can learn from the tea ceremony is the discipline of restraint. We need to reflect the essential loneliness of cyberspace in the electronic environments we create.

Jaku shares the *sei*'s fragility. Purity quickly drowns in clutter. Likewise, the initial serenity of cyberspace, its loneliness and focus, soon scatters with the noise of millions of messages. Cyberspace, especially in its newly found role as a source of commercial contacts, risks becoming bedlam. Concentration and focus will be impossible if cyberspace becomes a circus. To enjoy the circus, you will have to forget your purposes and go along for the ride. The serenity of vast cyberspace has been broken by the shouts of advertisers and the barkers who try to lure new customers. Perhaps the purpose of "knowbots," tiny programs with customized intelligence, is to keep down the noise. Knowbots can filter out distractions and remove the shouts of advertisers. The Internet already offers programs like Fast Forward, which invisibly removes advertising banners before they appear in the Netscape Web browser.

But advertising is not the only obstacle to *Jaku*. As I pointed out in *Electric Language*, the language system on computers is an essentially linked language.[9] Hypertext reading shows the linked nature of digital writing. The loneliness of the cyberspace void should not obscure the fact that computing solitude is essentially a social solitude. What we see on the computer screen may seem as intimate as the thoughts in our head, yet the on-screen vision links to millions of other computers, or—even if protected by firewalls—any screen may be recovered and viewed by thousands of anonymous others. Computer text is essentially linked text. When we write email, we may feel as though we are writing in a serene, private bubble, but in fact we might as well be shouting our message from the rooftop. Cyberspace offers no total privacy. Where there is no total privacy, there is no complete serenity.

Each of the four characteristics of the tea ceremony have a cyberspace correlate. These correlates appear to be metaphoric analogies between the virtues of the tea ceremony and the atmosphere of cyberspace, and they establish possible links between the two. What I am suggesting is that we apply the inspired qualities of the tea ceremony to our efforts to deepen computer-generated environments. Where we have a loose link or analogy today, we can have a rich experience tomorrow. Interface designers struggling to shape a sense of place on the Internet can lead this process of enrichment. Such a struggle will not be easy, however, as the analogy between cyberspace and the tea ceremony faces many challenges.

CHALLENGE OF THE TEA CEREMONY

Foremost among the challenges is the simple fact that cyberspace is dynamite. It is inherently dynamic and explosive. On-line communication accelerates the tempo of life. The faster our interpersonal communications, the faster will be all our other social interactions. As the cliché affirms, the very rate of change continues to change. Just look at someone browsing the World Wide Web, and see how the screens flash past, one after another. The television remote control has become the daily mode of reading. Reading is no longer contemplative but has become thoroughly dynamic. The dynamics of hypertext enter the user's psyche and alter the felt sense of the world. The world we feel is undergoing an ontological shift, a reconfiguration of the cultural tectonic plates that support all our other activities. Change the way we organize and access knowledge, and you eventually change the world under our feet. The world that is emerging from hypertext appears to be a "hyper" world in the sense that psychiatrists and health workers use the term: agitated, upset, pathologically nervous.

Cyberspace brings with it a pathology that I have called "Alternate World Syndrome." AWS breaks the harmony between the biological body and the cyberbody. The experiences in the virtual world bring the body out of sync with the ecology of planetary experiences. Alternate World Disorder (AWD) represents an illness of lifestyle. I discovered these disorders while researching the simulator sickness that appears in many virtual-reality systems. The military has done extensive research on simulator sickness, and much of that research points to serious problems ahead for a culture that frequently uses virtual reality. The high-speed dynamics and aggressive tempo of cyberspace brings with it a disharmony between the earth-rooted biological self and the digitally trained mind. The person is split between personal experience based on computer life and personal experience based on felt bodily awareness. The more we move into virtual worlds, the thinner becomes the umbilical cord that ties us to the earth.

The artist currently faces the challenge of creating electronic habitats for humans to dwell in cyberspace. Traditional design fields largely emphasize the art of composing static surfaces. Balance, focal point, and contrast are usually understood in static ways, from a steady, single point of view. Now, electronic design confronts artists with a dynamic, interactive, high-speed electronic environment. Traditional design skills need serious revision as transitions assume a more important role than static surfaces. Designers must ask: How does it feel to go from one screen to another? What is the atmospheric link that connects one flashing screen to another? How does a series of linked screens express the underlying knowledge base? Traditional design principles need revision in the face of a new medium. Film and video offer some clues, but interactivity still remains a challenge.

Even among filmmakers we see great caution about the dynamism of future media. In his film *Until the End of the World*, director Wim Wenders shows a population plagued by video disease. Eyes, minds, and hearts have become weary with continual exposure to powerful images that tap into and stimulate every aspect of the human psyche. Worn down by the pace of flickering images, the video-crazed protagonist of Wenders's film becomes literally blind. He seeks healing for his video disease by traveling to Japan and undergoing a Zen therapy treatment not unlike the tea ceremony. The therapy is reminiscent of what Taoists called "the sealing of the five senses." The Taoists believed that overuse of the senses, especially the eyes (the most yang-powered organs in the energy, or *chi*, of the body), depletes the powers of vision. The internal energies need occasional "sealing off" or closure by turning within to heal the senses and restore their power. Higher stages of meditation require that the senses be sealed so that the spirit (*shen*) can draw on the energy drained out of the senses by their daily use. I see the Wenders film as a parable about interface design in the age of virtual reality: We need the tea ceremony to heal the Western split between the body and the mind, between the overused, electronically stimulated sensibility and the earth-centered, serene poise of our natural good health. The tea ceremony can inspire, I think, such a crucial balance.

In this spirit, Muneharu Yoshida has developed a multimedia on-line tea ceremony. Using Macromedia Director and Adobe Photoshop he built a Shockwave application that invites the on-line browser to contemplate the contrast between the traditional tea room and the space of electronic habitation. The invitation to "take off your shoes" begs us to reflect on our body amnesia and the possible coexistence of cyberspace and the tea ceremony. The flat two-dimensional photos warn of the end of noninteractive representation, while the photorealism imposes the demands of texture, richness, and multi-sensory immersion.

I conclude with some comments on the famous Rock Garden at the Ryoan-Ji Temple in Kyoto, which has come to stand for the Zen esthetic. The Zen rock garden is a cousin to the tea ceremony, inspired by the same Zen culture that produced *sadô*. The Ryoan-Ji Garden reveals other aspects of the tea ceremony relevant to virtual reality.

Every garden, since the Garden of Eden, has been artificial, a creation, but there is none whose artificiality is more pronounced than that of Ryoan-Ji. Indeed, one is tempted to call it not a garden, but an abstract sculpture. It is more the pure idea of garden than any actual, messy garden. It is a product of elimination and pruning. While evoking the texture of water by means of raked white sand, and forested islands by fifteen dark, moss-covered rocks sunk into the sand, the garden stands as an artificial abstraction from the surrounding park of Ryoan-Ji Temple, with its abundant trees, bushes, and lagoons. The garden walls create an atmosphere of isolation that allows the inner to be highly stylized while still preserving a look beyond the walls at the trees and mountains surrounding the park.

On first seeing Ryoan-Ji, one is tempted to interpret it as a symbol or an abstraction of a garden. Yet the material elements, which Ryoan-Ji reduces to a minimum, should not be taken to "symbolize" anything at all, for the mountains in the garden are indeed rocks, and the watery sand is in principle an ocean, and the green growth on the rocks are miniature trees. This perception is especially true as it grows in the viewer who spends a couple of hours sitting within the restricted walls of the rock garden. Though minimal, these things are what they are in the same sense that William Blake's "world in a grain of sand" suggests that the world is built of earth and the earth is actually sand. The proportionate reduction of the world can compress it to a small size and make matter into a matter of relativity. "Pruning" or "trimming" (as the essence of aesthetics) happen in a radical way at this garden. By trimming back everything but the essentials, this garden allows us to contemplate the great earth and its oceans.

Moreover, Ryoan-Ji brings us to contemplate our own place as inhabitants of the great earth and its oceans. The garden at Ryoan-Ji presents the paradox of abode. Abode or inhabitable place becomes the puzzle of abiding as we sit on the wooden boards within the monastery walls. You do not "understand" the rock garden by stopping to look at it once. Rather, you encounter in it your own impatience as you feel the drive to go elsewhere, to turn from the stark, uncompromising scene. Our sense of presence and of being present wavers and fluctuates, and the garden confronts us brutally with our own fluctuations. We do not easily gain access to the garden as a place to dwell. It repels us again and again until we face our impatience and finally give up the effort to fit the garden into our preconceived categories (How many stones are there? What's the best point from which to view it?). Ryoan-Ji is clearly a place for practice in the German sense of *Übung* (disciplined, repeated contemplation). The garden forces us, if we take its challenge, to gain a deeper understanding of what it means to inhabit a world.

Inhabiting a world implies more than one superficial look, more than a glance from a single perspective. As we gaze on Ryoan-Ji, we are repeatedly drawn to organize its stones perceptually from many different angles. Each time our eyes catch a pattern in the clusters of asymmetrical rocks, we notice that even the slightest shift of position gives us another very different pattern to view from another vantage point. After many such experiences, we gradually realize that the garden is nothing other than a sequential presentation of a variety of viewpoints. All the perceived patterns viewed together— taken as an infinite number of slices—constitute the total garden. The implied perspective of the garden brings out the relativity of each viewpoint. The sequence of viewpoints can never be ordered once and for all for any finite viewer. The movement of human physiology guarantees random access and infinite variety. The world of the garden, its totality, exists only through simultaneous perspectives. The garden exists in the imagined totality of the multiple gardens glimpsed by an infinite number of sense perceptions. The garden exists only as the hidden oneness that eludes direct sensuous perception.

The optics of sensuous perception, so crucial for research in virtual reality and computer-generated telepresence, grow in importance as we contemplate the rock garden. No photograph, no picture can possibly convey the three-dimensional optical experience of Ryoan-Ji. By confronting us with the bare essentials of patterned landscape, the garden makes us painfully aware of our physical orientation in space and shows us how critical that orientation is for our visual field. Virtual reality systems—especially the immersive type of VR with full head-mounted display—work by coordinating the body's orientation in space with the visual display of computer-generated graphics. We turn the head slightly to the left, the Polhemus position-tracker sends feedback to the computer, which then updates the visual eye-display to show the scene from the perspective we now occupy. Precisely that connection between bodily and visual orientation constitutes an essential feature of virtual-reality telepresence. The unique aesthetic of Ryoan-Ji draws attention to this perspective-based, orientation-centered ecology of human presence. Our sense of reality is stimulated by Ryoan-Ji in such a way that we can better understand the challenge posed by telepresence. The harmony of bodily orientation and sensory perception belongs to our fundamental ontological experience.

Through patient practice, through long being present in the garden as an abode of contemplation, the rocks at Ryoan-Ji begin to move. The asymmetrical position of the stone clusters—from any number of seats at the garden's edge—sets the patterns in perceptual motion. The eye senses a play among the forms. This play belongs to the reality of the stones but also to the psychic atmosphere of the perceiver of the stones. They move in patterns as a play of the relaxed gaze that surrenders to the garden, to the place as an abode for dwelling. This intense breakthrough is a deepening of place, of being more fully present, of being present with alertness but without an ego will. It is a breakthrough to the harmony of perceiver and perceived.

In coming decades, we will build virtual realities in cyberspace. To create true places in cyberspace—places where we can dwell—we must soften the aggressive drive of our perceptual apparatus. No amount of willful visualization techniques can harmonize the perceived and the perceiver. The

Architecture in the Age

of Its Virtual Disappearance

AN INTERVIEW WITH PAUL VIRILIO

BY ANDREAS RUBY

PARIS, 15 OCTOBER 1993

ANDREAS RUBY: At your last seminar in the Collège International de Philosophie you stated: "Due to the continuous flow of optical appearances, it is becoming difficult, if not impossible, to still believe in the stability of the real, in the fixing of a visuality which is constantly fleeing away. The public space of the building suddenly vanishes behind the instability of a public image."

Should not one conclude then, that reality itself has become unstable today? That it is less defined by the materiality of architecture but rather by the ephemerality of the images with which we perceive the world?

PAUL VIRILIO: Obviously, stability has become less important than speed today. The French word for *to last* (*durer*) contains multiple meanings: *solid* (*dur*) and *to endure* in the sense of that which happens (*ce qui passe*). Now today, that which happens is much more important than that which lasts (*ce qui dure*)—and also than that which is solid (*ce qui est dur*). There is a dematerialization that goes parallel to deterritorialization and decorporation.

Centuries ago, matter was defined by two dimensions: mass and energy. Today there comes a third one to it: information. But while the mass is still linked to gravity and materiality, information tends to be fugitive. The mass of a mountain, for example, is something invariable, it is immobile; its information, however, changes constantly. For a prehistoric man the mountain is a nameless mass. Its information is to be an obstacle in his way. Later, the mountain slowly ceases to be an obstacle. It takes on other meanings, for instance that of the holy mountain, named Sinai. It gets painted in perspective, photographed, analyzed in its geographical layers, and exploited in its resources etc. Hence for us a mountain contains a whole world of information whereas for prehistoric man it was defined solely as an obstacle.

If the mass and the energy of a mountain is hence linked to the density of its matter, the information of the mountain evolves constantly through history. Today, information counts more than mass and energy. The third dimension of matter takes the place of the thing itself. Very much in the sense of Flaubert's phrase: "The image is more important than the thing of which it is an image." ("*L'image vaut plus que la chose dont elle est image.*") There is an inversion.

AR: Your writings about disappearance as a new mode of appearance are linked to a set of scientific approaches giving new emphasis to time, for example the theories of chaos, catastrophe, and complexity. Analyzing the development of forms, the theory of morphogenesis severely shakes up every discourse about form in architecture. It defines form no longer as something static but constantly changing and re-emerging in new configurations. Could this altered notion of form affect architecture?

ᴾⱽ: This development puts the architect in a rather difficult situation. At least if you concede that architecture, in a primary sense, has to deal with statics, resistance of materials, equilibrium, and gravity. Any architect works with the mass and energy of a building and its structure. But in terms of information, architecture still stays somewhat behind the present development.

It is not easy to answer this question since, for me, architecture is just about to loose everything that characterized it in the past. Step by step it looses all its elements. In some way, you can read the importance given today to glass and transparency as a metaphor of the disappearance of matter. It anticipates the media buildings in some Asian cities with facades entirely made of screens. In a certain sense, the screen becomes the last wall. No wall out of stone, but of screens showing images. The actual boundary is the screen.

What used to be the essence of architecture is more and more taken over by other technologies. Take a staircase: it becomes increasingly replaced by elevators which are no longer designed by architects but by engineers. When people in the past wanted to climb up to the sky, they built the Tower of Babel. Now you just take an airplane. Something of the tower became transposed to the airplane, but the tower has lost its interest. The same applies to the dissolution of the staircase in the elevator, or of the window vanishing in the facade screen.

Because of this increasing replacement of hitherto material elements of architecture by technical substitutes, a term like high-tech architecture appears tautological. "high technology" would be enough; it is unnecessary to add "architecture." It is certainly not by chance that many architects today use the vocabulary of airplanes or space shuttles. To design something immobile they apply the aesthetics of a vehicle—which bears some paradox in itself.

ᴬᴿ: You could also put it another way by saying that architecture today integrates elements that used to be part of something else. A hybridization of hitherto unconnected genres merging together into something new. As for example the encounter of tectonics and electronics in virtual space.

PV: One of the consequences of virtual space for architecture is a radical modification of its dimensions. So far, architecture has taken place within the three dimensions and in time. Recent research on virtual space has revealed a virtual dimension. Unlike the three known dimensions of space, this dimension can no longer be expressed in integer numbers but in fractional ones. It will be interesting to see how this is going to affect space. To some degree, virtuality has been haunting architecture for a long time. It announced itself in a set of spatial topologies. The alcove, for example, is a kind of a virtualized room. The vestibule could be called a virtualized house. A telephone booth then virtualizes the vestibule: it is almost not a space, nevertheless it is the place of a personal encounter. All these types of spaces prepare for something and engage a transition. Thus virtual reality tends to extend the real space of architecture toward virtual space. That's why it is no longer a question of simply putting on a head-mounted display, squeezing into a data-suit, promenading within virtual space—as Jaron Lanier, Scott Fisher, and many others do.

In terms of architecture it is important to create a virtual "room" in the middle of architectural space where electromagnetic spirits can encounter each other. This is an extraordinary transformation of the notion of three-dimensional space, because in this new space, you will be able to walk around in Alaska, to swim virtually in the Mediterranean sea, or meet your girlfriend who happens to be on the other side of the globe. This is a new, fractional dimension of space that should be built, just as one has built houses with living rooms or offices.

AR: This would be the space of the future?

PV: The space of the future would be both of real and of virtual nature. Architecture will "take place," in the literal sense of the word, in both domains: in real space (the materiality of architecture) and virtual space (the transmission of electromagnetic signs). The real space of the house will have to take into account the real time of the transmission.

> A R : But time in general appears to be one of the hidden issues in the history of architecture. Architectural design seems to focus more on the three dimensions of built space than the temporal dimension that emerges as we start to use that space—which is probably due to the traditional design tools of architecture.

P V : Absolutely. There is a dynamics of space, or of the space-time experience by the individual. And this dynamics escapes from the ordinary graphic representations of space such as plan, section, and elevation. But one needs to integrate time and movement as spatial parameters into the design of architecture. Together with my students, I have been thinking about using Labanotation (a kind of notation for dance movement established by German choreographer Rudolf Labour in the 1920s) not in order to work out choreographic notations, but to account in a more subtle way for the capacities in terms of movement that can unfold in a space. By "constructing" the dancer's movements in a certain space, the choreographer assigns a value to a movement. It would be a challenge to explore the potential of this approach for architecture, especially since there are now computer programs capable of analyzing complex patterns of movement in space.

> A R : Architects try increasingly to design space directly with spatial means (the model, for example) instead of taking the two-dimensional detour of the drawing. To reach beyond the limitations of ordinary computer aided design, there are attempts to apply virtual reality as a design tool for architectural design. After having defined a space within a conventional computer model on the screen, one enters this space virtually to continue its design "from within." It seems that this changes radically the role of the model in the design.

PV: The model clearly acquires a very important status. Up to now it has served mainly to deliver a miniature of the future building. But in virtual reality you can create models at a scale of 1 : 1. And as soon as you can build virtual spaces in which you can experience events that actually take place somewhere else, it will be possible to imagine the virtual model as an design tool of future architectural practice. This touches upon the question of mental images. I always try to make my students imagine their projects before drawing them. I almost force them to imagine the space they want to create only in their minds. What I ask them to do is in fact create nothing less than a mental virtual model. But it will soon be equally possible to make an instrumental virtual model. Obviously, this would push architecture still one step further into the realm of the virtual. And there is no point why such a virtual model would be confined to design purposes only. You would more than likely end up using it to also "live" in that space.

Again, this is a tendency that has a much longer history. It begins with the telefax or the telephone. During the first riots of the ex-Yugoslavian war, I remember how a friend called me to report the first military actions. You could actually hear the first shots in the air, another incident in the process of the virtualization of space that is now affecting architecture as a whole, beyond a simple object like a telefax or a telephone. These feed-back effects between civilization and architecture have never really been considered in architectural history. For a long time, the mainstream discourse pretended that it does not matter to architecture if houses are electrified, equipped with telephones and VCRs, etc. But today we can see that this is setting up a completely new condition for architecture.

AR: Eventually, the virtual model would inverse the "principle of reality" of architecture itself: building spaces that are no longer subject to the physical constraints of real construction—

PV: —which is exactly the specificity of virtual space; to be no longer subject to gravity but to electronics, electromagnetic waves, and electrical current. The transmission of these waves gives rise to an "electro-optics" that is subject to matter only in terms of waves. However, the optics of my glasses are subject to matter in terms of mass. It simply does not work if the glasses are not clean.

A R : To designate this splitting of spatiality you coined the term "tele-topology." Would not architecture itself be split up into two separate fractions? One branch of architecture to supply the spaces necessary for humanity's physical survival (which obviously would not need to be very sophisticated), and another branch to produce virtual spaces to cover our need for sensual experiences?

P V : It seems to be very likely. But in my point of view this is already the case in the relationship between, say, the royal palace and the peasant's house. The royal palace of the seventeenth and eighteenth centuries was full of virtual spaces—just think of the enormous number of mirrors used in this architecture! The Gallery of Mirrors in the Château of Versailles features a very clear form of spatial virtualization. And I think the mirror played an important role in the conceptual development of virtual space. How many Parisian cafés can only exist because of that false, fractional dimension of the space reflected on the mirrored walls of the café's interior. One can even go back to the Romans. Celebrating their parties during the night, they would cover the walls of their villas with glass (less reflective, obviously, than our glass today) to multiply the light flicker's in the reflections on the walls. The reflected light illuminated the night as an artificial setting for their orgies. Thus there were two societies: one living at day time (i.e.; the poor), under the sun, without virtuality and within a concrete corporality—and another society living at night time (i.e.; the rich), in the excess and the virtuality of an artificial light that was very expensive at that time.

Today's society is similarly split up, not by light but by speed: one part still lives in an electrical world, the other in an electronic world. That is, the first lives within the relative speed (of mechanical transportation, for example) while the second participate in the absolute speed (of the transmission of information in real-time, for example).

AR: It seems as if this process of virtualization is touching upon the very concept of space itself. Something of it can already be glimpsed in the work of J. J. Gibson. On demand of the U.S. Air Force during World War II, he conducted neuro-psychological experiments on dive-bomber pilots having orientational problems as they approached the earth at high speeds. Gibson's conclusion was to leave behind our traditional (Kantian) notion of space and to conceive of it instead as a succession of vistas producing a discontinuous space.

PV: That's the transition from three-dimensional to sequential space. There is a sequentialization taking place even in our gaze: twinkling with the eyes. If you can not twinkle, you get mentally ill. Taking off the eye's lid was a notorious torture in the old Chinese Empire.

We experience time through cuts. Without them you would fall into a state of hallucination. The first cut is sleep. Our relationship to the real acts along this cut between sleep and awakening. But even during the day, we fall asleep many times. It is a kind of a micro-sleep, a very short period of time during which we are actually absent without noticing it at all. If this takes too long, it is considered an illness (pycnolepsy). Our relationship to the world is already marked by a form of sequentialization that precedes that one of space Gibson was analyzing.

AR: Do you think that these transformations of space could make architecture "disappear"?

PV: First of all, the disappearance not only affects architecture but any kind of materiality: the earth (deterritorialization), the body (disembodiment) and architecture (deconstruction—in the literal sense of the word, not the architectural style). Any kind of matter is about to vanish in favor of information. You can see it also as a change of aesthetics. To me, to disappear does not mean to become eliminated. Just like the Atlantic, which continues to be there even though you can no longer feel it as you fly over it. Or like the body that continues to exist without actually being needed—since we just switch the channel. The same happens with architecture: it will continue to exist, but in the state of disappearance.

Arne Svenson, *Las Vegas, 1993 (Las Vegas Convention Center)*

Arne Svenson, *Las Vegas, 1994 (Convention Center Landscape)*

Arne Svenson, *Las Vegas, 1997 (Roller Coaster Track and Video Screen, Circus Circus Hotel Casino)*

Arne Svenson, *Las Vegas, 1997 (Roller Coaster at New York, New York Hotel Casino)*

Arne Svenson, *Las Vegas, 1997 (Hilton Hotel, Astroturf and trees)*

Arne Svenson, *Las Vegas, 1994 (Convention Center Booth)*

Stripping Architecture

MARK C. TAYLOR

AMERICA CANNOT BE understood today without understanding Las Vegas. The point is not that Las Vegas is the fastest growing city in the country, the most popular retirement destination, that it has ten out of the eleven largest hotels in the world with three more bigger than the rest currently under construction, or that it has built twelve new libraries and thirty new schools in the past five years. None of this discloses what is distinctive about Vegas in the 1990s. What is most important about Las Vegas today is the way in which the real becomes virtual and the virtual becomes real in this desert oasis. Approached from this perspective, Vegas becomes symptomatic of the radical transformations wrought by global postindustrial consumer society.

The effort to read Las Vegas as a reflection of broader social and cultural changes is not, of course, new. In the late 1960s, Robert Venturi, Denise Scott-Brown, and Steven Izenour not only saw the near future of architecture figured in the hotels and casinos of the Strip, but also viewed

Vegas as a sign of the times. In retrospect, what Venturi and his colleagues thought was the future about to emerge was actually the culmination of a past that had been unfolding since the end of World War II. Though written with all the gusto of a typical modernist manifesto, *Learning from Las Vegas* is more of a postscript than an introduction. What did Venturi miss? How does Las Vegas in the 1990s differ from Las Vegas in the 1960s? And what do these differences tell us about where we have been and where we might be heading?

Resolutely rejecting the sterile purism that characterizes much modern architecture, in *Learning from Las Vegas* Venturi and his colleagues call for a more "tolerant" architecture that accepts "existing conditions" rather than negates what is for the sake of what ought to be. The defining feature of the sixties Strip and its architecture, they argue, is the circuit joining car and sign.

> But it is the highway signs, through their sculptural forms or pictorial silhouettes, their positions in space, their inflected shapes, and their graphic meanings, that identify and unify the megatexture. They make verbal and symbolic connections through space, communicating—in a few seconds and from great distance—a complexity of meanings through hundreds of associations. Symbol dominates space. Architecture is not enough. Because the spatial relationships are made by symbols more than by forms, architecture in this landscape becomes symbol in space rather than form in space. Architecture defines very little: The big sign and the little building are the rules of Route 66. The sign is more important than the architecture.[1]

Here, the Strip is seen as the expressive embodiment of postwar American car culture. The form and location of buildings determine and are determined by patterns of traffic flow. For Venturi, these developments mark a decisive break with the foundational tenets of modern architecture.

Ever sensitive to complexity and contradiction, Venturi correctly maintains that modernists affirm in practice what they deny in theory. While insisting that form follows function, modern architects implicitly appropriate the iconography of industrialism in a way that transforms structure into ornament. "Modern ornament," Venturi points out, "has seldom been symbolic of anything non-architectural." Since the symbolism of modernism refers to other architectural symbols, it is reflexive or self-referential. By contrast, in Strip architecture, Venturi argues, signs point beyond themselves by communicating information necessary for orientation in an ever more complex world.

> From the desert town on the highway in the West of today, we can learn new and vivid lessons about an impure architecture of communication. The little low buildings, gray-brown like the desert, separate and recede from the street that is now a highway, their false fronts disengaged and turned perpendicular to the highway as big, high signs. If you take the signs away, there is no place. The desert town is intensified communication along the highway.[2]

Elsewhere Venturi underscores the communicative function of signs in a text that suggests the source of the design feature that distinguishes both his own Vanna Venturi House (1963–65) and Philip Johnson's AT&T Corporate Headquarters (1979–84).

> The sign for the Motel Monticello, a silhouette of an enormous Chippendale highboy, is visible on the highway before the motel itself. This architecture of styles and signs is antispatial; it is an architecture of communication over space; communication dominates space as an element in the architecture of the landscape....A driver thirty years ago could maintain a sense of orientation in space. At the simple crossroad a little sign with an arrow confirmed what was obvious. One knew where one was. When the crossroads becomes a cloverleaf, one must turn right to turn left....But the driver has no time to ponder paradoxical subtleties within a dangerous, sinuous maze. He or she relies on signs for guidance—enormous signs in vast spaces at high speeds.[3]

But are we sure signs still communicate? Can signs provide orientation and direction? Do signs point the way out of the labyrinth of daily life or take us even deeper into it? Can signs be trusted?

Venturi's postmodernist critique of modern architecture is, paradoxically, constructed around the quintessential modernist invention: the automobile. This is its strength as well as its weakness. Any theory or architecture that remains bound to the car cannot escape the regime of Fordism and everything it represents. As David Harvey insists, "Postwar Fordism has to be seen less as a mere system of mass production and more as a total way of life." In a circuit of exchange mirrored by the reflexivity of the work of art, mass production produces mass consumption, which, in turn, reproduces mass production. The automobile is, in effect, the incarnation of the structure of self-referentiality that informs both modern and modernist practices of production and reproduction. Automobility is, of course, self-movement. Like an ancient Unmoved Mover who descends from heaven to earth, the automobile is moved by nothing other than itself. The dream of automobility is autonomy. To inhabit the automotive machine is to be integrated within a closed circuit in which all production is auto-production. The very proximity of self and machine creates an insurmountable distance between self and world. When automobility becomes a way of life, machines for living become glass houses whose windshields function like screens of noninteractive television and non-immersive cinema. To drive down the Strip in such a glass machine is to watch passively as the film unwinds and the spectacle unfolds.

But the Strip of the 1990s, unlike the Strip of the 1960s, is not built around the automobile. While cars do, of course, remain, Las Vegas Boulevard has become a pedestrian promenade. The shift from driving to walking reflects broader changes that have taken place in Las Vegas during the past three decades. The early years of postwar Vegas were dominated by two legendary figures: Bugsy Siegel and Howard Hughes. It was Bugsy Siegel, Los Angeles representative of the Chicago mob, who first had the extraordinary vision of creating a spectacular oasis in the midst of the Nevada desert. Though the bosses remained suspicious of Bugsy's ambitions, his relentless pursuit of his dream eventually led to the completion of the first major casino resort hotel. In the years after Bugsy's murder, the crackdown on illegal gambling in California made Las Vegas increasingly attractive to mobsters. There were intermittent efforts to clean up Vegas, but mob ruled the town until the late 1960s. All of this changed when, in 1966, Howard Hughes stole into Vegas in the dead of night and took up residence in the isolated penthouse of the Desert Inn.

Hughes is best known for the idiosyncratic paranoia that dominated the later years of his life. Paul Virilio has gone so far as to describe Hughes as a "technological monk" whose life was a grotesque embodiment of the dystopic possibilities of contemporary culture: "Speed is nothing other than a vision of the world, and for me Hughes is a prophet, a monstrous prophet, moreover, and I'm not really at all crazy about the guy, but he's a prophet of the technical future of society. That absolute inertia, that bedridden man, a universal bedridden man as I called him, that's what we're all going to become."[4] This reading of Hughes not only represents a one-sided view of technology but also overlooks his important contributions to the transformation of Las Vegas. From his early involvement with Hollywood to his innovative development of flight simulators and high-tech amusements, Hughes projected a future for Vegas that broke with its seedy past. The realization of this future, however, required legislative actions that could only be initiated by someone with Hughes's power and influence. Prior to the 1960s, Nevada state law limited gambling licenses to individuals. This restriction created enormous financial difficulties for anyone who wanted to construct a casino. In most cases, individuals did not have the necessary capital to invest in an uncertain venture in the middle of the desert. Consequently, this state law had the unexpected effect of encouraging the illegal financing of casinos. One of the few organizations with enough money to bet on Vegas was the mob. Ever the canny businessman, Hughes recognized the financial opportunity created by legalized gambling. But he also realized that Vegas could not prosper as long as the mob ruled and legitimate business could not invest in the city. To create more favorable conditions for investment, Hughes developed a two-pronged strategy: first, he started buying hotels and casinos, and second, began lobbying state legislators to enact a law that would permit corporations as well as individuals to secure gambling licenses. When the Nevada legislature eventually succumbed to Hughes's pressure, the Las Vegas of the 1990s became not only possible but virtually inevitable.

As major corporations moved in, it immediately became obvious that financial viability required an expansion of Vegas's customer base. If there were to be any justification for the expenditure of funds necessary for the construction of new casinos and hotels, gambling would have to be made attractive to a broader range of people. To achieve this end, the new Vegas had to distance itself from its corrupt past. In devising strategies for developing Vegas, "legitimate" investors looked to Hollywood.

While Venturi and his colleagues recognized certain similarities between Disneyland and Las Vegas, they never could have anticipated the extent to which the thematization of urban space characterizes the city today. From frontier villages and tropical oases to Mississippi riverboats and Mediterranean resorts, from medieval castles and the land of Oz to oriental palaces and the New York skyline, every hotel-casino is organized around a theme. Fantasies fold into fantasies to create worlds within worlds. The spectacular MGM Grand Hotel, whose 5,005 rooms make it the largest hotel in the world, "literalizes" the thematization of Vegas by replicating Disney World. Though ostensibly miming Disney's "original," MGM's theme park is significantly different from its prototype. While the Disney "imagineers" who designed EPCOT Center take pride in accurately representing our "small world," the architects of MGM flaunt artifice by openly imitating an imitation for which there is no original. None of the nostalgia that pervades Disney World haunts Las Vegas. In the simulated environment of Vegas, the real becomes blatantly hyper-real.

The primary motivation for thematizing Las Vegas is economic. As we have seen, to attract people who had never considered gambling, illegitimate vice had to be turned into legitimate entertainment. Moreover, the city had to be made hospitable to the middle class and their families. The Disneyification of Vegas is intended to sanitize the city by white-washing its sin and corruption. Far from a den of iniquity, Vegas creates the facade of a user-friendly amusement park. When the architects of a new hotel-casino complex named New York, New York put a Coney Island roller coaster between the hotel-casino and the Strip, the strategy guiding recent development was put on display for everyone to see.

Shifting financial incentives bring changes in architectural programs. To create an environment appealing to a new clientele, architects have had to develop design tactics that would convincingly integrate the fantastic and the familiar. Between the 1960s and the 1990s, the pedestrian space of malls displaced the automobile space of the suburban strip. By the early 1980s, there were over 28,500 malls in North America. While most of these malls combined predictable design elements from arcades and department stores, which can be traced to the glass architecture that emerged in Europe during the nineteenth century, more venturesome developers sought to construct new environments for consumption by creating spaces in which shopping becomes spectacular entertainment. The 5.2-million-square-foot West Edmonton Mall, in Edmonton, Canada, for example, boasts eight hundred shops, eleven department stores, twenty movie theaters, thirteen nightclubs, 110 restaurants, a 360-room hotel, an ice-skating rink, nineteenth-century Parisian boulevards, and New Orleans's Bourbon Street. Vegas's new hotel-casino megaplexes borrow the most outlandish features of contemporary cathedrals of consumption and, as always, up the ante. Nowhere is this more obvious than in Caesar's Palace, where outside is brought inside to create an enormous mall that imitates an Italian village within the hotel-casino. Under an ever-changing Mediterranean sky, upscale shops line streets with quaint Italian restaurants and open-air cafes. In the middle of the piazza, there is a dramatic "marble" fountain whose figures are automatons that come alive every hour to tell the story of Bacchus and his drunken festivals. At Caesar's Palace, Hegel's "bacchanalian in which no member is sober" erupts before excessive rituals of consumption.

The Vegas mallscape, however, is not limited to the public interiors of giant hotels. In a certain sense, the entire Strip has become one big arcade or mall. No longer separated from the street by large parking lots, casinos crowd the sidewalk with facades that dissolve the boundary between inside and outside. Most of the casinos that are still set back from the street are framed by simulated movie sets depicting everything from erupting volcanoes and warring pirate ships to Italian lakes and New York skyscrapers.

As the car is left behind and pedestrians roam the set, the cine-mascape changes. No longer separated from the screen by a thin film of glass, viewers are consumed by a spectacle that knows no bounds. In this way, today's Strip creates an immersive environment in which the virtual becomes real and the real becomes virtual. In Vegas, as one of the city's leading citizens, Andre Agassi, proclaims from signs and screens, "image is everything." As display screens dissolve into display screens to reveal endless dataspace, images become consuming and "realities" are virtualized. Nowhere is the virtualization of reality more obvious than on the new Freemont Street. Long associated with the seedy side of old Vegas, "Glitter Gulch" recently has been transformed into what is, in effect, a gigantic computer terminal or virtual reality machine. Vegas city planners have converted the train terminal that was inspired by the glass architecture of Parisian arcades, into a computer terminal to create the new space of the virtual arcade. Freemont Street is now covered with a 1,500-foot computerized canopy with 1.4 million synchronized lights and lasers. To roam through Glitter Gulch is to discover the timely timelessness of terminal space.

The teletonics of Freemont Street suggest previously inconceivable architectural possibilities. If, as Toyo Ito suggests, the challenge of building in a simulated city—and what city today is not simulated?—can be met only by making "fictional or video-image-like architecture," that is undeniably "ephemeral or temporary," then it is once again necessary to learn from Las Vegas. But the lessons Vegas currently teaches are not the same as the lessons Venturi learned three decades ago. The issue is no longer modernism vs. post-modernism; nor is it simply a question of form vs. ornament, or structure vs. sign. Something else—something that is, in many ways, far more unsettling—is occurring. And this occurrence—this event as it were—involves a certain slipping away. Though Venturi no longer believes in the foundational structures of modernism, he still has faith in signs. In a world without foundations, he insists, signs provide orientation, direction, even meaning. But along today's Strip, even this faith comes into question. When signs consume the bodies that lend them weight, everything becomes a "matter" of light. The ground, which once seemed stable, becomes ground zero where nothing fixes meaning.

The more deeply one ventures into the superficial space of the Strip, the more it appears to be symptomatic of our current cultural condition. Las Vegas illuminates the ephemerality that is our "reality." People come to Vegas hoping to win and leave having learned how to lose. They wager expecting a return on their investment but discover that in the long run their expenditure is without return. In the casino economy, even when one "wins," loss cannot be amortized.

The loss the Strip displays is the strange loss of something we never possess. As reality is virtualized, we gradually are forced to confess that the real has always been imaginary. The bright lights of the Strip stage a virtual potlatch of meaning. Instead of communicating meaning, which can be read at a distance, proliferating signs immerse one in a superficial flux that never ends. Monuments built to stop the flux turn out to be glas(s) pyramids where the pointlessness of ancient sacrificial rituals becomes transparent. By simulating simulations, which have long been mistaken for real, the substance of our dreams is stripped away to expose the inescapability of time and the unavoidability of death. This insight need not lead to unhappy consciousness and ceaseless mourning, but can instead nourish a gay wisdom that freely accepts lack and embraces loss. In the game of life, it is necessary to wager everything with the expectation of receiving nothing in return. Absolutely nothing.

NOTES

1. Robert Venturi, Denise Scott Brown, and Steven Izenour, *Learning From Las Vegas: The Forgotten Symbolism of Architectural Form* (Cambridge, MA: MIT Press, 1972), 13.

2. Ibid., 8.

3. Ibid., 9.

4. Paul Virilio, "The Third Window," in *Global Television*, ed. Cynthia Scheider and Brian Wallis (Cambridge, MA: MIT Press, 1988), 194.

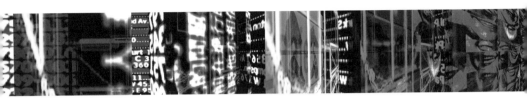

Ridzwa Fathom: *Demography-Dump*, still from QuickTime movie (1995)

Antitectonics:

The Poetics of Virtuality

WILLIAM J. MITCHELL

KENNETH FRAMPTON'S *Studies in Tectonic Culture* is self-exemplifying. It's a big, fat, weighty thing that lands with a satisfying thud when you drop it in the Book Return slot. The main structural element is a rigidly glued, inch-wide spine. The pages hinged to the spine are thick and shiny; they spring and riffle under your fingers, and close with a crisp snap. There's a rigorous grid, with an infill of graphic panels and blocks of Helvetica text—giving it an unmistakably retro-modernist look. The exterior cladding is fine gray cloth and a matte-varnished dust jacket. All these elements are cut and joined with precision. The production process consumed a lot of raw materials and energy and required the use of some very sophisticated, expensive, mass-production machinery. When this process was completed, the thousands of identical artifacts that resulted were warehoused, trucked to bookstores, and sold for fifty dollars apiece. It's a high-quality industrial-era job. The fine print at the front provides the publisher's address (Cambridge, Massachusetts), and announces that the volumes were printed and bound in the United States of America.[1]

A CD-Rom, by contrast, is made from immaterial, weightless bits.[2] These bits are not bound to some particular physical substrate, but can migrate freely from medium to medium; they can happily live on CD, on a Zip disk, on the hard disk of your personal computer, or in RAM. It's easy for anyone to make additional copies at any time, and these don't cost anything. Through the Internet, copies can be transmitted almost instantaneously to pretty much anywhere in the world. Nobody cares (or even knows, in most cases) about the physical organization of the information in whatever storage device currently happens to contain it; it's logical structure that matters. The format isn't fixed; you can load a copy into an editing program and change the layout and typography at will. And it kills far fewer trees.

This contrast illustrates a massive, fundamental shift that is taking place in the conditions under which artifacts—including works of architecture—are conceived, constructed, and consumed. It's a shift that suggests reading *Studies in Tectonic Culture* as an elegy—as a nostalgic tribute to the waning discourse represented by Perret, Wright, Kahn, Scarpa, Mies, and the other heroes of Frampton's narrative—not as the manifesto that it was probably intended to be.

MATERIALITY/VIRTUALITY

Frampton does not deny the volumetric character of architecture, but wants to resist modernist theory's marginalization of "the constructional and structural modes by which, of necessity, it has to be achieved."[3] Ironically though, at the very moment he chose to put forward this reassuringly traditionalist program, tendentiously buttressed with "of necessity," the avant-garde imagination was avidly flirting with a radical inversion of it—the anti to this thesis, the dys to his topia, the yin to his yang, whatever.

I mean, of course, the use of immersive virtual reality to create spatial experiences that are totally separated from physical construction, mass, and tactility. (Or, less dramatically, if you do not have the means or the desire to immerse yourself electronically, you can approximate the experience by peering into virtual spaces framed by your computer screen as a proscenium frames the space of a stage.) With this technology, you can walk or fly through virtual landscapes and virtual architecture, crash through enclosing surfaces without feeling a thing, and even encounter inhabitants represented by their virtual bodies. Because there is no material to transform, there is no weathering of surfaces with the passage of time. And the forms and relationships of the spaces are not necessarily stable; they can be programmed to shift and reshape themselves in whatever ways the designer wants.

Virtual spaces carry "less is more" to a provocatively anorexic extreme. They are not rooted in the ground, so they completely eliminate the "earthwork" that Gottfried Semper identified as the first of his four elements of architecture.[4] They don't need element two (the hearth), or element three (the framing), either. In fact, all that remains is a supremely attenuated version of Semper's fourth element—the lightweight enclosing membrane.

In this new architectural domain, joints just don't matter. (So, presumably, there are no Scarpas of cyberspace.) Surfaces have no thickness, and they can be fitted together with mathematical precision. You don't need nails, screws, or glue. There is no need to accommodate changes of material. Furthermore, there is no weather to keep out. In short, there is no room for ingenuity (or God) in the details; the game is entirely one of space and surface.

Ancient mainstays of architectural theory simply become irrelevant. There is no gravity (unless a programmer chooses to simulate it), so weights and loads do not create a rationale for member sizes, shapes, and proportions. Ideas of structural expression and honesty lose all meaning. Indeed, there is no necessary distinction between up and down, or between vertical and horizontal elements. Furthermore, you can forget the Modulor; in cyberspace, the body is just an arbitrarily proportioned and scaled avatar.

A virtual space, unlike a material construction, does not transform a specific site as, for example, Jørn Utzon's Opera House so memorably transformed Bennelong Point and Sydney Harbor. Instead, it masks a subject's physical surroundings and substitutes an electronically constructed one. And, as long as network connections and the necessary equipment are available, it can be instantiated anytime, anyplace.

MATERIAL REALIZATIONS/ELECTRONIC REALIZATIONS

Those who are troubled by this dematerialization—Marxists who take their materialism literally, Benjaminists in search of authenticity, real-estate developers in search of a buck, Martha Stewartists who just want everything to be nice—might want to deny such places the status of architecture. They might claim that these are things of another kind, and that their production and consumption belongs to a different and incompatible discourse. Maybe so. But I doubt that such a sharp distinction can usefully be sustained, for the material now appropriates from the virtual, and the virtual from the material.

Recall, for example, that many buildings (most major ones) are now designed on three-dimensional computer aided design (CAD) systems, and so can be visited virtually prior to construction. Conversely, with the appropriate electronic sensors, you can capture accurate, three-dimensional, digital models of physical objects and spaces. At the very least, then, we have to admit that exploration of virtual spaces now mediates the construction of physical ones, and that physical spaces may have indefinite numbers of virtual equivalents.

The purposes of these reciprocal appropriations vary, of course, and this variation affects both the characters and the roles of the resulting artifacts. Some virtual spaces are created as quick, inexpensive precursors to construction of their material equivalents. Thus they play a predictive role for the benefit of architects and their clients. The idea is to simulate as closely as possible the experience of the expected material realization.

In other cases—as in Kent Larson's superb electronic realizations of Louis Kahn's unbuilt Hurva Synagogue—creation of an electronic version serves as a substitute for material realization. Here, the electronic version may be understood as a counterfactual conditional; if this building had been constructed, then it would have been like this. Or, you may prefer to think of it simply as an alternative realization of the design using different means—much as a medieval musical composition performed with modern instruments, or Hamlet enacted under today's staging conventions, or even in radio or film versions.

Conversely, digital realizations that are constructed from existing physical ones are parasitic on their material precursors. They play roles much like photographs or measured drawings, allowing convenient inspection from other locations, and preserving "snapshots" of particular moments.

But an increasing number of virtual spaces are designed to be populated and experienced in their own right; there is never any question of physical realization. Sometimes, as in many virtual reality (VR) games and rides, the aim is to create dramatic spatial experiences that would be impossible in the physical world. Douglas Trumbull's motion-based VR ride at the Luxor pyramid in Las Vegas is a pioneering example of this genre; you "fly," at terrifying speed, through a complex three-dimensional space tightly packed with "solid" objects, feeling the accelerations, the shocks, and the shudders as you bang into and bounce off of obstructions. Alternatively, as in personal computer "desktops," and in the spaces that are created for social and commercial purposes in on-line virtual worlds, more traditional architectural forms are employed metaphorically (often in questionably literal and hokey ways) to provide familiar cues to users.

It seems most reasonable to enframe these diverse possibilities theoretically by saying that physically fabricated and electronically imaged versions are simply different realizations of a single architectural work that is specified by a set of drawings or a digital model—much as you can have different performances, by different performers with different instruments, of a single musical work that is specified by a score.[5] Some architectural works may have no realizations (that is, they remain unbuilt), some may have singular realizations, and some may have multiple realizations. Some may have only material realizations, some may have only electronic realizations, and some may have both. If material realization is intended, then the digital model should appropriately respond to physical constraints and the affordances of anticipated materials and production processes, but if only electronic realization is intended, then the less constraining logic of virtual space applies.

CRAFT/CAD/CAM

Even this common-sense distinction between material and electronic realization begins to fade, though, when computer-controlled production machinery is introduced; you simply employ the three-dimensional digital model to control different kinds of machines as appropriate to your current purposes. These machines define a continuum of possibilities. At one extreme, a cathode ray tube display yields a quick, ephemeral, inexpensive realization by employing an electron beam to excite a phosphor surface. A laser printer deposits tiny particles of toner on a paper surface; it takes longer, consumes a modest amount of material, is a bit more permanent, and costs a little more. A computer-controlled rapid-prototyping device, such as a stereolithography machine, deposits solid particles at specified locations in space to realize a small three-dimensional object; that's more time-consuming and expensive still. At larger scales, various kinds of CAD/CAM devices (computer-controlled cutting, routing, milling, and bending machines, for example) can automatically convert digital models into full-size architectural components—as brilliantly exemplified in the later work of Frank Gehry, such as the Guggenheim Museum in Bilbao.[6]

When artifacts are designed on the computer screen and the design is executed by means of some computer-controlled device, the capabilities of a local craft tradition no longer define the domain of possibilities that a designer can explore. This is established, instead, by the affordances of the CAD software and the production devices. You can see this most clearly, today, in graphic design—where, in a great many practical contexts, the design of print publications is now enframed at one level by the fundamental physical capabilities of laser printers, at a higher level by the constructs of the Postscript language that is employed to control these printers, and at a higher level still by the features of layout software such as QuarkXPress. (The Industrial Era gave us grids and Helvetica; the Digital Era gives us *Emigre* and *Ray Gun*.) In product design, the capabilities of CAD/CAM devices, of the languages used to program these devices, and of three-dimensional CAD software, may jointly play a similar role. And, in the early days of architectural CAD, software was often built around the vocabularies and syntactic properties of the industrialized component building systems that were popular at the time.

Typically, there is a complex reciprocal relationship between the shaping and arranging tools offered by CAD programs and the physical capabilities of CAD/CAM devices. On the one hand, for example, solid modeling software offers translational sweep operations that directly reflect traditional production processes such as the extrusion of molten plastics and rolling of steel sections, rotational sweep operations that recall the lathe and the potter's wheel, ruled surfaces that behave like twisted sheets of plywood or metal, and so on. On the other hand, multi-axis milling machines, stereolithography tanks, and other such advanced CAD/CAM devices impose few constraints on the production of three-dimensional shapes, so the tools provided by the CAD system become the principal determinant of the designer's formal repertoire. Thus there is an ongoing technical discourse in which the designers of CAD software try to reflect known production capabilities while the designers of production machinery try to create ever more flexible devices capable of realizing just about anything that a CAD system might specify.

In the context of this machine-mediated discourse, compositional principles that have long been taken as apodictic suddenly look arbitrary. Complicated curved surfaces may be no harder to produce than planar, cylindrical, spherical, and conical ones, so why stick to classical architectural geometries? Infinite variability may be as feasible as modularity; why not forget about grids, repetition, and symmetry? Truly three-dimensional compositions may be as easy to construct and manipulate as two-dimensional constructions of parallel bar, triangle, and compasses; the plan is no longer the generator, and the section may not tell us much. Algorithmically generated complexities become alternatives to simple ideas that can be held in a designer's mind; the idea of a procedurally expanded genome replaces that of a traditional *parti*.

Maybe there is, indeed, something fundamental about the old vocabularies and compositional precepts. But maybe, instead, these will eventually be seen as conventions established by a particular set of now-obsolete technological capabilities.

LOCAL/GLOBAL

The Digital Revolution is changing not only the nature of architectural production, but also its location. And this, in turn, redefines the connections of architectural production to the cultures of particular regions.

Once, it was perfectly reasonable to ask where an artifact was made and to expect a straightforward answer. Craftsmen had shops where they designed and built things. They used local raw materials to fabricate components, and assembled these components themselves. But the laptop computer on which I am typing these words was made in a very different way. Though it bears the imprint of a Silicon Valley company, it was actually put together on an assembly line in Taiwan. If you open up the gray plastic box, you find components stamped with the names and locations of manufacturing plants scattered globally. Similarly, subassemblies such as boards were put together at multiple locations. The software comes from Cupertino, Seattle, Cambridge, Sydney, and a multitude of other places. Design and integration of the hardware and software components and subsystems was carried out at innumerable, mostly anonymous locations. It has a brand name rather than a craftsman's signature; you cannot say who created it or where. It is a truly global product.

Though such globalization is most pronounced, so far, with relatively small, high-value artifacts such as electronic devices, it has increasingly affected the ways that buildings are made. In traditional cultures, buildings were designed and constructed on the spot, using whatever materials and processes the local economy afforded. With greater division of labor, architects distinguished themselves from craftsmen and moved off-site, and materials and components could be acquired through trade rather than created locally. With the Industrial Revolution, many architects were able to develop national and international practices, and materials and components were manufactured at relatively small numbers of specialized plants and distributed over wide areas by means of road, rail, sea, and air transportation systems. With the computer and telecommunications revolution, geographically distributed design and construction teams could effectively be created; an architect in Los Angeles might work with engineering consultants in Chicago and London, a general contractor in Tokyo, and specialist component fabricators scattered around the world, to construct a building in Shanghai. Such teams can be very competitive, since they can aggregate the best specialized expertise without regard to location, tap in to the most attractive labor markets worldwide, and make use of highly specialized fabrication skills and machinery.

To operate successfully in this context, architects need much more than knowledge of some particular, local craft tradition. They need to know about expertise and fabrication capabilities available globally, about worldwide labor markets and flows of capital rather than just local costs, and about technologies for supporting the collaborative work of geographically distributed, multidisciplinary teams. And they need, increasingly, to coordinate their design work with that of diverse and scattered materials, component, and subsystem designers.

Local conditions still matter a great deal, of course, but the response to them has to be different. Design and fabricate globally, assemble locally!

FACADE/INTERFACE

Bits also change the ways that buildings work. Works of architecture function as both shelter and symbol, and the introduction of digital technology opens up new ways to perform the symbolizing role. The resulting restructuring of a building's basic organization compares to that which resulted when artificial light appeared as an alternative to natural light.

Robert Venturi provides one insightful take on this. Decades ago, he and his associates infuriated stuck-in-the-mud modernists by pointing out that we should learn from Las Vegas rather than snobbishly disdain it; the electrical signs along the strip had effectively substituted for more traditional forms of architectural ornament and symbolism, and this division of roles suggested a new way to think about making buildings. Then times changed, Times Square acquired a Jumbotron, electronics increasingly replaced neon, and Venturi appropriately updated. In a pugnacious manifesto entitled "Sweet and Sour," he wrote that "the sparkle of pixels can parallel the sparkle of tesserae and LED can become the mosaics of today," and imagined "architecture as iconographic representation emitting electronic imagery from its surfaces rather than architecture as abstract form reflecting light from its surfaces only in the day." Conclusion: "Architecture was late in stylistically acknowledging the industrial revolution in the vocabulary of the Fagus Shoe Works around 1910: let us acknowledge not too late the technology of now—of video electronics over structural engineering: let us recognize the electronic revolution in the Information Age—and proclaim ourselves iconoclasts for iconography! Viva virtual architecture, almost!"[7]

As usual with Venturi, the sting is in the "almost." The interesting challenge is not just to replace atoms with bits, or presence with telepresence, but to learn from Luxor and the LED, and critically and thoughtfully to work out the subtle, complicated, problematic relationships of the material and the virtual. Several distinct approaches to this task are emerging.

Venturi himself harks back to ancient Egyptian, Early Christian and Byzantine, and Baroque traditions in which images are applied to sheltering surfaces, and plumps for "the electronic shed" with dynamic electronic ornament. At Harvard's Memorial Hall, for example, he constructed a dynamic LED frieze, and in his competition entry for the U.S. embassy adjacent to the Brandenburg Gate he created a facade from an LED board.

Bill Gates, on the other hand, sees electronic displays as virtual, reconfigurable windows. In his vast Lake Washington house he plans "twenty-four video monitors, each with a 40-inch picture tube, stacked four high and six across. These monitors will work cooperatively to display large images for artistic, entertainment, or business purposes. I had hoped that when the monitors weren't in use they could literally disappear into the woodwork. I wanted the screens to display wood-grain patterns that matched their surroundings. Unfortunately, I could never achieve anything convincing with current technology, because a monitor emits light while real wood reflects it. So I settled for having the monitors disappear behind wood panels when they're not in use."[8] Another scenario: "If you're planning a visit to Hong Kong soon, you might ask the screen in your room to show you pictures of the city. It will seem to you as if the photographs are displayed everywhere, although actually the images will materialize on the walls of rooms just before you walk in and vanish after you leave."

But all this is tinkering. More radically, we can recognize that inhabitation involves continuous interchange of information between a building and its inhabitants, and that the introduction of electronics requires us to rethink this interchange. Any part of a building, from a doorknob to a floorboard, can now be embedded with sensors. Conversely, any dynamic element, from a light fixture to a garage door, can be controlled by computer. All these things can be networked together, equipped with processors and memory, and programmed. You may read displays and operate controls, or you may just upload and download bits between the building net and your body net. The difference between computer network and structure elides. Interface becomes architecture, and architecture becomes interface.

In this context, infrastructure and interface are the crucial elements. Buildings still have supporting structures and enclosing surfaces, but privileging these as the focus of architecture, and insisting that they should carry most of the cultural freight, becomes as quixotic as similarly privileging the chassis and the beige box of a personal computer.

TECTONICS/ELECTRONICS

Electronics now rule. The architectural profession can face this new condition as an increasingly irrelevant, resistant rump—insisting on materiality and practicing a nostalgic modernist revivalism while potential clients vote with their feet. Theorists can take solace in Heidegger, and construct loftily disdainful texts about all things technological. But it is more productive, and certainly a lot more fun, simply to retire the exhausted dogma of architectural composition and construction as our world is rewired. Here, for those who want to try it, is my top-ten checklist:

RETIRED	REWIRED
Tectonics	Electronics
Craft	CAD/CAM
Hand tools	Software
Local tradition	Global organization
Facade	Interface
Ornament	Electronic display
Helvetica	*Emigre*
Parti	Genome
Permanence	Reconfigurability
Learning from Luxor (stone)	Learning from Luxor (VR)

1. Kenneth Frampton, *Studies in Tectonic Culture* (Cambridge, MA: MIT Press, 1995).

2. My *City of Bits* (Cambridge, MA: MIT Press, 1995), which appeared simultaneously as a hardback book and as a Web site is a hybrid. Increasingly, though, publishers are taking virtuality all the way. I no longer need access to the heavy, bulky, print version of the *Oxford English Dictionary*, for example; I simply surf to the on-line version that is available through the MIT library.

3. Frampton, *Tectonic Culture*, 2.

4. Gottfried Semper, *The Four Elements of Architecture and Other Writings*, trans. Francis Mallgrave and Wolfgang Herrmann (Cambridge: Cambridge University Press, 1989).

5. This line of argument is originally due to Nelson Goodman. See Nelson Goodman, *Languages of Art,* 2nd ed. (Indianapolis: Hacket, 1976).

6. The acronym CAD/CAM stands for Computer-Aided Design integrated with Computer-Aided Manufacturing. For an introduction to architectural applications of this technology, see William J. Mitchell and Malcolm McCullough, "Prototyping," in *Digital Design Media,* 2nd ed. (New York: Van Nostrand Reinhold, 1995), 417–40.

7. Robert Venturi, *Iconography and Electronics: Upon a Generic Architecture* (Cambridge MA: MIT Press, 1996), 5.

8. Bill Gates, *The Road Ahead* (New York: Viking, 1995), chap. 10, "Plugged In at Home," 205–26. Gates introduces his discussion by announcing, "My house is made of wood, glass, concrete, and stone.... My house is also made of silicon and software."

There will be no further need for cities
or castles. There will be no further
reason for roads or squares. Every point
will be the same as every other...

—Superstudio, circa 1968

Envisioning Cyberspace:

The Design of On-Line Communities

PETER ANDERS

INTERNET AS SITE

Multi-User Domains (MUDs) are mediated social environments on the Internet. Originally intended for role playing games such as Dungeons and Dragons, they have since developed into elaborate social settings serving on-line social and professional communities. Despite the spatial qualities of MUDs, few of them are presented graphically. Instead, they are text-based virtual realities that require the user to rely on descriptions of space and motion to create an image of the domain.[1] The use of text is dictated by the MUD software. Currently there are a variety of MUD types differing largely in their programming code. MOOs (MUDs Object Oriented), MUSHs (Multi-User Shared Hallucinations), MUSEs (Multi-User Simulated Environments) are among the many hundred MUDs currently operating on the Internet.[2] The text interface is an efficient medium. It limits memory requirements for the computers and speeds up real-time interaction. It can also conjure an image with a well-crafted description. As a result, MUD users often prefer the verbal environment, arguing that it allows them freedom of interpretation. Some users insist that the introduction of graphics will reduce, rather than enhance, the MUDing experience.

Use of MUDs involves logging onto a computer server, often using Telnet or Gopher programs. Once on, the user types responses to text on the screen—say, the description of a room they have "entered." The user might type "N" to leave the room by going north. The scene then changes as a new space description is offered. Users move from place to place by using sequential commands or by teleporting directly to their destination.

Conversation on MUDs is formatted to simulate dialog in a book. If a user, Fred, types "Hey, there!," the computer configures this to read as "Fred says, 'Hey, there!'" The result is that the user appears engaged in both the reading and creation of a novel. As users become more familiar with the commands, they gain a greater range of expression and action within the MUD.[3]

Graphic MUDs are still a technical novelty and their success is mixed. Preliminary efforts (the Palace, World Chat, and Alphaworld) are disappointing. The schematic quality of the contents and their graphics lack the poetry found in text MUDs. The ephemerality of MUDs also argues for spaces that are dynamic, responsive to their social and subjective nature. While text-based environments have an implicit, logical structure, their image as architecture is highly subject to the user. Current graphic MUDs, on the other hand, lose this depth by literally illustrating architectural environments. In many cases their illustration comes at the expense of poetry.

MUD ARCHEOLOGIES

In the spring and fall semesters of 1995, graduate and undergraduate students at the New Jersey Institute of Technology's School of Architecture surveyed ten MUDs on the Internet. The study was largely conducted in a CAD supported design studio and was carried out as a semester-long design assignment. The MUDs selected were social domains not overtly used for role-playing games.[4] Their selection was limited to text-based MUDs in order to maximize the students' design opportunities.

1 & 2: Logical adjacency model for MediaMOO. Michael

Lissowski and George Paschalis

The students, in teams of two, became citizens of their selected MUDs and explored the spaces described by the text. Typically, the team would divide the work between a navigator and cartographer. One operated the machine, "moving" from place to place within the MUD. The other charted locations of the places they visited. As the domains were mapped, these diagrams grew increasingly complex. This information was carefully documented to produce a log/sketchbook and a three-dimensional logical adjacency model of the MUD (FIGS. 1 & 2). These models, perhaps the first spatial documentations of these MUDs, formed a schematic diagram of the domains' spaces. Their coding was intentionally simple. Cubes represented spaces that were accessed directionally, using N, E, S, W or Up and Down commands. Spheres indicated spaces accessible by teleporting or by invoking their names. Points of MUD entry were colored red. Spaces were linked with simple rod connections appropriate to the directions indicated. Other symbols varied from model to model depending on the specifics of the MUD.

The final results were surprising in their complexity. Resembling extremely large molecular models, they documented hundreds of spaces. In many cases the models had to remain unfinished since the MUDs contained many more spaces beyond their main structure. Since MUD structure is dynamic, many of them grew and evolved throughout the study.

Most MUDs mapped easily as flow-chart diagrams. Some, however, had spatial anomalies. A room in DreaMOO described as being west of another, was entered by going east from that room. The nested arrangement of the Chatting Zone spaces did not translate easily into the ball and stick model. The rigorous structure of HoloMUCK forced the creation of "stepping stone" spaces used for navigating the MUD. Users pausing in one of these spaces would receive descriptions of different viewpoints within a larger space. Often these texts reflected changing perspectives or approaching views.

DOMAIN STRUCTURE

The logical adjacency model of each MUD has a distinct form, like a fingerprint. Often MUDs begin as a verbal diagram of a neighborhood (Jay's House), an existing town (The Chatting Zone) or even the Earth (Meridian). Once in place, citizens of the MUDs are invited to build their own rooms and buildings. Over time the configuration of the domain changes to the point that not even its operators, known as wizards, know the current shape of the community.[5]

It is a participatory architecture, a kind of "architecture without architects."[6] There are constraints on building, however. The degree of freedom that builders have largely depends upon each MUD's wizards. Some MUDs, like HoloMUCK or Jay's House, have stringent codes enforcing the "realism" of proposed additions. Each citizen is allotted an amount of memory to build objects.[7] This increases with the status of the citizen. Getting memory or status in a MUD is a symbolic and social issue, often a result of "who you know." In the study, some researchers achieved high-ranking builder status and eventually became wizards themselves.

Some domains were clearly based on physical models, often the hometowns of the administrating wizards. For example, The Chatting Zone is a cyberspace mapping of Ipswich, Ireland, hometown of the MUD's founder. While Meridian maps the entire planet, its point of entry is in Norway, home of its wizard. Oddly, Meridian's server is in Morristown, New Jersey.

Basing MUDs on actual physical models is an expeditious first step in starting the domain. It saves the wizard the effort of creating the spaces from scratch and lets him or her make a "home" out of the domain. It also allows easy navigation of the space, keeping the directions simple and places memorable for its users.

JupiterMOO, developed by Pavel Curtis, is based on the layout of XeroxPARC in Palo Alto, California.[8] Its mapping is so accurate that MUDers who visit the actual facility can find their way around the campus. LambdaMOO, one of the largest operating MUDs, was originally based on Curtis's personal apartment. In yet another case, MediaMOO incorporates the architecture of MIT's Media Lab. Its founding wizard, Amy Bruckman, whimsically added a floor to the building to provide space for a ballroom and party facilities.

As a MUD community develops, the original structure is elaborated, sometimes leaving the real-space reference behind. The resulting geometry can become complex and difficult to map. Most MUDers are allowed to build their own rooms once they have citizenship. These rooms are often independent of the main logical structure, hovering outside the domain. In DreaMOO, for instance, linking new construction to the main structure requires permission. Not only must the builder petition the wizards, but the creators of connecting spaces. It is a complicated affair, and none our investigators were able to link their work to the main structures.

The result of this difficulty of finding space in which to build is that many constructions have nondirectional connections to the main MUD. Most private spaces, which are often quite elaborate, can only be accessed by teleporting, and guests may enter these spaces only if they are invited to do so by the owner. As a result, many of the private spaces of the MUDs remained unmappable because they were inaccessible. Often, even the addresses for teleport access were simply unavailable.[9]

The freedom allowed by wizards directly affects the MUD's structure. BayMOO, a San Francisco based MUD, has a laissez-faire approach and over time has evolved into a free-form branching structure. Its logical mapping reflects its incremental and unplanned growth. In contrast, Jay's Place has such severe "reality" requirements that descriptions of nearby cliffs had to be rewritten to reflect the actual rock composition.

Generally, MUDs in which wizards exert the most control are more rigorously geometrical and easier to map. The looser structure of more participatory communities—like MediaMOO—make them initially more difficult to navigate. In MediaMOO organizing spaces like Curtis Commons were later added to provide orientation for the users.

HoloMUCK, whose server is located at McGill University in Montreal, Canada, illustrates the extremes of control. HoloMUCK's predecessor, Flux, was originally developed as an open MUD, placing minimal restrictions on building proposals. As the MUD developed, the configuration became more and more complex. The founding wizards eventually came to feel that the illogical nature of the spaces made the MUD unusable: navigation depended more and more on teleporting and the illusion of the larger MUD structure was lost.

HoloMUCK was recreated using geometry clearly derived from a generic Canadian small town. Two main roads and a river intersect to provide orientation. The wizards have created one of the most controlled MUD environments found in the study. As in Jay's Place, HoloMUCK's planning stresses the realism of the domain. If a closet were opened to reveal an aircraft hangar, the wizards would not allow its construction in the main MUD structure.

If the failure of the original HoloMUCK was due to its spontaneity, the new MUD suffers from its stifling control. HoloMUCK's wizards have tried to resolve this by letting builders do what they like outside the "city limits." Lying outside the main structure is a free-zone in which spaces may follow any or no logic at all. As a result, most new construction lies outside the rigorous and isolated core, known as TANSTAAFL.[10]

"REALITY" CHECKS

The failure of some MUDs is due to problems other than politics. MUD size is largely determined by the number of spaces and objects programmed by the citizens. The number of rooms vastly outnumbers the users—especially the number logged on at any one time. A paradoxical result is that MUDs with the greatest number of builders seem to have the lowest density population. This explains the apparent vacancy of many MUDs. While there are pockets of activity, large portions of the MUD often remain unused and rarely visited.[11]

Unsuccessful rooms are like unsuccessful Web home pages. Once built they are rarely modified. Visitors may "hit" on a space once or twice, but without novelty or companionship to engage them, they rarely return. Our researchers found that few fellow MUDers knew the domains as well as they did. Many citizens had not explored the main structure since their first few visits.

MUD activity centers on the entry, where users begin their sessions. In the MUD it often appears as a lobby, a town square or visitor center. In LambdaMOO, it is a closet. The area immediately around the entry is also populated but occupancy drops off sharply thereafter. MUDers often prefer teleporting to their destinations rather than sequentially moving through the labyrinth of rooms.

The problem is exacerbated by privatization; private spaces are often not spatially linked to the main MUD structure. The Chatting Zone and the University of MOO apparently have a great number of rooms in which private socializing occurs. Many citizens enter the MUD only to teleport directly to their rooms. In some MUDs citizens enter directly into their rooms, often staying there to monitor the MUD. This depletes the activity in the public portions of the MUD. There usually aren't enough users logged on to support this stratification.

This polarization between entry and private rooms results from poor spatialization and design. Real cities don't have single points of entry. Their periphery is open to the traffic of commerce and the population. Even the most private spaces in a city are part of its spatial structure. MUDs, while seemingly based on reality, ignore some fundamental truths of community planning. Teleportation is a symptom of the problem, but not its cause. HoloMUCK forbids teleportation because its wizards feel teleporting destroys the sense of physical community. This solution, however, is ill-conceived, as teleportation is merely a user's way around a problem of design.

The graphic representation of a domain offers solutions to these problems. If visitors can "see" the extent of the MUD, they might be more inclined to explore it. Presently, the text medium blinds users to distant spaces and blinkers their experience. It limits their exploration to sequential plodding from space to space. They are only aware of the rooms immediately adjacent to their current positions.[12]

Teleportation is preferred to this movement once destinations are known and citizens are familiar with their domains. However, social activity diminishes as teleporting increases. Teleportation does not allow for the chance encounters and discoveries offered by the illusion of actual movement.

One possible resolution is to incorporate the private spaces into the main structures of MUDs. By limiting access to these spaces to spatial motion, activity in the main structure may also improve. Additionally, the burden of access should be lightened by providing more access points to the MUD. This would shorten the distance to a destination. If more than one entry is used, each will serve as a node of activity, creating the equivalents of neighborhood pubs and hangouts.

Random entry at these points would also stimulate exploration and interaction. Once the main entry has a critical mass of occupants, additional visitors could be let in elsewhere to spread activity to the lesser frequented areas. It could revitalize the MUD community.

ENVISIONING CYBERSPACE

The next phase of the study was to create two visions of the MUDs: one from a consensus of the subject MUD community; the other a personal interpretation by each investigator. In both cases the ambiguities of the text were used to spark the design process.

After the creation of the logical adjacency models, the investigators interviewed several of their fellow MUD citizens. This came naturally from the mapping phase. Many friendships had been made in the course of charting the domains, and other MUDers were curious about the project and would periodically check on its progress. The wizards were impressed, at times flattered, by the dedication of the researchers to their domains. The citizens were generally enthusiastic about helping with the study.

The results of the interviews were mixed and initially disappointing. The original aim of this phase was to arrive at a consensus vision of what the MUD would be like as a three-dimensional environment. By having the MUDers elaborate on their domains, it was hoped that enough detail would be generated to visualize the spaces. This proved difficult at best.

In only a few cases did respondents provide useful information. When asked to elaborate on a series of spaces, one woman faxed sketches she had made to illustrate what she imagined them to be. This was an exception to the rule. Largely, the responses, though well-meaning, generated no more than the descriptions already provided by the MUD itself. The MUDers were not prepared to embellish these texts and were bemused by the researchers asking such "obvious" questions.

This phase of the study contrasted the researchers' interests with those of their fellow MUDers. The project had been created with the aim of envisioning these cyberspace communities. Most MUDers don't question the use of text, treating it as a given while logged onto the domains. Some feared losing the richness of text to the newer graphical MUDs. To them the MUD is about social interaction, not the setting. [13]

Many MUD citizens value the subjectivity of the text and bridle at the definition of the MUD space with a fixed design. This became a theme many of the researchers incorporated into their own designs. Some projects merged text with graphics to provide a hybridized environment, others developed methods to allow MUDers to customize their image of the domains.

In the final phase of the project, the researchers were to individually generate a vision of their MUDs. They were to incorporate anything they might have learned in the course of the study, but were not bound by the information generated in the interviews. Each student was asked to use this opportunity to express a unique quality of being on-line. This was an effort to define the qualities of cybereal architecture. [14]

The sequence of spaces encountered in the rendition had to match the layout of the logical adjacency model. The models became the focus of much debate since the illusion of space and motion had not been challenged to that point. The logic of the MUD structure (orientation, connection, and location) is verifiable, but the nature of the spaces and connections is subject to debate.

POETRY IN MOTION

Motion in a MUD is an illusion created by the text sequence. MUDers issue directional commands to get from place to place. If no directional options are available, they can use the name of the destination to get there. Teleporting differs little from conventional MUD movement. Both result in a spatial description with options for exits.[15]

Motion by the user is entirely symbolic. The symbolism of motion is crucial to the MUD experience. It implies that the user is situated and complicit within the MUD environment. Movement brings the user into the MUD psychologically. It is integral to the MUD's immersive nature.

The investigators were encouraged to view this motion critically, seeing themselves as stage managers in a play. This manager has a unique position in a production. Unlike the actors or audience, the manager is not immersed in the environment. He is charged with realizing the illusion. The students were to create the illusion of motion without necessarily mimicking it.

Several students explored motion in their visualizations. In all cases, the work was presented as computer animations rendered with Autodesk's 3D Studio. While CAD (Computer Aided Design) animations are still a novelty in architecture schools, the dynamic, ephemeral qualities of MUDs demanded the medium. Fades, pans, animation, the changing of viewing angles, morphing, and other cinematic methods became common practice by the end of the study.

These techniques were specifically used to address the illusion of motion. For example, fading into another scene is similar to the experience of reading the description of a space. Entering into an unknown space was also presented as though the user had backed into it—as if a video camera were pointing out the back of a car. The viewer doesn't know where he or she is until the room has already been entered.

Some investigators interpreted motion relativistically. Rather than the viewer moving around the space, the space would move around the viewer. This reflected the actual user sitting in a chair while manipulating the MUD environment.

In other cases morphing techniques were used to transform distant buildings into closer buildings, providing a dreamlike quality to the motion. One project, by George Wharton III, proposed that the MUD was always the same space and that the viewer was fixed. The illusion of motion was provided by a continual morphing of the MUD envelope. "Architectural" ripples in the envelope internally created the illusion of passing buildings.

Morphing can create motion effects in other ways. If rooms transform themselves into a user's destination, a nonspatial movement is effected. One researcher, Susan Sealer, devised buildings that changed shape at the user's whim. Going from one space to another was equated with reshaping the point of departure. In another experiment she changed the focal length of the software cameras. By dynamically reducing the focal length, the original scene was reduced to a point, and the succeeding scene seemed to engulf it as it came into view, ultimately replacing it.

Another investigator, Tom Vollaro, presented his MUD as empty space filled with flying shards of matter (FIG. 3). When the user wanted to enter a space, the shards would collect around him as though drawn by a magnet until the space was formed. This resulted in a graceful ballet of fragments shattering and reforming as the user "moved" through the MUD.

3. Formation of rooms from available data

"shards." Sequence by Thomas Vollaro

4. Crowd of abstract avatars in a setting without architecture. Dana Napurano

The user's identity while on line is represented by a character called an avatar. Avatars often do not have the same name as their owner, disguising the user's identity. The result is a masque that retains the role-playing character of the earlier MUDs.[16]

Several researchers focused their work on the avatar's presence in the MUD. As with motion, presence can be viewed relativistically. Presence is a subtle interaction between the self and the environment and several avatars were designed to manifest this relationship.

One investigator, Dana Napurano, associated light with the avatar. When moving from place to place in a text-based MUD, the user activates the descriptions of the rooms. That space is "illuminated" by reading the text. This illumination would remain constant until one avatar met another and engaged in conversation. At that point the light emanating from one avatar focused upon the other, casting the rest of the space into shadow. Attention and focus were both illustrated by this simple gesture.

While many avatars in the study were humanoid in shape, there were significant exceptions. In an independent project by one student, the setting of the MUD was invisible and avatars were abstract, illuminated forms (FIG. 4). When an avatar entered a new space, its color changed. Groups of avatars in a space formed constellations of light, intensifying their color while in dialog. Cyberspace was envisioned as a universe of human constellations.

In another case an investigator created a user interface for MUDing. One side of the screen offered a menu of masks, the other showed a nightclub scene populated with floating masks of various colors (FIG. 5). By selecting a mask from the menu, the user could take on the point of view of any of the avatars in the night club. The user could theoretically maintain a dialog with himself by shifting between masks.

Despite the personal mediation of the avatar, MUDs can be surprisingly affecting. Communication seems intimate because of its unearned familiarity. Typing messages to another person on line is similar to having a phone conversation. As a result, the researchers made a number of friends and acquaintances on MUDs throughout the study period. Some continue to maintain contact.

On a larger scale, these bonds can create subgroups within a larger MUD. These can operate as special interest groups and develop political power. For example in the University of MOO, the wizards' capricious pranks were causing the MUD citizens to call for their removal. Some were even planning to create a new MOO in protest. In other MUDs, social harmony can create enduring loyalties.

The researchers of DreaMOO discovered that a number of their on-line compatriots were refugees from the now-defunct Metaverse MUD. Metaverse, a fairly elaborate MUD, charged its members a fee for use. Apparently, it was not successful and the server was reassigned. The stranded population of Metaverse was then left to wander cyberspace looking for a new home. Our researchers discovered a number of refugees reminiscing about their old domain.

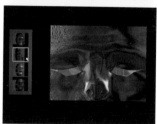

As a tribute to their many MUD compatriots, the researchers presented their analyses and video animations over the Internet on March 8, 1996. Each team presented its results as part of an on-line dialog with the remote onlookers. The home page used for the presentation will be used as a gallery for the products of the study. It is planned to have links to the entry points of all MUDs in its display. In this way, MUDers may enter other domains by passing through the home page way-station. This form of cybereal stepping stone is intended to provide a larger structure for MUDing.

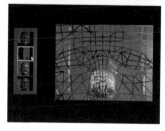

5. MUD interface showing avatar options and setting. Avatars may be selected to take on the viewpoint of another citizen. George Wharton III

The development of a truly spatial cyberspace will draw on the talents of many disciplines including the fine arts, theater, and architecture. The work done by these students offers the possibility of a new area of architectural endeavor. Architects, trained in spatial design, community planning, aesthetics, graphic communication, and the use of computers are in a unique position to contribute to this effort. As spatial MUDs are being created, the input of these skills will be vital to creating a rich, cultural setting for future mediated societies.

NOTES

This essay would not have been possible without the assistance and research of Brian Booth, Mike Buldo, Ian Dorn, Sean Edwards, Keelin Fritz, Keith Kemery, Michael Lisowski, Raymond McCarthy, Tom Mesuk, Dana Napurano, Melanie Pakingan, George Paschalis, Susan Sealer, Kevin Spink, Eric Syto,Thomas Vollaro, George Wharton III, and Robert Zappulla, who participated in a seminar on MUDs conducted by the author at the New Jersey Institute of Technology in 1996.

1. "MUD" and "domain" are used here to generically refer to these types.

2. The acronyms can be whimsical. The investigators of a MUCK were told that it stood for Many Unemployed College Kids. It actually stands for Multi-User Collective Kingdom.

3. The following is taken from a sample session held by researcher Mike Buldo on his MUD, HoloMUCK. Naima and Dex are the avatar names of other MUD citizens. "You" refers to Mike and is used only on the machine he is logged onto. Other MUDers' screens see the name of his avatar, Kilian. The "page" command is used to address another remote user of the MUD. Spelling errors reflect the real-time speed of interaction:

Time> Tue Oct 31 19:53:04 1995

page naima= we d got them on Monday!!, thanx alot

You page, "we got them on Monday!!, thanx alot" to Naima.

You head west...

Main Street (800W)

This once-desolate section of Main Street is looking busier these days.

To the north, at 800 W. Main St., stands the Red Dragon Inn.

[Obvious exits: north, w, e]

4. Many MUDs operate as game-playing environments, following the example set by Dungeons and Dragons in the early 1980s. The appeal of these games lies in their setting and participant role-playing. They act as a form of theater, or masque, in which MUDers may take on one or many identities in the course of play. Brenda Laurel and Sherry Turkle have written extensively on the psychological and social implications of this activity.

5. Note the reference to Dungeons and Dragons.

6. The electronic equivalent of earlier cultures whose buildings inspired Bernard Rudofsky's study by this name. Bernard Rudofsky, *Architecture Without Architects: A Short Introduction to Non-Pedigreed Architecture* (New York: Hacker Art Books, 1969).

7. In most MUDs, particularly MOOs, all objects are descendants of other objects. This is a result of

object-oriented programming that allows replication of code modules for editing and reconfiguration. Even the avatars that represent MUD citizens fall into this category of objects. The entire MUD structure is related in this curiously genetic way.

8. Curtis, one of the pioneers of MOOs, has investigated the use of MUDs as social and professional environments. AstroVR, for example is a MUD used by professional astronomers, providing them with a "timeless place" for gathering and displaying their findings.

9. This points up one of the advantages of graphic MUDs. Navigation is difficult if one needs to memorize specific addresses. Browsing and discovery are facilitated by visual, nontextual spaces.

10. TANSTAAFL is an acronym for "There Ain't No Such Thing As A Free-Lunch." This may be an ironic reference to the surrender of freedom implicit in HoloMUCK's building codes.

11. This experience is often like moving through a series of underground chambers. The creation of rooms is often referred to as "digging" a space. This combined with the acronym MUD seem to make MUDing earthbound. The opacity of the Internet for many users belies the term "cyberspace." One of the objectives of building the logical adjacency models was to see the MUD components in relationship to one another. This is only possible if the rooms are seen from the outside, as objects. Mostly, however, MUD spaces are experienced from inside, without seeing the outer context.

12. An example of this is MediaMOO. This MUD, at the Massachusetts Institute of Technology, was developed as a learning tool, and its many spaces and student experiments extend far beyond its original configuration. As a result, the investigators often found it largely vacant when they visited. This does not necessarily reflect on the success of the MUD. MediaMOO's spaces are largely navigable with conventional commands. Problems arise when the bulk of a MUD is invisible to its users and only accessible via teleportation, as in University of MOO and portions of BayMOO.

13. While there is no denying the effectiveness of text, graphic on-line environments can have their own poetry. If we accept MUDs as "virtual theater," we have to acknowledge the importance of the set. Actors use the set and props to convey subtle information. Leaning on a wall has different implications than facing it, for instance. Sets and props are distinguished by their evocative potential. Visualizing them would allow a subtler manipulation of these devices, "broadening the bandwidth" of the theater.

14. "Cybereal architecture" here refers to virtual objects within the computer's illusive space. Unlike CAD drawings or models, they are not part of a design process that culminates in a physical presence. Instead, they operate autonomously within cyberspace to define information content. Common examples of cybereal objects would be computer icons and windows. They act as symbols of information structures (files, directories). Once spatialized these objects could define meaningful space for the location of information, much as architecture is used to define institutions, organize contents, and orient people.

15. Other means of motion are available. Many MUDs—like Purple Crayon and Meridian—have modes of public transportation, such as trains or boats, that take MUDers on preselected routes. Some MUDs offer planes or taxis, modes of teleportation in which the destination, once known, can be called out. The experience is sequential and textual, the vehicles a camouflage for the paradox of bodiless movement.

16. On the subject of identity and MUD communities, see: Brenda Laurel, *Computers as Theater* (Reading, MA: Addison Wesley, 1991); Allucquere Rosanne Stone, *The War Between Desire and Technology at the Close of the Mechanical Age* (Cambridge, MA: MIT Press, 1993); Sherry Turkle, *Life on the Screen: Identity in the Age of the Internet* (New York: Simon & Schuster, 1995); and Howard Rheingold, *The Virtual Community: Homesteading on the Electronic Frontier* (Reading, MA: Addison Wesley, 1993).

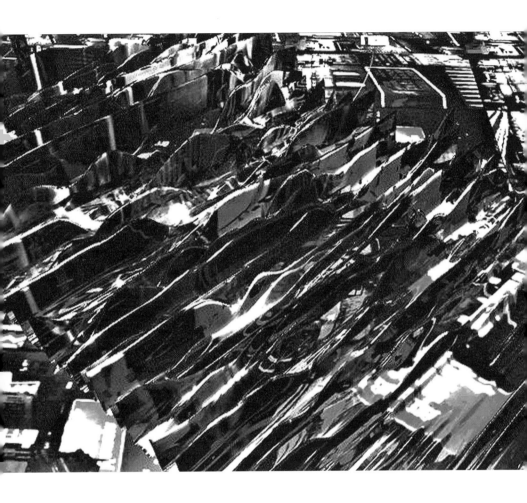

Times Square, human agency, 1995 (with Rebecca Carpenter)

Hypersurfaces: Socius Fluxus

STEPHEN PERRELLA

THE VIRTUAL DIMENSION may be understood as an immanent manifestation of instrumental reason in late-Western culture. The operation of the technologically virtual produces new realms of human interface, ones far more complex than the casual separation between the fields of the real and virtual. Rather than as an added "dimension" to the Cartesian construct, the virtual dimension unfolds as an escaped mutation of the State, whose tacit mandate includes military dominance, technological mastery over nature, and the pursuit of social progress. This indictment of virtuality's collusion with instrumentality reveals a logic of assumptions carried forth in the name of Enlightenment humanism, but it also belies technology's inherently schizophrenic modalities. Technology simultaneously liberates as it undermines and reconfigures.[1] Teletechnology creates possibilities, but also ingests and redefines according to its methodologies and industries. For example, the way that issues of identity are manufactured in what is called "Generation X" is inconceivable without sampling and integrating—both consumer technologies. Here, identity is problematic because the mode of production is complicit with economics. The pursuit of authentic identity involves a subjugation to the technologies of difference. As technology becomes the dominant mode of production (approaching a majority of the gross domestic product by the year 2011), the way that a virtual dimension unfolds into the "reality equation" should be more clearly investigated. The virtual dimension also deterritorializes institutions of collectivity; in actuality, the virtual, instead of being a tool for the extension of man's control, has begun to fold back onto itself in a process of duplication and generation of a complex, mutant socius, a productive yet schizophrenic condition, one that Felix Guattari calls, "Chaosmosis."[2] If this description has any rigor, it means we can no longer rely on foundational, traditional notions of space and time, the existing dimensions of Cartesianism, especially as they ground our understanding of architecture and urbanism. At the very least, this implosive effect raises questions about where and how those traditional notions are established.[3] Nor can we rely on the provisional divisions between the real and the virtual to contain the enormous degree of reciprocal contamination that each holds for the other, stemming from an erosive and disseminating dynamic of a lifeworld out of which has arisen deviations of virtuality.

To better understand the significance and consequences brought about by the virtual dimension, consider a diagram of a configuration that discloses a superposed and interspersed "reality." This diagram attempts to present how a new mixture of electronic horizons configures an "infrastructure." Not a literal infrastructure, in the sense of transportation routes and backbones for distribution, but a diagram for new modalities of human agency, one that supersedes a now outmoded Cartesian paradigm. This diagrammatic infrastructure is constituted of seams and interstitial folds resulting in fluxing lines of demarcation, converting separate realms into grafted ones. Once a virtual dimension appears, the provisional layers of existing fabric implode, engendering fluid interpermutations. Our cultural "ground," then, becomes a continuous zone of inflections whereby the "real" is subject to fluctuation and interfoldings into a systemic of dynamic interrelations; a systemic of transversality.[4] The effects of this condition erupt from very specific machinations within praxis, not outside of it. There is no outside or inside. In this diagram, what is being drawn is the implosion of structures of transcendence into radically mutable superpositions. Instead of the real and the ideal being separate realms, the divisions sustained by transcendental metaphysics, the divisions now become fused. This is significant because previous constructs have brought about different paradigmatics and thus another modality of experience is to be expected. For instance, a world dominated, indeed determined, by television, creates an affect of transcendentality; that is, the effect of a governing metaphysic that through technologized structures of ideation, give the effect of an outside or an upper-realm, or "the concrete realization of Hegel's Absolute Spirit."[5] And it is precisely this sort of dynamic that leads Brain Massumi (in this book and elsewhere) to discuss a radical empiricism and proprioperception as ways of explaining how we will experience these new modalities.

In our existing technologically saturated context there are horizons through which our lives are drawn. The emergence of a virtual dimension attenuates a further layer beyond two current electronic strata. Respectively,

they are the "Free Space Horizon," the "Signification-Infrastructure Horizon," and most recently, the "Internetted Horizon." Combined, these three horizons organize layers of activity or inhabitation but should not be considered mutually exclusive. Increasingly, capitalism drives a world culture of consumption forcing these layers to become increasingly dense and interwoven. The process and logic of pervasion stemming from teletechnology intermixes television within the Internet, the Internet impacts upon built infrastructure, and so forth, creating a convergent, infolded, organization. From this condensed condition arises

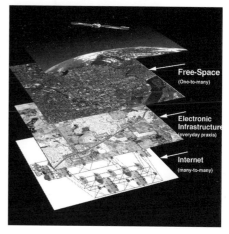

Haptic Horizon, diagram, 1995,

Haptic Horizon, 1995

new and emergent phenomenon. The action of this recombinant schema seems to occur from the middle out. For instance, it was originally thought that the electronic revolution would replace print media. But instead what has actually happened is that the virtual dimension has increased and saturated the media even further. From this construct, specific relationships may be understood as hypersurfaces, a term that attempts to characterize the complex way new interfaces will occur and reconfigure us.

Within this three tiered interpretation of technologized culture, what critical dynamic brings about the virtual dimension? It seems historically that the middle layer, the electronic infrastructure, packed with programs of communications, advertisements, print media, telephonic discourse, transportation, commerce, and all of the other trappings of an industrialized and postindustrialized infrastructure is an urbanized society that operates as a plane of immanence. The affect of that plane is best described as an urban complex, a bustling metropolis with centers of industry, an affect well expressed in early genres of cinema, specifically the German cinema of the 1930s. With the advent of television in the early 1950s, another layer is generated out of the "middle," seemingly above the metropolis, extending beyond and in effect creating a vast sub-urban terrain, where the one-to-many logic of broadcast media effects a generalized narrative simultaneity controlled by the military industrial complex. Its effect on culture is closer to social engineering, as the spread of advertisement and entertainment stand in place of meaningful social discourse, or, more specifically, a media insinuated within social discourse. With the advent of free-space there is no real possibility for an unmediated dialog.

What is the real? At what point was anything real? How is the real tied to social discourse and was there ever a state of unconstrained social discourse? How does the Internetted horizon effect that? What kind of space does the Net produce? Is virtuality the opposite of broadcast space, thereby doubling the logic of simulation? Simulation, considered as a doubling, gives the effect of realism but is the height of a debased culture, perhaps at its most precarious moment.

These interpenetrating layers, fueled by consumer capitalism, will reconfigure the topology of human agency. Emergent forms of representation will unfold due to the radical interweavings that create both commensurate and incommensurate juxtapositions of varying fields. This condition may perhaps be best understood as a surrealism imbedded within the everyday.[6] The way that it will effect the architecture/culture mix is a thematic being taken up under a thematic called Hypersurface, and may be what results from the exigencies of the virtual dimension.

NOTES

STEPHEN PERRELLA

1. Alison Gill and Freida Riggs, "The Angst and the Aura," in *R/U/A/TV?*, ed. Tony Fry (Sydney: Power Publications, 1993).

2. Felix Guattari, *Chaosmosis: An Ethico-Aesthetic Paradigm* (Bloomington: Indiana University Press, 1995).

3. Mark Wigley, *The Architecture of Deconstruction: Derrida's Haunt* (Cambridge, MA: MIT Press, 1996).

4. Gianni Vattimo, *The Transparent Society* (Baltimore, MD: The Johns Hopkins University Press, 1992).

5. Stephen Perrella, ed., *Architectural Design Magazine: Hypersurface Architectures* (London: Academy Editions, 1998).

240

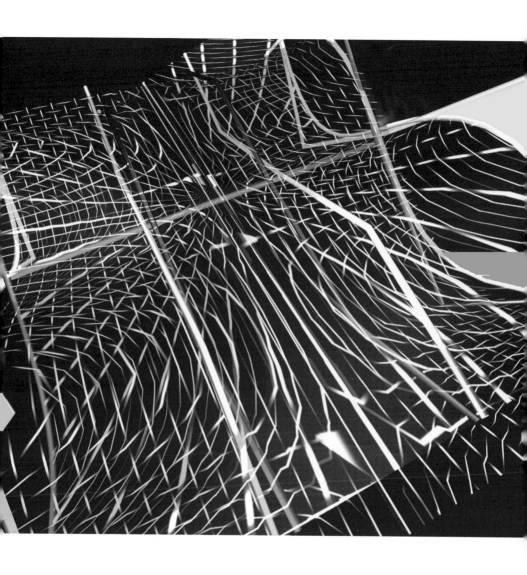

Hypersurface panel, study, 1998

Terminal Velocities:

The Computer in the Design Studio

STAN ALLEN

Oh but it's not the fall

that hurts him at all—

It's that sudden stop.[1]

DURING THE HOT summer months in New York City cats begin to fall, or throw themselves, out of high windows. Nobody quite knows why, but researchers studying the phenomenon have uncovered a curious pattern. While a cat falling one or two stories has some chance of landing safely, a cat falling from three to six stories is unlikely to survive. Surprisingly, a cat falling from more than six stories is quite likely to survive. Apparently, by twisting into proper position and completely relaxing, the cats develop enough resiliency to survive the impact. Beyond fifteen floors the chances of survival drop again. Too much time in the air, and the cats reach terminal velocity—in the most literal sense.

Speed is fundamental to the rhetoric of the computer. Bigger is better, but faster is best. In advanced imaging and animation programs, for example, it is processing speed and not disk space that is the limiting factor.

High-end personal computers already run at inconceivably fast speeds—x^n calculations per second, and improving all the time. Mainframe supercomputers and parallel processing promise even greater speed. In part this is bound up with questions of marketing and efficiency. The immense capital expenditure for software development and the large-scale implementation of computer aided design (CAD) systems in design and production would have been impossible without measurable gains in speed and productivity. The same Taylorizing impulse at work in early modernism—the elimination of obsolete and inefficient work methods—is still visible today.[2]

But in the rhetorical fictions of the computer, speed brings something else: a future not only more fully integrated with technology, but a promise to recover precisely that which had been destroyed by modernity in the first place. Claims are made for the recuperation of community, self, political space, precision craft, and local identity.[3] The rhetoric of accessibility in turn depends upon the capacity of the computer to simulate reality. And it is speed that guarantees the seamlessness (and thereby the realism) of these new simulations. But between the promise of a digital future and the realities of the present there are complex questions to be answered. In *Pure War*, Paul Virilio has signaled his skepticism about the depletion of time as technologies of speed are everywhere put into place: "There again it's the same illusory ideology that when the world is reduced to nothing and we have everything at hand, we'll be infinitely happy. I believe it's just the opposite—and this has already been proven—that we'll be infinitely unhappy because we will have lost the very place of freedom, which is expanse." Control and concentration are the inevitable counterparts of these new technocratic regimes: "The field of freedom shrinks with speed. And freedom needs a field. When there is no more field, our lives will be like a terminal, a machine with doors that open and close."[4]

Virilio distinguishes between metabolic speed—the speed of the living being, reaction time—and technological speed—the artificial speed of machines. Significantly, what differentiates recent technologies from modernist machines (the aircraft, the telegraph, or the automobile) is a blurring of the boundary between technological speed and metabolic speed. Computer speed is microspeed, invisible in its working, visible only as affect. With the computer, technological speed approaches metabolic speed. Genetic algorithms can simulate hundreds of thousands of years of evolution in a few minutes; artificial life programs bring responsiveness and adaptivity to the technological environment. For Virilio, what distinguishes metabolic speed is its inconsistency: "What is living, present, conscious, here, is only so because there's an infinity of little deaths, little accidents, little breaks, little cuts..."[5] It is through these interruptions that the field is reconstituted—not as seamless continuity, but, through a shift in scale, as a finer grained texture that allows local connection and continuity; an order that accepts discontinuity and difference without encoding it as catastrophic disjunction. Hence, as Sylvere Lotringer (Virilio's interlocutor in *Pure War*) notes: "All is not negative in the technology of speed. Speed, and that accident, that interruption which is the fall, have something to teach us on the nature of our bodies or the functioning of our consciousness."[6]

What is at stake for architecture in all this? The computer in the design studio provokes both extravagant claims and high levels of anxiety. Is there, as with the cats falling through the hot summer air, a window of opportunity between an initial state of dismay or confusion, and the endgame of "terminal velocity"? Questions of identity politics and the real effects of new technologies on the spaces of the city are issues that urgently need to be addressed. But before this is possible, it will be necessary to look more closely at the paradigms and protocols at work in the use of the computer as a design tool.

A legitimate skepticism toward both the technocratic drive for efficient production as well as the vague promise of a utopian future is a start. But a positive program is required as well. This would begin with a speculative and open-ended investigation of the possibilities and potentialities of these new technologies within the specific demands of the discipline of architecture. It is important not to lose sight of the instrumentality of the computer. The computer is not "just another" tool, but it is a tool nonetheless—a tool with very specific capabilities and constraints. What are the specific opportunities for new modalities of geometrical description, spatial modeling, simulation of program and use, generation of formal and organizational systems, or rapid prototyping? A careful reassessment of the implications of these new tools in their theoretical and conceptual context is warranted. By questioning the rhetoric of the new, it is possible to rethink both the new technology and architecture's own persistent paradigms of order, geometry, and organization. The luddite option, for all of its rhetorical attractiveness, is untenable, and, finally, uninteresting. What is required is to become familiar enough with the technology so as to be able to strip away its mythological veneer. Don't count on "being digital"; rather, work on becoming digital. The interruption and the accident need to be cultivated; software systems must be used against the grain. Established protocols need to be tweaked.[7]

FIRST HYPOTHESIS: DIGITAL ABSTRACTIONS

One of the curious aspects of digital technology is the valorization of a new realism.[8] From Hollywood special effects to architectural rendering, the success of the new technology is measured by its ability to seamlessly render the real. Even so-called virtual reality has not so much been used to create alternative realities but to replicate those already existing. In architecture this is evident in "visualization" techniques. The promise here is that if computer technology can create more and more realistic simulations, design mistakes will be avoided. This too is clearly market driven, answering a need to predict what something will look like before spending the money to build it.[9] The fallacies of this position are almost too numerous to specify. For one, it assumes that a very narrow range of perceptual mechanisms come into play in the experience of architecture: a tunnel-like camera vision, ignoring the fluidity of the eye and the intricacies of peripheral vision—not to mention the rest of the body.[10] But more significantly, it ignores what has traditionally given architectural representation its particular power of conceptualization—that is to say, its necessary degree of abstraction, the distance interposed between the thing and its representation.[11]

The story of Diboutades is often evoked as an account of the origins of drawing: The daughter of a Corinthian shepherd traces the shadow of the head of her departing lover as a memento (FIG. 1). The drawing is a substitute, a partial record of the absent, desired thing. This story of origins is consistent with classical theories of mimesis, but problematic from the point of view of architecture. In architecture, the object does not proceed its representation in drawing. Rather, the built reality is both imagined and constructed from accumulated partial representations. As codified in systems of mechanical drawing, the object is imagined inside a transparent box—the materialization of the Cartesian coordinate system (FIG. 2). On the surfaces of the box are registered the traces of the lines of orthographic projection. Traditionally, the architect works on the two dimensional surfaces of this box, not on the object itself. The architectural project is a virtual construction, a whole created from abstract parts interpreted and combined according to shared conventions of projection and representation.

1. P. Devlamnyyk, *The Invention of Drawing*, after a painting by Joseph Suvée, 1791

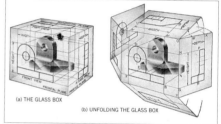

2. *The Glass Box*, from *Technical Drawing* by Giesecke, Mitchell, and Spencer, 1958

Now the computer simultaneously collapses and increases the distance between the architect's two-dimensional representations and the building's three-dimensional reality. That is to say, in as much as computer representations are more immaterial than conventional drawings, the distance is increased; in as much as it is possible to work directly in three dimensions, the distance is collapsed. The vector of representation is reversed; the glass box is turned inside out. In computer modeling, the architect works directly on a three dimensional representation of the object itself. In the virtual space of the computer, it is possible to go quickly back and forth (or even to work simultaneously) on the two-dimensional projection and the three-dimensional object. (Of course, another system of projection/representation intervenes—the two-dimensional display of the screen itself—but the ease with which it is possible to move the object and to move around in that space can provisionally suspend its presence as intermediary.) That object is a collection of commands as opposed to the result of a series of projections. Instead of a finite number of representations constructing an object (either in the mind or in the world) there is already an object (itself made up of a nearly infinite number of discrete elements) capable of generating an infinite number of representations of itself.

As a consequence of this, the effect of working on the computer is cumulative. Nothing is lost. Elements and details are continuously added, stored, and filed in perfect transparency. Instead of proceeding from the general to the specific, the designer moves from detail to ensemble and back again, potentially inverting traditional design hierarchies.

The status of the drawing, and in turn the process of design itself, undergoes a transformation. A new kind of abstraction emerges: abstraction not as final result of operations of idealization or reduction, but of the indifferent order of bits. Interestingly enough, a sense of casualness, a paradoxical lack of precision, is one result of this. Computer abstractions are radically provisional, open to infinite revision. If the power of the computer lies in its ability to handle large amounts of information, multiple variables, and abstract codes, it is worthwhile to be attentive to an emerging sensibility for diagrammatic and loose organizational paradigms: a contingent, "conditional" abstraction. This in turn implies a shift away from the false certainties of visualization toward the generative capacities of the computer as an abstract machine. Today, this is expressed not so much as a mandate as a possibility. Abstraction is no longer a categorical imperative, but one choice among many. When working with the computer, however, it is a logical choice as it is something that the computer does well.

SECOND HYPOTHESIS: DIGITAL FIELDS

Analog technologies of reproduction work through imprints, traces, or transfers. The image may shift in scale or value (as in a negative), but its iconic form is maintained throughout. Internal hierarchies are preserved. A significant shift occurs when an image is converted to digital information. A notational schema intervenes. "Digital electronic technology atomizes and abstractly schematizes the analogic quality of the photographic and cinematic into discrete pixels and bits of information that are transmitted serially, each bit discontinuous, discontiguous, and absolute—each bit 'being in itself' even as it is part of a system."[12] A field of immaterial ciphers is substituted for the material traces of the object (FIG. 3). Hierarchies are distributed; "value" is evened out. These ciphers differ one from the other only as place holders in a code. They have no materiality, no intrinsic value. Already in 1921, Viktor Shklovsky had anticipated the radical leveling effect of the notational sign: "Playful, tragic, universal or particular works of art, the oppositions of one world to another or of a cat to a stone, are all equal among themselves."[13]

3. Digital code: text file print

out of image file

This evening out of value has implications for the traditional concept of figure/field. In the digital image "background" information must be as densely coded as foreground information. Blank space is not empty space; there is empty space throughout the field. If classical composition sought to maintain clear relations of figure on ground, which modern composition perturbed by the introduction of a complicated play of figure against figure, with digital technologies we now have to come

AXIAL SYMMETRY		PERIPHERAL COMPOSITION
COLLISION/ASSEMBLAGE		LINKED ASSEMBLIES
STRIATED		STRIATED 2
PATCHWORK 2		FIELD VECTORS
CLUSTER		OPEN CLUSTER
LOOSE GRID		FELT

to terms with the implications of a field/field relation (FIG. 4). A shift of scale is involved, and a necessary revision of basic compositional parameters is implied.

A moiré, for example, is a figural effect produced by the superposition of two regular fields (FIG. 5). Unexpected effects, exhibiting complex and apparently irregular behaviors, result from the combination of elements that are in and of themselves repetitive and regular. But moiré effects are not random. They shift abruptly in scale, and repeat according to complex mathematical rules. Moiré effects are often used to measure hidden stresses in continuous fields, or to map complex figural forms. In these cases, figure and field can never be separated as distinct entities, producing an uncanny coexistence of a regular field and emergent figure.

Comparing these field formations to the organizing principles of classical architecture, it is possible to identify contrasting principles of combination: one algebraic, working with numerical units combined one after another; and the other geometric, working with figures (lines, planes, solids) organized in space to form larger wholes. In algebraic combination, independent elements are combined additively to form an indeterminate whole. The local syntax is fixed, but there is no overarching geometric scaffolding. Parts are not fragments of wholes, but simply parts. (As Jasper Johns has remarked: "Why take the part for the whole; why not take the part for the part?") Unlike the idea of closed unity enforced in Western classical architecture, algebraic combinations can be added onto without substantial morphological transformation.[14]

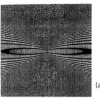
(a)

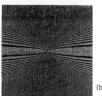
(b)

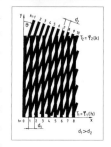

5. top: Moiré fringes formed by the superimposition of a circular grating and two linear gratings with period (a) larger than and (b) equal to the period of a circular grating

bottom: parametric description of moiré fringes formed by two linear binary amplitude gratings

The diagrams produced by the Christaller model of urban growth (FIG. 6), which ignores large-scale accidents of history or geography but incorporates fine-grained difference in the form of multiple variables and nonlinear feedback, demonstrate how the interplay between laws and chance produces complex but roughly predictable configurations of a nonhierarchical nature. The whole of the city is never given at once. The city is a place of contingency, a whole that is not bounded and closed, but capable of permutation, open to time and only provisionally stable.

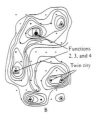

6. Christaller diagrams

In the late 1980s, artificial life theorist Craig Reynolds created a computer program to simulate the flocking behavior of birds. Reynolds placed a large number of autonomous, birdlike agents (which he called "boids") into an on-screen environment. The agents were programmed to follow three simple rules of behavior: first, to maintain a minimum distance from other objects in the environment (other agents, as well as obstacles); second, to match velocities with other agents in the neighborhood; third, to move toward the perceived center of mass of agents in its neighborhood. As Waldrop notes: "What is striking about these rules is that none of them said 'Form a flock'…the rules were entirely local, referring only to what an individual boid could do and see in its own vicinity. If a flock was going to form at all, it would have to do so from the bottom up, as an emergent phenomenon. And yet flocks did form, every time."[15]

The flock is clearly a field phenomenon, defined by precise and simple local conditions, and relatively indifferent to overall form and extent.[16] Because the rules are defined locally, obstructions are not catastrophic to the whole. Variations and obstacles in the environment are accommodated by fluid adjustment. A small flock and a large flock display fundamentally the same structure. Over many iterations, patterns emerge. Without repeating exactly, flock behavior tends toward roughly similar configurations, not as a fixed type, but as the cumulative result of localized behavior patterns.

One of modern architecture's most evident failings has been its inability to adequately address the complexities of urban context. Recent debates have alternated between an effort to cover over the difference between the old and the new (the contextualism of Leon Krier or the so called "New Urbanists") or a violent rejection of context (deconstruction, and related stylistic manifestations). These two examples, the Christaller model of urban growth and Reynolds' simulations of flocking behavior (others could be cited as well), dissolve the traditional opposition between order and randomness. They offer a way out of this polarized debate, acknowledging on the one hand the distinct capabilities of new construction, and at the same time recognizing a valid desire for diversity and coherence in the city. Logistics of context suggests the need to recognize the limits to architecture's ability to order the city, and at the same time, to learn from the complex self-regulating orders already present in the city. And it should be pointed out that the computer is especially well suited to the mapping and simulation of these systems—registering the cumulative effects of incremental changes, recursive and reiterative strategies, these are all inherent to the logic of the processor. Attention is shifted to systems of service and supply, a logics of flow and vectors. This implies close attention to existing conditions, carefully defined rules for intensive linkages at the local scale, and a relatively indifferent attitude toward the overall configuration. Architecture needs to learn to manage this complexity, which, paradoxically, it can only do by giving up some measure of control.

1. Bobby Russell, "Sudden Stop," recorded by Percy Sledge, 1968.

2. Our tendency to privilege the new and the optimal, along with the popular idea that every new form of technology renders existing technologies obsolete, needs to be rethought. Two simple examples demonstrate why: the first is the development of high-speed trains in Europe and Japan. A nineteenth-century technology, railroads were supposedly made obsolete long ago by air travel, but they now emerge as a logical alternative from ecological and urbanistic points of view. Similarly, AM talk radio—a technology supposedly made obsolete by television—along with the Internet and other advanced forms of communication, has acquired extraordinary political power in the United States in recent years.

3. Many examples could be cited; see, for example, Michael Benedikt, ed., *Cyberspace: First Steps* (Cambridge, MA: MIT Press, 1991), as well as the more recent emergence of academic and popular books on the subject. Scott Bukatman has coined the term "cyberdrool" for this kind of terminal identity fiction; he cites Vivian Sobchack's observation of the "peculiar oxymoronic cosmology" linking "high technophilia, 'new age' anamism, spiritualism, and hedonism, and Sixties counter-cultural 'guerrilla' political consciousness." Scott Bukatman, *Terminal Identity: The Virtual Subject in Post-Modern Science Fiction* (Durham, NC: Duke University Press, 1993), 189.

4. Paul Virilio and Sylvere Lotringer, *Pure War* (New York: Semiotext(e), 1983), 69.

5. Ibid., 33.

6. Ibid.

7. Brian Eno has proposed a simple formula: "If you want to make computers that really work, create a design team composed only of healthy, active women with lots else to do in their lives and give them carte blanche. Do not under any circumstances consult anyone who a) is fascinated by computer games b) tends to describe silly things as "totally cool" c) has nothing better to do except fiddle with those damn things night after night." Kevin Kelly, interview with Brian Eno, *Wired*, May 1995, 150.

8. The use of the computer in the design studio has facilitated two important shifts in design practice that have yet to be examined critically. First is a renewed use of perspectives, which once had to be laboriously drawn by hand but can now be generated effortlessly by clicking a button. Second is the use of color. Color in the computer is either extravagantly false or attempt to simulate photographic representations

of reality through sophisticated rendering programs incorporating reflection, transparency, and texture mapping. In both cases, the ease of achieving seductive effects has as yet overwhelmed any impulse to question the relationship between the means of representation and the architectural intention.

9. This is to ignore for a moment those who think that architecture will simply disappear in a future dominated by "virtual" realities. As they have never been really interested in architecture anyway, there's no great loss.

10. "I ask myself, What is pissing me off about this thing? What's pissing me off is that it uses so little of my body. You're just sitting there, and its quite boring. You've got this stupid little mouse that requires one hand, and your eyes. That's it." Kelly, interview with Brian Eno, 149.

11. See Robin Evans, "Translations from Drawing to Building" *AA Files* 12 (1986).

12. Vivian Sobchack, "The Scene of the Screen: Towards a Phenomenology of Cinematic and Electronic Presence," *Post-Script* 10 (1990): 56. Cited in Bukatman, *Terminal Identity*, 108.

13. Viktor Shklovsky, "Theory of Prose," (1921) cited by Manfredo Tafuri in "The Dialectics of the Avant-Garde: Piranesi and Eisenstein," *Oppositions* 11 (winter 1977): 79.

14. In this context it is interesting to note that the Turing machine—the hypothetical computing machine that is the conceptual basis of the modern digital computer—performs complicated relational functions, (multiplication or division, for example) by means of serially repeated binary operations. Paradoxically, it is only when the individual operations are simplified as far as possible that the incredible speed of the modern computer is achieved.

15. Ilya Prigogine and Isabelle Stengers, *Order out of Chaos Man's New Dialogue with Nature* (New York: Bantam Books, 1984), 197ff.

16. M. Mitchel Waldrop, *Complexity: The Emerging Science at the Edge of Order and Chaos* (New York: Simon and Schuster, 1992), 240–1.

17. "One of the essential characteristics of the dream of multiplicity is that each element ceaselessly varies and alters its distance in relation to the others...These variable distances are not extensive quantities divisible by each other; rather, each is indivisible, or 'relatively indivisible,' in other words, they are not divisible above or below a certain threshold, they cannot increase or diminish without changing their nature." Gilles Deleuze and Felix Guattari, *A Thousand Plateaus* (Minneapolis, MN: University of Minnesota Press, 1988), 30–1.

Dream house, 1996

A Capacity for Endlessness

BEN VAN BERKEL AND CAROLINE BOS

OFTEN, IN ORDER to understand our ambitions and secret desires, we revert to history—and if we don't, others will do it for us, pointing out which architects of the past were already engaged in the subjects that intrigue us now. In this individuated approach to history Frederick Kiesler has achieved a special significance in recent years. A new sympathy has emerged for the hopeless enormity of his architectural ambition, and the distressing contrast it makes with what he managed to produce. Craggy surfaces and rickety constructions serve as the improvised envelopes of the most grandiose spatial intentions. But even as we slowly learn to read those atrophied exterior crusts as topological mappings, it remains the effort to create a supreme spatiality within his buildings that evokes an affinity with contemporary architecture.

Others in history have impressed later architects with their advanced spatial imaginations; in the 1970s and 1980s Piranesi fulfilled the role of unexpectedly topical precursor. The renewed interest in Piranesi's drawings

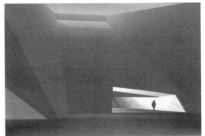

Ethnological Museum, Geneva, 1996

at that time announced a growing fascination with more complex architectural space, providing an indirect indication of the end of modernism. Reintroducing Piranesi meant that space was again shown to be subject to evolution, expansion, inversion, and other contortions and manipulations that went beyond the generic space that was the ultimate achievement and ideal of modernist architecture.

Like Piranesi's drawings, Kiesler's work contains an additional significance because it is mostly unrealized, so that nothing stands in the way of the magnanimity of its vision. But Kiesler also confronts contemporary architecture with something else; an idea of endlessness that amounts to a fully saturated spatiality, if such a condition can be imagined. While the full extent of Kiesler's spatial aspirations is unknowable, the computational techniques now at our disposal enable the deepest understanding of Kiesler ever possible. The tantalizing new spatial conditions suggested on every computer screen result in a general familiarity with the potential of a multidimensional spatial experience. Generic space—which used to be an expression of the sum of spatial conceptualization—seems rigid, static, and limited compared with the potential of spatial arrangements that follow the diving, swooping, zooming, slicing, folding motions that take place on computer screens. Special effects in films, silly cartoons, even screen-savers express a delight in explorative spatial conditions, leading to a rapid increase in the capacity for spatial conceptualization that architecture should absorb.

The first of three recent projects that we would like to present in this context and that engage in an experimental, expansive spatiality, is the competition entry for the anthropological museum of Geneva. The museum revolves around seven deep light wells that integrate the constructive, programmatic, infrastructural, lighting, and organizational aspects of the building. Analogous to pyramids, the concrete shafts simulate monoliths, extending from the ground plane like reliefs emerging from the desert. Within the mass of accumulated material, space is contained. The structure generates rooms without ceilings, rooms with sloping walls. The distribution of the program follows the structure of the wells, winding its way along the sloping walls of the shafts over three floor levels. In an architectural ensemble of this sort there is no structural core around which programmatic and routing properties fly. Routing and the distribution of the program organize the substance and construction in one integral gesture, enabling new spatial identities.

Our entry for the Cologne Diözesan Museum was developed simultaneously with the Geneva competition. Here too the ground plane forms an essential basis for the project, although it is materially disconnected from an extension which hovers above the ruins of a cathedral. Our proposal to occupy the ruins and create a free plaza is a reversal of the condition of the past thirty years or so, and entails the completion of the block, thereby generating new relations within the surrounding area.

Materially and organizationally, the model for the museum is basalt lava that has solidified around pockets of air, voids organizing the field. In the evolution of the site a pattern was recognized, and this became the basis for a grid with four foundation points for the new construction. The spaces in between the four points hover beneath the structural roof, allowing for a free division of space in between the ruins and the roof.

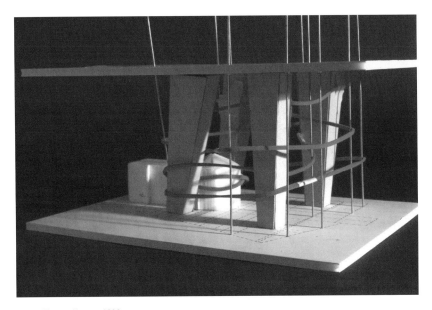

Cologne Diözesan Museum, 1996

The voids take the form of light shafts dropping from the roof and niches rising up from the ruins. The volumetric wrapping of these two elements creates the museum envelope, which consists of a variety of tightly interwoven spaces with different light sources, different heights and sizes, different organizations, but overlapping qualities. Vitrine becomes wall, light shaft becomes floor—views, voids, outside/inside spaces tend to ambiguity. The condition of overlapping qualities is intrinsic to the project's conception as one porous volume, differentiated, yet homogeneous.

An image that sums up the contemporary acceptance of the simultaneous existence of different identities within one cohesive organization is that of the manimal. As a computer image of the hybridization of a lion, a snake, and a human, this work provides another example of the capacity of

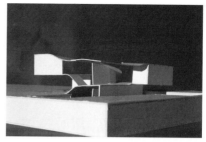

Dream House, 1996

endlessness. The manimal is so loose in its identity that it does not divulge any information about its original component parts. All traces of the previous identities have been seamlessly absorbed within the image. Architecturally, the manimal could be read as an amalgamation of several different structures that generate a new notion of scale and identity. The process that generates the image is potentially as interesting as its effect. The seamless, decontextualizing, dehistoricizing combination of discordant systems of information can be instrumentalized architecturally. As an effect, the image makes you wonder how something like this would translate spatially. As a technique, it excites because it has been produced in a manner that is radically different from all pictorial techniques that have been employed by artists before.

Research, technique, and effect are the three steps that are central to architecture. When the imagination is stimulated by something exterior to architecture, techniques will be developed to realize that effect in architectural substance. The capacity for endlessness that we recognize in Kiesler and in the manimal, we search to apply to the way in which a structure could incorporate all aspects of a building—time, the distribution of the program, construction—in one single gesture. The third project that we would like to cite in this context is the Dream House in Berlin, which has a column-free structure unfolding in a single surface organization. The concept of the Dream House is to achieve a fluid continuity between landscape and interior. This is achieved by introducing diagonal space, thereby blurring transitional zones. The spaces between inside and outside, or the representation of horizontal and vertical spaces, are dissolved diagonally.

The smooth transition between spaces is the result of the diagonal organization of function and infrastructure; the living room flows out into the garden in the same way as the garden extends into the living room. Stairs become ramps and the ramps merge with the landscape. The floor plans are expressed as undulating layers rather than planar surfaces so that the horizon and variations in light levels can be perceived differently and endlessly throughout the house. The core of the house is not formed by a staircase, but by a void, around which layers of spaces wrap themselves. The central positioning of the void enables light penetration into the core of the house, and allows the landscape to enter the rooms. The inclusiveness of the architectural organization complies with a notion of consistency, within which fragmentation and difference occur. This is in contrast to an architecture that is based on techniques of fragmentation and collage, which imply incoherence in the organization itself.

The freedom to assume different identities is an achievement of the condition of endlessness. Almost as expressively as in his projects, Kiesler's capacity for endlessness is conveyed in a series of photographs in which he takes on another persona: Kiesler as a Surrealist, as a minotaur, as Willem de Kooning, as a chess player, as Mies van der Rohe. These are just some of his incarnations. The message that can be read in those photographs is: imagine, invent, expand, pretend. With this variety of poses, the contemporary reading of Kiesler is that of multiplicities constituting a cohesive identity. For us, the whole Kiesler is found in this wide-ranging series of Kieslers. Kiesler-as-Kiesler is a manifold, generating, proliferating and projecting an infinite measure of possible identities.

Dream house, 1996

freshH^{2}O eXPO

NOX/LARS SPUYBROEK

FRESHH^{2}O EXPO (1993-97) is a water pavilion and interactive installation created for WaterLand Neeltje Jans. It is the result of a private/public partnership with the Dutch Ministry of Transport, Public Works, and Water Management, and is located in Zeeland, in the southwest of the Netherlands.

It is a turbulent alloy of the hard and the weak, of human flesh, of concrete and metal, of interactive electronics and water. A complete fusion of body, environment, and technology. The design was based on the metastable aggregation of architecture and information. The form itself is shaped by the fluid deformation of fourteen ellipses spaced over a length of more than 65 yards. Inside the building, which has no horizontal floors and no external relation to the horizon, walking becomes akin to falling. The deformation of the object extends to the constant metamorphosis of the environment, which responds interactively to visitors through a variety of sensors that register the constant reshaping of the human body.

This building does not "contain" an exhibition in the classic sense, nor does it have a program.

Next to non-interactive events—ice, spraying mist, water on the floors, rain, and an enormous well—there are seventeen sensors connecting different visitor actions to fluidity. Light sensors for crowds, touch sensors for individuals, and pulling sensors for groups create, respectively, waves, ripples, and blobs in real-time projections and sound manipulations.

top left: Hamarikyu Garden

top right: Fish Market

middle left: JR apartment house

middle right: Shimbashi Station-sandwich man

bottom: World Trade Center

10_DENCIES

KNOWBOTIC RESEARCH

10_DENCIES EXPLORES THE possibilities of intervening and acting in complex urban processes taking place in distributed and networked environments. The project looks at urban environments, analyzes the forces present in particular urban situations, and offers experimental interfaces for dealing with these force fields. The aim, however, is not to develop advanced tools for architectural and urban design, but to create events through which it becomes possible to rethink urban planning and construction. 10_DENCIES challenges the potentials that digital technologies might offer toward connective, participatory models of planning processes and of public agency.

In Tokyo, the central Shimbashi area was analyzed in collaboration with local architects. Several "zones of intensities" were selected. In these zones, qualities of urban movement (architectural, traffic, human, information, economic) were distinguished. These movements and flows and their mutual interferences are represented by dynamic particle flows that can be observed

above left: Hinode Passenger Terminal

above right: Hinode Passenger Terminal, remote attractor

opposite, top: Shimbashi Station, economic qualities

opposite, bottom: Ginza Shopping Center

and manipulated through an Internet interface. In a Java Applet users can deploy a series of specially designed movement attractors, each of which has a different function in manipulating or modifying those processes. These are functions like: confirming, opposing, drifting, confusing, repulsing, organizing, deleting, merging, weakening. Participants can collaboratively develop hypothetical urban dynamics. As soon as one participant starts working on and modifying the urban profile by changing the particle streams with movement attractors, a search engine in the background starts looking for other participants with similar manipulation interests and connects to them. If another participant is found, the data movements can be changed collaboratively; they can be made stronger, weaker, more turbulent, denser, and so forth.

Streams of urban movement can shift between dynamic clusters of participants. Participants can develop new processes or react to already existing, ongoing ones. The streams of the manipulated movements are visualized in the activated segment of each participant, however, each participant will work on and experience a singular and different segment. The software modules allow for the variation and transformation of data by connective activities. This is seen as an approach to a discursive object, where aesthetic and action-oriented interests occupy and reappropriate urban sites.

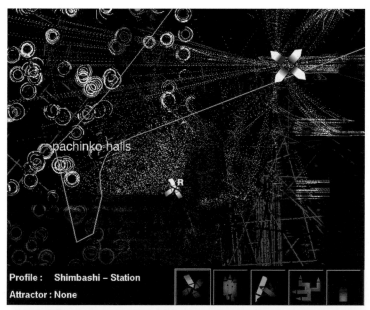

Profile :   Shimbashi – Station

Attractor : None

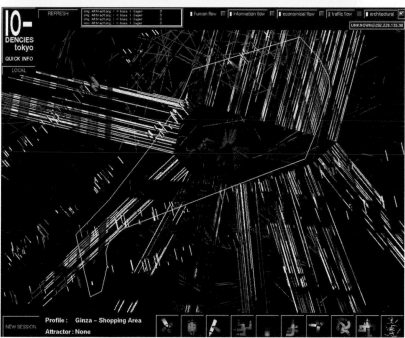

REFRESH

chg Attracting : 0 hces 1 layer   3
chg Attracting : 0 hces 1 layer   3
chg Attracting : 0 hces 1 layer   3
mov Attracting : 0 hces 1 layer   3

■ human flow   ■ information flow   ■ economical flow   ‖ traffic flow   ‖ architectural

UNKNOWN@202.228.135.98

IO-
DENCIES
tokyo

QUICK INFO

LOCAL

NEW SESSION

Profile :   Ginza – Shopping Area

Attractor : None

10_DENCIES creates a topological cut through the heterogeneous assemblage of physical spaces, data environments, urban imaginations,
connective agencies, and individual experiences. It forms a model for the complex way in which network topologies will have to be questioned.

above: Small, hand-held devices that display visual and textual notations of the Shimbashi area.

opposite, top: Energetic metallic field of Internet Applets, sounds, and strobe lights.

opposite, bottom: Data about physical concentrations in the exhibition space

was used to influence certain profiles in the Java Applet.

Meshworks, Hierarchies,

and Interfaces

MANUEL DE LANDA

THE WORLD OF interface design is undergoing dramatic changes that promise to rival those brought about by the use of the point-and-click graphical interfaces popularized by the Macintosh in the early 1980s. The new concepts and metaphors that are aiming to replace the familiar desktop metaphor all revolve around the notion of semiautonomous, semi-intelligent software agents. To be sure, different researchers and commercial companies have divergent conceptions of what these agents should be capable of, and how they should interact with computer users. But whether one aims to give these software creatures the ability to learn about the user's habits, as in the noncommercial research performed at MIT autonomous agents group, or to endow them with the ability to perform transactions in the user's name, as in the commercial products pioneered by General Magic, the basic thrust seems to be in the direction of giving software programs more autonomy in their decision-making capabilities.

For a philosopher there are several interesting issues involved in this new interface paradigm. The first one has to do with the history of the software infrastructure that has made this proliferation of agents possible. From the point of view of the conceptual history of software, the creation of worlds populated by semiautonomous virtual creatures, as well as the more familiar world of mice, windows, and pull-down menus, has been made possible by certain advances in programming language design. Specifically, programming languages needed to be transformed from their historically rigid hierarchies to the more flexible and decentralized structures that they have gradually adopted as they have become more "object-oriented." One useful way to picture this transformation is as a migration of control from a master program (which contains the general task to be performed) to the software modules that perform all of the individual tasks. Indeed, to grasp just what is at stake in this dispersal of control, I find it useful to view this change as a part of a larger migration of control from the human body first to the hardware of the machine, then to the software, then to the data, and finally to the world outside the machine.

The first part of this migration, when control of machine-aided processes moved from the human body to hardware, may be said to have taken place in the eighteenth century when a series of inventors and builders of automata created the elements that later came together in the loom invented by Joseph Marie Jacquard, a machine that automated some of the tasks involved in weaving patterns in textiles. The Jacquard loom used a primitive form of software in which holes punched into cards were coded to some of the operations in the creation of patterned designs.[1] This software, however, contained only data and not control structures. In other words, all that was coded in the punched cards was the patterns to be weaved and not any directions to alter the reading of the cards or the performance of the operations, such as the lifting of the warp threads. The machine's hardware component "read" the cards and translated the data into the motion in which control of the process resided. Textile workers at the time were fully aware that they had lost some control to Jacquard's loom, and, on several occasions, they manifested their outrage by destroying the machines.

276

Though the idea of coding data into punched cards spread slowly during the 1800s, by the beginning of the twentieth century it had found its way into computing machinery, first in the tabulators used by Herman Hollerith to process the 1890 United States census, then into other tabulators and calculators. In all these cases control remained in the machine's hardware. Even the first modern computer, the imaginary computer created by Alan Turing in the 1930s, still kept control in the hardware, the scanning head of the Turing machine: the tape that his fictional machine scanned held nothing but data. But this abstract computer already had the seed of the next step, since, as Turing himself understood, the actions of the scanning head could themselves be represented by a table of behavior, and the table itself could be coded into the tape. Although people may not have realized it at the time, the coding of both numbers and operations in side by side digits on tape was the beginning of computer software as we know it.[2] In the 1950s Turing created the notion of a subroutine, that is, the notion that the tasks that a computer must perform could be embodied in separate subprograms all controlled by a master program residing on tape. With this, the migration of control from hardware to software became fully realized, and from then on computer hardware became an abstract mesh of logical gates, its operations fully controlled by software.

The next step in this migration took place when control of a given computational process moved from the software to the very data that the software operates on. For as long as computer languages such as Fortran or Pascal dominated the computer industry, control remained hierarchically embedded in the software. A master program would surrender control to a subroutine whenever that subtask needed to be performed, and the subroutine could itself then pass control to an even more basic subroutine. But the moment the specific task was completed, control would revert back up the hierarchy until it reached the master program again. Although this arrangement remained satisfactory for many years—and indeed many computer programs are still written that way—more flexible schemes were needed for some specific, and at the time, esoteric applications of computers, mostly in the field of artificial intelligence.

Trying to build a robot using a hierarchy of subroutines meant that researchers had to completely foresee all the tasks that a robot would need to do and then centralize all decision-making into a master program. But this, of course, would strongly limit the responsiveness of the robot to events occurring in its surroundings, particularly if those events diverged from the predictions made by the programmers. One solution to this was to decentralize control. The basic tasks that a robot had to perform were still coded into programs, but unlike subroutines these programs were not commanded into action by a master program. Instead, these programs were given some autonomy and the ability to scan the database on their own. Whenever they found a specific pattern in the data they would perform whatever task they were supposed to do. In a very real sense, it was now the data itself that controlled the process. And, more importantly, if the database was connected to the outside world via sensors so that patterns of data reflected events outside the robot, then the world itself was controlling the computational process, and it was this that gave the robot a degree of responsiveness to its surroundings.

Thus, machines went from being hardware-driven to being software-driven, data-driven, and finally event-driven. The typical Macintosh computer is indeed an event-driven machine even if the class of real-world events that it is responsive to is very limited, including only events happening to the mouse (such as position changes and clickings) as well as to other input devices. But regardless of the narrow class of events that personal computers are responsive to, it is in these events that much of the control of the processes now resides. Hence, behind the innovative use of windows, icons, menus, and the other familiar elements of graphical interfaces, there is a deep conceptual shift in the location of control embodied in object-oriented languages. Even the new interface designs based on semiautonomous agents were made possible by this decentralization of control. Indeed, simplifying a little, we may say that the new worlds of agents, whether those that inhabit computer screens or, more generally, those that inhabit any kind of virtual environment (such as those used in artificial life), have been the result of pushing the trend away from software command hierarchies ever further.

The distinction between centralized and decentralized control of given processes has come to occupy center stage in many different contemporary philosophies. Economist and artificial intelligence guru Herbert Simon views bureaucracies and markets as the human institutions that best embody these two conceptions of control.[3] Hierarchical institutions are the easiest ones to analyze, since much of what happens within a bureaucracy in planned by someone of higher rank, and the hierarchy as a whole has goals and behaves in ways that are consistent with those goals. Markets, on the other hand, are tricky. Indeed, the term "market" needs to be used with care because it has been greatly abused over the last century by theorists on both the left and the right. As Simon remarks, the term does not refer to the world of corporations, whether monopolies or oligopolies, since in these commercial institutions decision-making is highly centralized, and prices are set by command.

Indeed the sense of the term can be limited even more to refer exclusively to those gatherings of people at a predefined place in town, and not to a dispersed set of consumers catered to by a system of middlemen (as when one speaks of the "market" for personal computers). The reason for this is that, as historian Fernand Braudel has made clear, it is only in markets in this true sense that we have any idea of what the dynamics of price formation are. In other words, it is only in peasant and small town markets that decentralized decision-making leads to prices setting themselves up in a way that we can understand. In any other type of market economists simply assume that supply and demand connect to each other in a functional way, but they do not give us any specific dynamics through which this connection is effected.[4] Moreover, unlike the idealized version of markets guided by an "invisible hand" to achieve an optimal allocation of resources, real markets are not in any sense optimal. Indeed, like most decentralized, self-organized structures, they are not hierarchical, they have no goals, and they grow and develop mostly by drift.[5]

Herbert Simon's distinction between command hierarchies and markets may turn out to be a special case of a more general dichotomy. In the view of philosophers Gilles Deleuze and Félix Guattari, more abstract classes, which they call strata and self-consistent aggregates (or trees and rhizomes), are defined not so much by the locus of control as by the nature of elements that are connected together. Strata are composed of homogenous elements, whereas self-consistent aggregates articulate heterogeneous elements.[6] For example, a military hierarchy sorts people into internally homogenous ranks before joining them together through a chain of command. Markets, on the other hand, allow for a set of heterogeneous needs and offers to be articulated through the price mechanism without reducing diversity. In biology, species are an example of strata, particularly if selection pressures have operated unobstructed for long periods of time, allowing the homogenization of the species' gene pool. On the other hand, ecosystems are examples of self-consistent aggregates, since they link together into complex food webs a wide variety of animals and plants, without reducing their heterogeneity. I have developed this theory in more detail elsewhere, but for our purposes here let's simply keep the idea that besides centralization and decentralization of control, what defines these two types of structure is the homogeneity or heterogeneity of their composing elements.

As both Simon and Deleuze and Guattari emphasize, the dichotomy between bureaucracies and markets, between hierarchies and meshworks, should be understood in purely relative terms. In the first place, in reality it is hard to find pure cases of these two structures: even the most goal-oriented organization will still show some drift in its growth and development, and most markets, even in small towns, contain some hierarchical elements, even if this is just a local wholesaler who manipulates prices by dumping (or withdrawing) large amounts of a product on (or from) the market. Moreover, hierarchies give rise to meshworks and meshworks to hierarchies. Thus, when several bureaucracies coexist (governmental, academic, ecclesiastic) in the absence of a superhierarchy to coordinate their interactions, the whole set of institutions will tend to form a meshwork of hierarchies, articulated mostly through local and temporary links. Similarly, as local markets grow in size, as in those gigantic fairs that have taken place periodically since the Middle Ages, they give rise to commercial hierarchies, with a money market on top, a luxury goods market beneath and, after several layers, a grain market at the bottom. A real society, then, is made of complex and changing mixtures of these two types of structure, and only in a few cases will it be easy to decide to what type a given institution belongs.

A similar point may be made about the worlds inhabited by software agents. The Internet, to take the clearest example first, is a meshwork that grew mostly by drift. No one planned either the extent or the direction of its development, and indeed, no one is in charge of it even today. The Internet, or rather its predecessor, the Arpanet, acquired its decentralized structure because of the needs of the U.S. military for a command and communications infrastructure that would be capable of surviving a nuclear attack. As analysts from the Rand Corporation made clear, only if the routing of the messages was performed without the need for a central computer, could bottlenecks and delays be avoided, and, more importantly, could the meshwork put itself back together once a portion of it had been vaporized in a nuclear attack. But on the Internet only the decision-making behind routing is of the meshwork type. Decision-making regarding its two main resources, computer (or CPU) time and memory, is still hierarchical.

Schemes to decentralize these aspects do exist, as in Drexler's Agoric Systems, where the messages that flow through the meshwork have become autonomous agents capable of trading among themselves both memory and CPU time.[7] The creation by General Magic of its Teletext operating system, and of agents able to perform transactions on behalf of users, is one of the first real-life steps in the direction of a true decentralization of resources. But in the meanwhile, the Internet will remain a hybrid of meshwork and hierarchy components, and the imminent entry of large corporations into the network business may in fact increase the number of command components in its mix.

These ideas are today being hotly debated in the field of interface design. The general consensus is that interfaces must become more intelligent to be able to guide users in the tapping of computer resources; both the informational wealth of the Internet and ever more elaborate software applications. But if the debaters agree that interfaces must become smarter, and even that this intelligence will be embodied in agents, they disagree on how the agents should acquire their new capabilities. The debate pits two different traditions of artificial intelligence (AI) against each other: symbolic AI, in which hierarchical components predominate, against behavioral AI, where the meshwork elements are dominant. Basically, while in the former discipline one attempts to endow machines with intelligence by depositing a homogenous set of rules and symbols into a robot's brain, in the latter one attempts to achieve intelligent behavior from the interactions of a few simple task-specific modules in the robot's head and the heterogeneous affordances of its environment. Thus, to build a robot that walks around a room, the first approach would give the robot a map of the room together with the ability to reason about possible walking scenarios in that model of the room. The second approach, on the other hand, endows the robot with a much simpler set of abilities, embodied in modules that perform simple tasks—such as collision-avoidance—and walking-around-the-room behavior emerges from the interactions of these modules and the obstacles and openings that the real room affords the robot as it moves.[8]

Translated to the case of interface agents, for example a personal assistant in charge of helping a user understand the complexities of a particular software application, a symbolic AI program would attempt to create a model of the application as well as a model of the working environment, including a model of an idealized user, and then make these models available in the form of rules or other symbols to the agent. Behavioral AI, on the other hand, gives the agent only the ability to detect patterns of behavior in the actual user, and to interact with the user in different ways so as to learn not only from his or her actual behavior, but also from feedback that the user gives it. For example, the agent in question would be constantly looking over the user's shoulder, keeping track of whatever regular or repetitive patterns it observes. It would then attempt to establish statistical correlations between pairs of actions that tend to occur together. At some point the agent would suggest to the user the possibility of automating these actions; that is, that whenever the first occurs, the second should be automatically performed. Whether the user accepts or refuses, this gives feedback to the agent. The agent may also solicit feedback directly, and the user teach the agent by giving some hypothetical examples.[9]

In terms of the location of control, there is very little difference between the agents, and in this sense the two approaches are equally decentralized. The rules that symbolic AI would put in the agents head, most likely derived from interviews of users and programmers by a "knowledge engineer," are independent software objects. Indeed, in one of the most widely used programming languages in this kind of approach (called a "production system") the individual rules have even more of a meshwork structure than many object-oriented systems that still cling to a hierarchy of objects. But in terms of the overall human-machine system, the approach of symbolic AI is much more hierarchical. In particular, by assuming the existence of an ideal user, with homogenous and unchanging habits, and of a workplace where all users are similar, agents created by this approach are not only less adaptive and more commanding, but they themselves promote homogeneity in their environment. The second class of agents, on the other hand, are not only sensitive to heterogeneities, since they adapt to individual users and change as the habits of their users change, but they promote heterogeneity in the work place by not subordinating every user to the demands of an idealized model.

One drawback to the approach of behavioral AI is that, given that the agent has very little knowledge at the beginning of a relationship with a user, it will be of little assistance until it learns about his or her habits. Also, since the agent can only learn about situations that have occurred in the past, it will be of little help when the user encounters new problems. One possible solution, is to increase the amount of meshwork in the mix and allow agents from different users to interact with each other in a decentralized way.[10] Thus, when a new agent begins a relation with a user, it can consult with other agents and speed up the learning process, assuming that is, that what other agents have learned is applicable to the new user. This, of course, will depend on the existence of some homogeneity of habits, but at least it does not assume a complete homogenous situation from the outset, an assumption that in turn promotes further uniformity. Moreover, endowing agents with a static model of the users makes them unable to cope with novel situations. This is also a problem in the behavioral AI approach, but in this model agents may aid one another in coping with novelty. Knowledge gained in one part of the work-place can be shared, and new knowledge may be generated out of the interac-tions among agents. In effect, a dynamic model of the workplace would be constantly generated and improved by the collective of agents in a decentral-ized way, instead of each one being a replica of each other, and operating on the basis of a static, centrally created, model.

The degree of hierarchical and homogenizing components in a given interface is a question that affects more than just events taking place on the computer's screen. In particular, the very structure of the workplace and the relative status of humans and machines are at stake. Western societies have undergone at least two centuries of homogenization, of which the most visible elements are the assembly-line and related mass production techniques whose overall thrust has been to let machines discipline and control humans. In this circumstance, the arrival of the personal computer was a welcome antidote to the development of increasingly more centralized computer machinery, such as systems of numerical control in factories. But this is hardly a victory. After two hundred years of constant homogenization, working skills have been homoge-nized via routinization and Taylorization, building materials have been given constant properties, the gene pools of our domestic species homogenized through breeding, and our languages made uniform through standardization.

The solution to this is not simply to begin adding meshwork components to the mix. Indeed, one must resist the temptation to make hier-archies into villains and meshworks into heroes. This is because they are con-stantly turning into one another, because in real life we find only mixtures and hybrids, and the properties of these cannot be established through theory alone but demand concrete experimentation. Certain standardizations—say, of electric outlet designs or of data-structures traveling through the Internet—may actually turn out to promote heterogenization, in terms of the appliances that may be designed around the standard outlet, or of the services that a com-mon data structure may make possible. On the other hand, the mere presence of increased heterogeneity is no guarantee that a better state for society has been achieved. After all, the territory occupied by former Yugoslavia is more heterogeneous now than it was ten years ago, but the lack of uniformity at one level simply hides an increase of homogeneity at the level of the warring ethnic communities. But even if we managed to promote not only heterogeneity, but diversity articulated into a meshwork, that still would not be a perfect solution. After all, meshworks grow by drift and they may drift to places where we do not want to go. The goal-directedness of hierarchies is the kind of property that we may desire to keep at least for certain institutions. Hence, demonizing centralization and glorifying decentralization as the solution to all our problems would be wrong. An open and experimental attitude toward the question of different hybrids and mixtures is what the complexity of reality itself seems to call for. To paraphrase Deleuze and Guattari, never believe that a meshwork will suffice to save us.[11]

NOTES

1. Abbot Payson Usher, "The Textile Industry, 1750–1830," in *Technology in Western Civilization*, vol. 1, ed. Melvin Kranzberg and Carrol W. Pursell (New York: Oxford University Press, 1967), 243.

2. Andrew Hodges, *Alan Turing: The Enigma* (New York: Simon & Schuster, 1983), ch. 2.

3. Herbert Simon, *The Sciences of the Artificial* (Cambridge, MA: MIT Press, 1994), 43.

4. Fernand Braudel, *The Wheels of Commerce* (New York: Harper & Row, 1986), ch. 1.

5. Humberto R. Maturana and Francisco J. Varela, *The Tree of Knowledge: The Biological Roots of Human Understanding* (Boston: Shambhala, Boston 1992), 47, 115.

6. Gilles Deleuze and Félix Guattari, *A Thousand Plateaus* (Minneapolis, MN: University of Minnesota Press, 1987), 335.

7. M. S. Miller and K. E. Drexler, "Markets and Computation: Agoric Open Systems," in *The Ecology of Computation*, ed. Bernardo Huberman (Amsterdam: North-Holland, 1988).

8 Pattie Maes, "Behavior-Based Artificial Intelligence," in Jean-Arcady Meyer, Herbert L. Roitblat, and Stewart W. Wilson, *From Animals to Animats*, vol. 2 (Cambridge MA: MIT Press, 1993), 3.

9. Pattie Maes and Robyn Kozierok, "Learning Interface Agents," in *Proceedings of AAAI '93 Conference* (Seattle, WA: AAAI Press, 1993), 459–65.

10. Yezdi Lashari, Max Metral, and Pattie Maes, "Collaborative Interface Agents," in *Proceedings of 12th National Conference on AI* (Seattle, WA: AAAI Press, 1994), 444–9.

11. Deleuze and Guattari, *A Thousand Plateaus*, 500. Their remark is framed in terms of "smooth spaces" but it may be argued that this is just another term for meshworks.

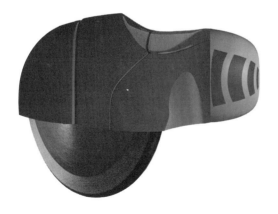

The Difference-Scape

ASYMPTOTE

IN RELATION TO architectural and spatial practices the use of digital technologies posits a number of interesting questions regarding notions of futility, conceptual artifice, and representation. Even if we think of the computer as a (neutral) tool embedded into the complex procedures of design, it is still capable of dismantling our conventional modes of making, reading, writing, communicating, and, inevitably, comprehending. Digital technologies, themselves being the foundation of computing, the Web, the mass media, and a vast array of other so-called advances are no less tools of expression and form-givers to desires as they are sociopolitical instruments. The digital machine makes it possible to operate simultaneously on infinite scales of meaning formation. Within the digital machine we strive to be simultaneously located within and dislocated from a community, and through the digital interfaces we manufacture, perception is now perpetually in a state of flux where the only dominant landscape is one of difference.

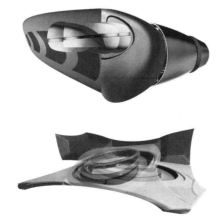

It is ironic that the prospect of community on such a large scale (where cultural boundaries are physically erased) is more often than not accompanied by an attempted erasure of cultural identity. In the end, however, despite the apparent common ground shared by diverse factions, an opportunity is provided for deciphering precisely the opposite. For instance, through a reading of one culture's misappropriations of another, it is actually possible that one could begin to measure such (spatial) difference. A good example of this is Japan's sense of its own cultural and iconographic makeup as a mediated inflection of American and Western European pop culture. Elvis, Marilyn, Superman, Nike, Tin Tin, and the like are all iconographic assemblies absorbed, reworked, and distributed globally in various forms and embodiments ranging from Anime to bullet trains. The icons that comprise this new landscape of difference are essentially mediated reflexes of similarity and diversification (constructs that are mirrored endlessly over computer networks, home pages, televised imagery, advertising campaigns).

The notion of modernity that emerged from postwar Western Europe called for a fabricated perfection, instigated in part from a obsessive interest in hygiene, homogeneity, and the relentless export of idealism. Much in the same manner that the international style in architectural and design venues was perfectly engineered, so are the hysteria and propaganda that herald the Web as a utopian entity. The Web is being peddled as a place where we are all happily plugged-in with complete and uncensored access to all information. The utopian communities that are seemingly latent exist on the fringes, providing ability to access goods, sex, news, lifestyles and other forms of desire. It, too, is proposed as a hygienic, pristine, open, and free terrain for all those with an access code. And all this is ostensibly carried out without censorship, persecution, or fear of reprisal. A veritable melting pot for a new humanity, the communal farm without the sweat, the absolute vacation without the trouble.

Ultimately, the reality that belies the digital machine is that no matter how entrenched in our daily lives it becomes, it will never achieve complete familiarity. The distance that the electrosphere has to us will always be a chasm. This impossibility of dominance is perhaps where the most potential lies for new spatial entities that are now only beginning to surface.

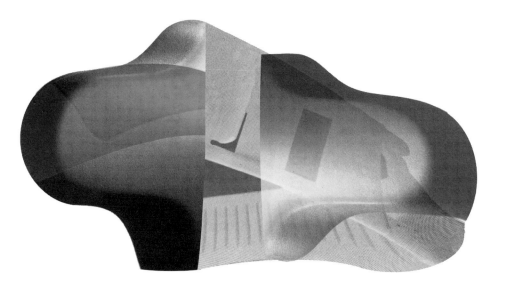

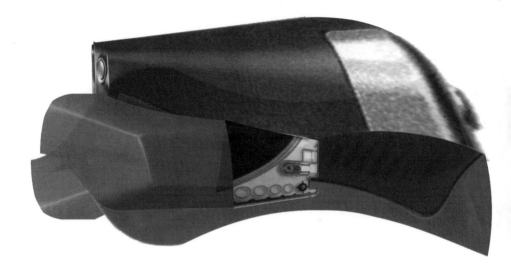

Bernard Cache, Bistro Table, 1997.

Framing the Fold: Furniture,

Architecture, Geography,

and the Pursuit of the Virtual

BERNARD CACHE

INTERVIEWED BY MICHAEL SPEAKS

The following discussion between Michael Speaks and Bernard Cache took place in New York City in August, 1994.

MICHAEL SPEAKS: One of the things that interests me most about your work is its connection to the work of Gilles Deleuze. What is striking about the relationship between your furniture production and Deleuze's philosophical production is that you started out to do architecture and became dissatisfied with architecture in a way that one imagines Deleuze became dissatisfied with philosophy. Deleuze is a philosopher, trained as a philosopher, but he does philosophy in a different way—he draws conceptual lines. You were trained as an architect and yet you don't do architecture in a traditional kind of way. There seems to me to be parallels between the way you generate furniture forms and the way Deleuze generates philosophical forms. Can you say something about your personal relationship with Gilles Deleuze?

BERNARD CACHE: I have met him only a few times, but to me Deleuze is a respiration, a breath. Deleuze wrote some things about a famous French actor, Alain Cuny, and he talked a lot about his voice. But Deleuze is not even a voice; he is, I think, a respiration, and that's why it is difficult to catch him and give a definition to what he is doing. When I read him, I can hear him breathing. For me anything he has written is really enjoyable because it puts me in touch with a certain way of feeling.

MS: How would you say Deleuze's way of doing philosophy is different from what we understand to be traditional philosophy.

BC: I think that Deleuze was able to catch the blow from traditional philosophy, something like the wind of Spinoza, or the pneuma of the Stoics.

MS: Can you explain that?

BC: We have a very impoverished idea of philosophy when we think only of the academies. Deleuze understands philosophy as a living thing. Most people think that intellectuals are cut-off from life. But there is a real, life affirming hollow in philosophy, and Deleuze was able to catch the wind that resides there.

MS: For most North American intellectuals who are interested in the work of Deleuze, and particularly those of my generation—aged twenty-five to thirty-five—what has been important about his thought is that it is systematic and rigorous, and yet it's not scholarly. It moves, it lives, it is something that you can do things with. It works. For Deleuze philosophy is a way of producing that obviously is not the way one normally understands philosophy.

BC: Deleuze's courses were simply called "Explications." Every year you had "Text Explanations." It was a very funny way of avoiding the pretense of being overly academic, of writing new things without making a show of it. He'd just say, "Let's explain this."

> **MS:** In a number of works that we know here in this country, *The Fold* and *What is Philosophy*, written with Félix Guattari, Deleuze mentions some of your own work as important to his understanding of the concept of the fold. Could you say something about the way in which you first came to be involved with Deleuze and his thought.

BC: One day I was just browsing around in a seminar—I didn't even know Deleuze—and I began to hear his voice. The way he was dealing with things just amazed me. I thought, "this is philosophy to me." It was obvious. Deleuze really had a very sensitive touch.

> **MS:** Did this understanding of philosophy make sense to you because of or in spite of your architectural training?

BC: When I was young, philosophy seemed the most difficult thing to study. I did not dare study philosophy after my baccalaureate. Then I started to do architecture. It was really by way of the theory of architecture I was taught in school that I came in contact with philosophy; it was bad philosophy, of course, and not even interesting with respect to architecture. Most of the people doing theory of architecture are not involved in producing drawings. When you start studying architecture, you first exchange your vision of the things you already know; as in any place, you are already in the middle, just as you can be in the middle of a landscape, which also has a relationship to architecture. So that's the first thing. Then you think, "How would I design it? How would I put something in it?" You must really have a relationship to the lines that need to be drawn for architecture, a feeling for how these lines connect with other lines, with philosophy, for example. Deleuze draws lines in philosophy, and those lines for me were really important.

ms: In the 1988 deconstructivist exhibition at the Museum of Modern Art in New York, the philosophical production of Jacques Derrida was used as a selling point for a new style that came to be known as "deconstructivism." Whether Derrida's work was read and understood by this group of architects, his philosophical production was used to give substance to the architecture on display. Now there are all kinds of reasons for that— some are interesting and some aren't—but the point is that within contemporary architecture Derrida's work has been very important. Recently, however, there has been a shift in interest away from Derrida's work and toward Gilles Deleuze's. Many of the architects who have become interested in Deleuze have done so for reasons that seem not so philosophical. Derrida is interested in issues of representation, and in reading and writing; his philosophical work might in fact be described as a practice of reading and writing older texts and offering new readings of those. Similarly, deconstructivist architecture understands buildings as texts that are read and rewritten in built form. Deleuze's work is philosophically very different from that. Whereas Derrida reads and rewrites an existent tradition, Deleuze begins in the middle and produces new things by way of a pragmatic-constructivism. Deleuze produces concepts as if they were forms or as if they were new things in the world. Many architects, especially those interested in "the fold," have simply represented Deleuze's concept of the fold in architectural form, and this seems to me very un-Deleuzian. It strikes me that the relationship between the way that Deleuze produces concepts and the way that you produce furniture images is different from that.

B C : What your question requires is a very close examination of the relationship between what is writeable and what is visible. Michel Foucault has of course written about this. Anyway, this question still puzzles me; certainly it is not an easy one to answer. There is a way to think with images and so the problem is not to represent that thinking; it is that thinking is already in the images themselves. I am very interested in the mathematician Roger Penrose, whose work deals with the way we think, the way we create mathematics. He insists that at the moment of discovery, mathematicians are thinking neither with formulae nor with language, but instead they are thinking with images. The problem of representation is one between things that are thought as language and things that are reality, what we visually intend as reality—I mean objects that are visible. My problem—and it's the way I deal with Deleuze's philosophy—is that part of the thinking is already images, so it's just normal that they become visible in an object, and thus it is the nature of thinking that is puzzling in this. Rather than the classical question of representation, I am instead interested in the relation between language thinking and image thinking. In his books on the cinema, for example, Deleuze does not criticize or make interpretations of film directors; instead he classifies the various ways directors think with images, and this is a very puzzling question. What is interesting even in the work of someone like M. C. Escher is to see how he addresses the question of the limits of the visible and how this can be compared with the limits of language.

> *M S :* If, as you say in your book, *Earth Moves: The Furnishing of Territories*, architecture is "the art of the frame," what is the relationship between architecture and furniture? If architecture is the art of the frame, then what is furniture?

B C : There are several ways to answer this question, but one has to do with what it means to be an architect today. Given the current means of architectural production—the way we produce buildings—it is perhaps easier to be an architect in fields other than architecture, fields whose production is lighter than buildings. For instance, producing photographs today is a very light way of practicing architecture. When I started to produce furniture, the first connection I discovered between furniture and architecture was the problem of how to frame the landscape. I can show you one of the models I made of the landscape while I was studying architecture. Suddenly it occurred to me that this model was a beautiful piece of furniture. I used plywood, and the relationship between this object and the lines in the landscape was remarkable. When you drill a curved surface in plywood, the lines that appear are the equivalent of topographical lines. Plywood gives me a direct connection with what is our usual representation of geographical forms. That was the beginning. After that it was crucial to understand geography as what is exterior to architecture; and as such geography remains outside the control of human beings. Imagine New York as a perfect quasi-crystal or a quasi-frame that the buildings make visible. All around I can feel it, as if I were living in a Sol LeWitt environment, and the buildings are everywhere filling in parts of this crystal and making it visible. But here in New York very little geography remains. Thus what is important in New York is to develop a new relation to this essential configuration of images, the inflection. Today we must make our own geography at home instead of having it outside in the city. As we sit here in New York, we are surrounded by the crystal.

MS: How does furniture differ from geography?

BC: Furniture is an unusual geography, but it's our own personal geography. It's our landscape and that's why I worked on models of waves, and became attentive to the effect of the wind on the dunes.

> *MS:* So if architecture is the frame itself and geography initially is that which is outside the frame, geography becomes interior as furniture images, which could be said to run the continuum from the very personal to the geographical.

BC: Furniture is what remains geographical in us, but it is more like the state of the desert than a landscape dotted with little churches and little villages. In the desert there is no frame to actualize identity; this landscape of dunes is also an image very important for the English painter Francis Bacon.

MS: It's a remarkable connection that you seem to have happened onto in material form—your use of plywood, I mean. It seems accidental and yet that was maybe a moment of inflection.

BC: Yes, you are right that it's an accident. I think there is no necessary connection among philosophy, aesthetics, and mathematics. But suddenly you find connections. They remain accidental but that's precisely one of the additional reasons why they are beautiful.

MS: Would you say that architecture actualizes a virtual image that is the possibility of singularity.

BC: No, because there are several ways of organizing the relation of the vector. Often architecture tends to isolate the inflection from the environment of vectors, for instance the wind, the direction of the sun, and so on; these are the concrete images of vectors all architects use in their daily practice. There are two different kinds of architecture: one that selects the vector to make appear an identity on the inflection; and another one, which on the contrary, tries to isolate the inflection from any vector so that it remains a virtual singularity. But of course there is always something that imposes itself on the inflection that results in the disappearance of the virtual singularity.

MS: Is it not the case that architecture can never actualize a virtuality, that it can never truly actualize a singularity because a singularity in a sense always remains outside the frame?

BC: Also because the singularity is impersonal and is out of our control.

MS: And therefore it is outside the framing device itself?

BC: Yes. There are two aspects: one is that singularity cannot exist without losing its character of virtuality. Its existence as virtuality, as soon as it is perceived by us, introduces a relation of *rapport de force*. This produces an identity without which we would be unable to perceive things; we are unable to perceive things without shaping them into identities. That's my concern. So the fact is that you will never have enough frame to protect the inflection, to prevent it from becoming an identity. That's why in baroque architecture they start doubling frames. There is never enough frame in architecture. We are surrounded by the frame but it's never enough. And even if it were enough, we probably couldn't live inside it.

MS: If architecture couldn't do that, it wouldn't be a framing device anymore either. It wouldn't be architecture anymore.

BC: Yes.

MS: How then is furniture different?

BC: Furniture is not at all architecture. I'm not an architect simply because I'm a graduate of an architecture academy. Let's take hunting as an example. The hunter is the one who holds the gun, but the hunt is also dependent on what is aimed at, the object on the other end of the gun. Instead of framing things, I am manipulating things and images that are supposed to be framed. I see the thing from the other way but I am not practicing architecture because I am doing precisely the contrary—I am at the other end. I know that architecture surrounds me and I am doing it in relation to the frame it provides.

ms: If furniture images are the interior of architecture and if architecture is a framing device that, by definition, can never fully account for the actualization of a virtuality, a singularity that's outside it, is geography that very virtuality that we can't frame entirely?

bc: Yes, yes.

ms: If that's the case, then in a very perverted and interesting way furniture images are much closer to singularity than architecture.

bc: Yes, clearly. Architecture is just here to help things either to become an identity or to protect the singularity. There are many ways of using the frame. These are simply the most obvious, but surely there are others. And these might lead to an architecture that is different from the way we understand it.

ms: Would you say something about your own production process, which seems to me to have something to do with your own dissatisfaction with the state of architecture. It strikes me that the way you produce can't be done in architecture as it presently exists. With the exception of accidental occurrences like discovering the relationship between plywood and geography, you seem to control the entire production process from the generation of the content, to the drawings, to the designing of the software, to the designing of the software for the machinery to generate the forms. Can you say something about this processes?

bc: At present we have new possibilities with the computer. I want to know less about computers and more about how to use them. Until very recently we used software like AutoCad and so on; only circles and squares and things like that could be easily manipulated. Even Form•Z only allows us to create squares, so it's not a new thing. Of course, besides the manipulation of primitives, you can also pull the key points of approximation curves like Béziers, Splines, or Nurbs. But if there is anything new with computers it is the mathematical use of the computer that enables you to draw anything. You can do many things with the computer but surprisingly architects are behind in their use of it.

MS: How does this affect your design of furniture?

BC: The problem is that with existing software and with the organization of the means of architectural production as well as the organization of the intellectual world, there are architects who draw a sketch on paper and give it to other people who just enter them into the computer. The computer allows nothing more than a translation, nothing more than what can be done with a pencil. It's not new, just more efficient. Perhaps it's everything you want, but it's still the same thing. But if you start using the computer as a conceptor, and if we become something more than simple operators, real possibilities begin to emerge.

MS: What do you mean by conceptor?

BC: Both drawer and user of the computer. The architect who uses the computer must know a bit of mathematics because the problem with the software industries is that they are working at an industrial level, on a large scale. And if you look at most people using the computer, they are operators not conceptors. They are asked only to pinpoint what is drawn on paper, and that is a very stupid use of the mouse I think. The mouse is really the most stupid interface; of course it's user-friendly, but in many ways it causes us to overlook the real capacity of the computer to calculate. We must learn to think with the computer in mathematical terms; we must develop mathematical formulae and not use the computer to pick points. If we can begin to do that, then inflection becomes a mathematical function. That is how I design my furniture.

MS: Not by drawing forms?

BC: I never draw. I can be very unclever with a pencil in my hand.

MS: So none of your forms, none of the drawings are drawn?

BC: No. What I am doing presently is all calculated. I can give you an analytic function for all my images.

MS: But with this computational model of design are you still dealing with virtuality?

BC: Yes, and that's why I am very much against the uncritical use of what many call the art of the virtual. If you look at the use of the term virtual in virtual reality and multimedia and things like that, what is meant is a model of a space, as in a flight simulator. If you give the coordinates of your position, you can create a view that is simply the actualization of the model that is inside the computer; that's the technical way virtual reality works. Many say the work of art is no longer what you see but I disagree, for not all that comes out of the model is interesting.

MS: But in the end is your work any less determinable or deterministic than these simplistic approaches to virtual reality?

BC: Oh, yes. These furniture objects are strictly reproducible, purely reproducible, but they are also purely deformable—I only have to change the value of certain variables and it gives me new forms. And that is what is new and what is the real purpose of my work: to develop a nonstandard mode of production.

Line Parable for the Virtual

(On the Superiority of the Analog)

BRIAN MASSUMI

1. TOPOLOGY

The virtual, as such, is inaccessible to the senses. This does not, however, preclude figuring it, or constructing images of it. To the contrary, it requires a multiplication of images. The virtual that cannot be felt cannot but be felt, in want of potential, outside possibility: in its effects. When expressions of its effects are multiplied, the virtual fleetingly appears. Its fleeting is in the depths between and the surfaces around the images.

Images of the virtual make the virtual appear, not in their content or structure, but in fleeting, in their sequencing or sampling. The appearance of the virtual is in the twists and folds of content, as it moves from one sampled structure to another. It is in the ins and outs of imagistic content or structure. This applies whether the image is verbal, as in an example or parable, or whether it is visual or aural. No one kind of image, let alone any one image, will do the trick.

Since the virtual is in the ins and outs, the only way an image can approach it alone, with its own content and structure, is to twist and fold on itself, to multiply itself internally, knotting at a certain point. Doublings and foldings, punctualities rejoining encompassments, prospection buckling into retrospection, expanding contractions and contracting expanses. The virtual can perhaps best be imaged by superposing these deformational moments of repetition, instead of sampling differences in content and structure. Think of each image receding into its deformation, as into a vanishing point of its own twisted versioning.[1] That vanishing into self-variety is the fleeting of the virtual—more appearingly than in the in-between and around of the single-image contents and structures, however thoroughly resequenced. The folding-vanishing point is the literal appearance in words (or vision or hearing) of a virtual image center. Take the images by their virtual centers. Superpose them. You get an over-image of images of self-varying deformation: a unity of continuous separation from self. It is there that the virtual most literally, parabolically appears.

This is to say that the virtual is best approached topologically. Topology is the science of self-varying deformation. A topological figure is defined as the continuous transformation of one geometrical figure into another. Imagine a pliable coffee cup. Join the surfaces of the brim, enlarge the hole in the handle, and then stretch it so that all its sides are equally thick. You get a doughnut. You could then tie the doughnut into complex knots. All of the geometrical figures you can create in this way are versions of the same topological figure: topological unity is, in and of itself, multiple. Of course it is impossible actually to diagram every step in a topological transformation.[2] Practically, only selected stills can be presented. Once again, the need arises to superpose the sequencings. It is only in that superposition that the unity of the figure can be grasped as such, in one stroke. That one stroke is the virtual image center of the figure. It is virtual because you cannot effectively see it or exhaustively diagram it. It is an image because you can, for all of that, figure it, more or less vaguely, in the imagination. Imagination is the mode of thought most precisely suited to the vagueness of the virtual.[3] It alone manages to diagram without stilling. Imagination can also be called intuition: a thinking feeling. Not feeling something. Feeling thought—as such, in its movement, as process, on arrival, as yet unthought-out and unenacted, postinstrumental and preoperative. Imagination is felt thought, thought only felt, felt as only thought can be: insensibly unstill. Outside any given thing, outside any given sense, outside actuality. Outside coming in. The superempirical feeling of the insensate. The mutual envelopment of thought and sensation, as they arrive together, pre what they will have become, as they are, just beginning to unfold from the unfelt and unthinkable outside, of contingency, of process, of transformation in itself.

Whatever medium you are operating in, you miss the virtual unless you carry the images constructed in that medium to the point of topological transformation. The approach to the virtual is necessarily topological. If you fall short of the topological, you will still grasp the possible (differences in content and structure considered as predictable alternatives). You might even grasp the potential (the tension between superposed possibilities and the advent of the new). But never will you come close to the virtual.

2. ON THE SUPERIORITY OF THE ANALOG

Topology is a purely qualitative science. It has no empirical (predictive) value.[4] It is more apparitional than empirical. It is by nature analogic. A topological image center makes the virtual literally appear, analogically, in felt thought. Sensation—always on arrival a transformative feeling of the outside, a feeling of thought—is the analog, matter in analog mode.[5] An analog process is the continuous transformation of an impulse from one qualitatively different medium into another. Electricity into sound waves. Or heat into pain. Or light waves into vision. Or vision into imagination. Or of noise in the ear into music in the heart. Of the outside as a coming in. Sensation is the analog processing by the body of impinging forces. Its substance is topological deformation.

Both possibility and potential can be approached quantitatively, the latter through probabilities. Although they lend themselves to quantification, it must remembered that they only lend themselves. Every possibility and potential, however calculated, retains an irrevocable residue of qualitative difference, to which it owes its distinctness. That residue or reserve (more insistent in potential than in possibility) is virtuality, as enveloped in the given: the virtual in its empirical presentation (as the possibility or potential it is not, but in and out of whose expressions it appears, in effect).

Possibility, potential, and virtuality are modes of reality of the inactual. Quantification and qualitative transformation (the analog) are processes of deactualization, or envelopment. Each of these deactualization processes is a mode of thought, defined as a processual excess over the actual.

Quantification pertains to the mode of thought commonly called instrumental reason. Its media are possibility, and potential to a less certain (probabilistic) degree. Qualification pertains to what was earlier called operative reason. Its media are the potential (shed of what René Thom calls the "imposture" of probability, accepted as the unpredictability it is), and more vaguely (residually and reservedly) the virtual. When most attentive to the virtual, qualification deforms into the topological exercise of contingent reason (imagination or intuition).

The actual is the interpenetration of the three modes of thought, the process of their meeting, mixing, and reseparation. The actual is sensation in its widest connotation. Although centered on potential, sensation stretches from limit to limit, from the advent of the virtual to the run-down of possibility, from the insensibly given to the out-worn, from emergence to entropy. As does thought, though differently, and centered on the virtual. Images of the ins and outs of the possible, the potential, and the virtual are images of thought (sensation). An image of thought is an imaging of the imageless, as always analogic (the greater the degree of deformation, the better; the more twisted the truer).[6]

There is a third deactualization process: codification. The digital is a numerically based form of codification (zeros and ones). As such, it is a close cousin to quantification. Digitality is a numeric way of arraying alternative states so that they can be sequenced into a set of alternative routines. Step after ploddingly programmed step. Machinic habit.

"To array alternative states for sequencing in alternative routines." What better definition of the possible? The medium of the digital is possibility, not virtuality, and not even potential. Digital coding is possibilistic to the limit.

Nothing is more destructive for the thinking of the virtual than equating it with the digital. All arts and technologies envelop the virtual, in one way or another. Digital technologies in fact have a remarkably weak connection to the virtual, by virtue of the enormous power of their systemization of the possible. They may yet have a privileged connection to it, far stronger than that of any preceding technology. But that connection has yet to be invented. It is the strength of the work of Pierre Lévy (against Jean Baudrillard) to emphasize the participation in the virtual of earlier technologies—in particular writing—and (following Gilles Deleuze) to insist on a distinction between the actual, the possible, and the potential as an integral part of any thinking of the virtual. Equating the digital with the virtual reduces the apparitional to the artificial, with the "simulacrum" taking the place of the phantasm ("phantasm" being a good-enough substantive for the process of the imagination).[7] This forgets intensity, brackets potential, and in that same sweeping gesture bypasses sensation, the actual envelopment of potential. Multiple miss.

Digital technologies have a connection to the potential and the virtual only through the analog. Take word processing. All of the possible combinations of letters and words are enveloped in the zeros and ones of ASCII code. You could say that entire language systems are numerically enveloped in it. But what is processed inside the computer is code, not words. The words appear on screen, in being read. Reading is the qualitative transformation of alphabetical figures into figures of speech and thought. This is an analog process. Outside its appearance, the digital is electronic nothingness, pure systemic possibility. Its appearance from electronic limbo is one with its analog transformation. Now take digital sound: a misnomer. The sound is as analog as ever, at least on the playback end, and usually at the recording end as well (the exception being entirely synthesized music). It is only the coding of the sound that is digital. The digital is sandwiched between an analog disappearance into code, and an analog appearance out of code.

Take hypertext. All possible links in the system are programmatically pre-arrayed in its architecture. This has led some critics to characterize it not as liberating, but as downright totalitarian. While useful to draw attention to the politics of the possible, calling hypertext totalitarian is inaccurate. What it fails to appreciate is that the coding is not the whole story: that the digital always circuits into the analog. The digital, a form of inactuality, must be actualized. That is its openness. The freedom of hypertext, its potentialization, is in the openness of its analog reception. The hypertext reader does something that the copresence of alternative states in code cannot ever do: accumulate, in an unprogrammed way, in a way that intensifies, creating resonances and interference patterns. For the reader, the link just left overlaps with the next. They are not extensively arrayed, beside and outside each other, as alternatives. Neither are they enveloped in each other as coded possibilities. They are copresent in a very different mode. The analog process of reading translates ASCII code into figures of speech enveloping figures of thought, taken in its restrictive sense of conscious reflection. The relation between signification and conscious reflection to sensation is reversible. Sensation (in this case predominantly visual) envelops the envelopment of thought in signification, and conversely the envelopment of thought in signification envelops sensation. There is no thought that is not accompanied by a physical sensation of effort or agitation (if only a knitting of the brows or quickening of heartbeat).[8] The sensation is that of thought arriving, situating itself—in virtual situation. Thought-sensation—the only-felt thought of the event calling attention to itself—is a germ of potential. Incipient action.[9] Germinal tendency, a sprouting of the tendency to tendency. The situational sprouts are integrations of sensations not restricted to the visual. The visual envelops the tactile, and the tactile the aural, and the prioproceptive the visual. Virtual situations are synaesthetic germs about to bloom into potential. They are multiple unities, so many virtual centers in impassive tension. Each virtual situation is a tensile field. In moving from one link to the next, the reader moves from field to field, but since each field involves the same virtual centers, in variation, the movement is a dopplering, an accumulation of phasings in and out, crescendoing and tapering off. The movement, in other words, is intensive: deformational. Self-varying. The moments of the reading are copresent to each other in a lived topology of virtual interpenetration which edges on the actual, appearing to experience where the virtual twists into the germ of the actual.

The synaesthetic twist each reading puts on the deformational process of digitally-assisted virtual phasing introduces the element of the new. For in the actual play between the digital system of the possible and its virtual analog, new thoughts may be thought, new feelings felt. These may translate into veerings into and out of actual situations outside the reading. Full-fledged potentialization. Digital processing doesn't possibilize—the digital is already exhaustively possibilistic. It can however potentialize, circuitously. The digital may be virtualized, in the process of its analog appearing, and that virtualization may be expressed in a potentialization. This is a scrambling of the order followed in my earlier parables. The relations between actuality, possibility, potential, and virtuality, it seems, are also reversible. In this case, it is the virtual that can be said to envelop the expression of potential, rather than the expression of potential enveloping the virtual. The thinking of the digital might begin with the way in which, in circuiting into the analog, the digital reorders the modes of reality of the inactual in their relation to the actual; the way in which it reorders modes of thought.

The crucial point is that the digital is virtualized and potentialized only in its integrative circuiting with the analog, in the way in which it is integrated into the analog or integrates the analog into itself. This is the guiding insight behind the bluster of the MIT Media Lab, and its director's phantasms of a ubiquitous interface seamlessly relaying impulses into and out of the body: infinitely reversible analog-digital circuiting on a planetary scale.[10] The ultimate immersive environment. The more traditional immersive environments that have become synonymous in the popular press with with the "virtual reality" of digital technology will become truly virtual as opposed to possibilistic, phantasmic as opposed to merely simulacral, only when mechanisms are found to effectively integrate other senses alongside vision, or through vision (for example, by finding ways to pack other sensations—in particular tactile and proprioceptive—into visual sensation; by finding ways to make felt the synaesthetic field in which the virtual center of vision participates, as one tensile attractor among others; by more intensively integrating the analog). Neural nets, probabilistic creatures living off programmed randomness, take a step in the direction of potential and the unpredictable while remaining digital. But the ultimate "virtual reality" phantasm is the supersession of neural nets with neuronal computers. But by then—if then ever actually arrives—the processing will no longer be digital. Possibilization and probabilization will have given way to synaptic indeterminacy: the unprogrammed randomness of pure chance. And its functional/symbolic capture. Which, of course, is an analog transformation. The "digital revolution" will be truly on the way to potentialization and virtualization when it rebecomes analog, in becoming-brain.

The path to the digital virtual is not through increasing cleverness in systems design or programming. Quite to the contrary, the digital will only rejoin the virtual when it raises itself to the highest powers of brainy vagueness.

3. DESCRIPTION OF A STRUGGLE

Potential can be thought of in terms of what chaos theory calls "bifurcation points" or "critical points." Criticality is when what are normally mutually exclusive alternatives pack into the materiality of a system. The system is no longer acting and outwardly reacting according to physical laws unfolding in linear fashion. It is churning, running over its own possible states. It has folded in on itself, becoming materially self-referential, animated not by external relations of cause and effect but by an intensive interrelating of versions of itself. The system is a knot of mutually implicated alternative transformations of itself in material resonance. Its possible futures are present, in the system, in its matter. In *effect*: incipient effect (resonance and interference, vibration and turbulence, unfoldable into an array, an order). Possibility has, in effect, materialized. The matter of the system has entered a state where it does not extrapolate into an abstract possibility, and instead effectively absorbs possibilities, *en masse*, into its animated matter.

It is serviceable but inaccurate to say that what will be the possible states of a system (as retrospectively arrayed) were actually copresent to each other (prospectively) at the critical point of self-referential potential. The alternate states are only present as felt. They were present not so much to each other as in sensation. They were enveloped or infolded in sensation. It would be stretching things to say that they were individually felt, even though, when arrayed, they are sequentially thinkable. It was their superposition was felt—vaguely, en masse, as the intensity of an impinging force. The vagueness was the presence of something more than any pre-established array of possibility: potential (systemic change, the new). Potential is an intensely felt, superpositive vagueness of infolded transformations, known and new, impinging en masse. The even-more-vague of the virtual, the in-itself of in-folded transformation, can be neither felt nor thought. In its in-itself it is impassive, insensible (void). It simply arrives, comes to. Its coming to, for its part, cannot but be felt-thought. Shockingly. Singularly. The arrival of the virtual is the advent of thought, its coming to being, as impingement: the force of thought.[11] Being felt. Thought-being. The forced entry of the virtual into actuality, as sensation, force as thought.

Possibility concerns degrees of clearness and distinctness (simplicity). Potential is a multiple-vague (complexity). The virtual is a singular multiple-vague (complication, emphasizing the etymological meaning of "plica," fold).

The mass of transformations in potential can be seen to fall along a continuum stretching from the possible to the virtual, from the clear and simple to the impossibly vague. They also fall into a continuum of degrees of feltness. The overall intensity of the sensation is a complex of subintensities that are not individually felt. Although they are differentiated in relation to each other, they register in sensation only in their mutual envelopment. Like Peirce's Firstness, the sensation is the indivisible effect of a multiplicity (a "manifoldness") that imposes itself in the manner of a force (unrefusable impingement).[12] "All the mind's materials without exception are derived from passive sensibility."[13] Potential is a First unfolding from pure arrival, upon impact.

       Imagine the transformations arrayed on a plane receding in all directions from the actual conjuncture of criticality. The most forceful are almost upon the situation, bunching up on it in a rush. The forcing frenzy settles down as you look away from the critical point. The bunching flattens into the tranquility of the plane. But then way off in the distance, the plane curls in on all sides. It coils out of sight, into a ring of vagueness slanting down and around back toward the critical point from underneath. At a point directly beneath the bunch-up around the critical point, the edges of the plane meet and swirl together. Now draw parallel lines through the flatness of the plane, and watch them curling into a knot at the critical point, forming arabesques of unimaginable complexity. Try to imagine the unimaginable arabesque beneath the critical point, where the edges meet. Imagine it rejoining the knot of the critical point from below, so that its vagueness is inestimably compounded by an under-vagueness. Now make the lines tensile, like elastic bands. The calmness of the plane is a mirage. It is actually where the lines are pulled most tautly by the bunching and curling on either end. Suddenly, something gives. A tension line snaps at the critical point. There was a weak point in the tensile web somewhere in the folds of the critical conjunction, and a line whips out and up. Above the critical point, it intersects with a plane running parallel to the first. This plane is composed of parallels and perpendiculars, and continues infinitely in all directions without noticeable bunching or knotting, only a distant fade-out. If you looked down on the point at which the snapped line intersected the second plane, you wouldn't see a knot, but an infinitesimal hole where its leading point cut into the webbing. The snapped tension line seems to come up into the plane at the cut, and run into one of the lines on the second plane. Above, where you look down from, there is no third plane. Just empty space.

Call the second plane, of perpendiculars and parallels, extension (emphasizing the etymological sense of "ex-": out-(of)-tension). Every point of intersection between a perpendicular and a parallel is a situation. On the second plane, each intersection is situated *vis-à-vis* the others in a manner accessible to calculation and, where there is movement between situations, to prediction of varying degrees of accuracy. The intersections are positioned, enabling trajectories through them to be plotted.

The connection between the situated intersection and the too-complex knot of potential is the actual. For ease of expression, the intersections on the plane, and the plane itself, may be referred to as "the actual," provided that it is remembered that it is not the structure of the plane and its calculability that qualify it as actual, but the relation between these and potential (and what potential continues and envelops).

Now from any given point of actual intersection, run an x- and a y-axis along the perpendiculars that form it. The set of all of the points at which the x-axis is intersected by other lines comprises the present. The set of all points at which the y-axis is intersected by other lines, to the left of the x-axis, is the past. The y-intersections to the right of the x-axis are the future. The x-axis is the dimension of actual copresence, of juxtaposition. The y-axis is the dimension of actual succession. Now imagine that a snapped line on the first plane leads to each and every actual intersection, past, present, and future. Since potential has a connection to every situation at once, it is incalculable and unplottable. It is transpositional. The connection between it and any actual point is a nonlocalizable relation across the cut of the snap-line.

Go back to the first plane, and call it intension. The parallels composing the plane of intension or intensity do not extend infinitely in a linear fashion. The plane has two topological limits, where it infinitely folds in on itself. If the knotting at the critical point is potential, then the knot formed beneath it by the curling under at the edges is the virtual. Call the free-floating view from above the second plane down onto a cut where a snapped line from the first plane hits it, the perception of a possibility. Potential and virtuality are connected. They form a continuum of intensity, potential at one tensile extreme (the tumultuous breaking point), the virtual at the other (the impassive, unsnappable, but no less knotted and tensile). Since the extremes knot together, at the limit the potential and the virtual meld. Using either term to designate the unity of the continuum would therefore not be misleading. But for convenience, "potential" could be reserved for the end of the continuum knotting up toward the cut into the actual, and "virtual" could be reserved for the end knotting out-under.

The knot of potential impinges on the plane of the actual, cuts forcefully into it, at a snap point. All its tension hits there and is released: a lowering of intensity, not to impassivity—which is a qualitative limit of intensity rather than its diminution—but to repetition: the predictable, periodicity, rhythm, habit, pattern, structure, law. The knot of the virtual is impassive in the sense that it is in no way felt. It is not seen by the view from above, to which only the cut and the plane of the actual is visible. The potential end of the continuum is felt—it snaps to experience. The virtual end is insensible, the limit of sensibility. It is in reserve. Unseen and unfelt, it is at the limit a pure ideality, even though its knotting in itself is not vague but infinitely fine-threaded. The virtual limit is the unthought of thought, where felt-thought continues to unfeeling. The potential end is sensation at its limit of felt intensity. If the cut-connection of the potential to the plane of the actual is every-present and transpositional, the continuation of potential in the virtual is a-positional as well as a-temporal, at the limit. Eternal. The forever of transformation, in itself, folding infinitely in, outside actual time and space: matter-energy.

Now consider that the fade-out of the plane of the actual is an optical illusion. The foggy ring of vagueness on its horizon is in fact a many-threaded cascade. Beyond the edge, the situation plummets—onto the ring of vagueness below, and from there, from the edge of the plane of potential, into the under-knot of the virtual. Unfeelable eddies of residual tension form at the confluent edges of the planes of the actual and of potential. Certain residualized situational junctures backwash along the plane of potential toward the snapping point, while others descend into the virtual, whose reserve is therefore also a residue. It is the "form" of the situations that virtualize and repotentialize: the situations relieved of their situation, outside positioned and plottable matter, where the future runs down, dissipating into the mists of matter.[14] Imagine each situation-form as a dissipated point of actual intersection swept up in the impassive turbulence of the eternity of matter in its energetic state. Consider those run-down points—at the limit, at the confluent edge, and underneath in the virtual—attractors or virtual centers. Some eddy back through the tensile lines leading to the snapping point of potential, and are tumultuously reintensified. Call these tendencies: regerminating situations blooming forth from the virtual. Beyond the critical point in the other direction, toward what would be the past on the plane of the actual, there is another confluent edging, eddying, and tendency. Now notice that at every actual point in-between, on the upper plane, there is subtle leakage, like condensation. Some of these run-down points join the tendency lines in the rush back to the critical point, while others drip straight into the underknot. The drip lines and cascades that rejoin the virtual reintensify in a different way. Since they do not snap, they continue to knot. They fold so infinitely in on themselves and each other that at the limit each contains all. At that processual limit, each moment of infolding is present to all the others, as if the knotting were perpetually repeating itself at infinite speed, so fast that the speed blurred stroboscopically into an immobility of absolute motion.[15] The tensile tranquility of the plane of potential taken to its extreme. At that extreme, where movement stands still in endless involution, each situation-form is refracted in all the others, as in a virtual prism. Each is a monad, containing all of the others, all situation, a whole world, from a certain angle of infolding, from a certain prismatic perspective. Now say that a monad can, for no apparent reason, rise, weightlessly, to make a surprise reentry into the critical potential from underneath. When that happens, it brings with it a whole-world-perspective, the unity of an enveloped world, enveloping all, like no other. The vaporous rise and reentry of a monad is contingency or singularity: pure unheralded, worlding chance. The irruption into potential of an attractor. The "energetic" attractor state of matter-at-the-edge and in the virtual underneath is "impassive" because it is not a force even though it is in absolute motion. It is unfelt, in itself. It is only felt as enveloped in an actual sensation. In dynamic terms, it does no work. Thus it would be just as fair to call it nonenergetic (ideal).[16]

It is simply beyond that duality (among others). It is zero-point energy.[17] It is a quantum of situation. At the quantum level, matter is impassive and insensible, expressing no force and doing no work. It is extensively active, and can be said with accuracy to exist only as captured by calculation, extracted from its qualitative difference, from its pure arrival, and arrayed on the plane of the arrived-at, the quantifiable; only as drawn out of itself, into structure, snapped-to and actualized. In itself, it insists. The quantum is the in-itself of force: the envelopment of structure in utter complication and infinitely residual tensile reserve. For "envelopment" read "onto-topo-logical transformation." For "structure" read "the functional distinguishability of situated space (position) from plottable time (trajectory)"; or, "the geometry of instrumental reason." For "residual tensile reserve" read "virtual reality"; or, the ideality of matter-energy (the zero-point energy of the quantum void).

Earlier it was said that the order of the plane of the actual—the parallels and perpendiculars defining situated intersection points, and the axial movement through sets of these—was perceptible only from above. But if a view from above zoomed into an intersection point, it would see an endless descent into the infinitesimal depths of a mathematical point. Any actual situation automatically resolves itself into a mathematical point, by virtue of the infinite quantitative divisibility characteristic of time as distinguished from space, and space as distinguished from time. Take the duration of the situation, and cut it in half, and in half again, and so on. You end up with a temporal point-void. Take the height, depth, and breadth of the situation and cut them in half, and in half again, indefinitely. Look at the cuts. You get a trio of point-cuts contracting into a single point. If you could look down on the repeatedly calculated situation, it would be like peering into a bottomless cone plunging endlessly into the infinitesimal. If you looked down at a number of situations, whether in spatial juxtaposition or temporal succession, their point-cuts would all converge, cones funneling into an ur-cone. The point of the ur-cone would be a monad, any monad. The monad would be a virtual world, whatever world.

If it were possible to see the actual from potential, the actual would be virtual: situations in and out of situations, perspectives within perspectives, galaxies of worlds. Monad(s). The actual is the virtuality of potential's perspective on its own abyssal-monadic cut-in. The actual is the virtual self-referentiality of potential. Fold over. Potential folding over on itself as it folds out into actual structure and at the same time shines through its plane to rejoin the virtual cosmos.

But it is not possible. There is no godlike eye in the sky, any more than there exists a virtual sewer rat. No, vision is always ground-level, on the plane of the actual, where potential cuts in. And it is always mixed, folded synaesthetically into other senses. There is no such thing as vision from a distance. There are only degrees of an unfolding tactile-proprioceptive-visual proximity. A view, says Bergson, is a virtual touch. The tactile, proprioceptive and visual are extensions into and out of each other, separable only as limit-states, infinitely tended to, never reached, of the same essentially synaesthetic experience. The most distilled vision still carries traces of the tactile, through its connection to a virtual center (run-down point or reimpassive—and regerminable—synaesthetic attractor). The "senses" are multiple dimensions of a singular proximity (being in the midst of things, being in situation), rather than measures of spatial disjunction. Degrees of multidimensional contact, rather than measures of distance.

Place yourself where you always are: at the cut-in. In situation. Where the sub-cones meet the ur-cone. You are concerned. What, poised in mid-abyss, will your next step be? As you pace the void, place the lens of your concerning eye across the ur-cone, its edges coinciding with the circumference of the cone. Feel-think it an experiential prism that refracts the senses, separating them out from each other and into their respective components. Tactility, proprioception, smell, and the others it disperses horizontally, so that they quickly melt back together into a ring of proximate vagueness. The visual part of the sensory spectrum it sharpens, projecting it upward into the distance, in a rainbow of converging rays. Not an infinite distance. The rays from every situation effectively converge, forming a single cone mirroring the cone plunging infinitesimally into the virtual. At the apex is a mirror: visual limit-state, where refraction folds back, in reflection. Call that visual limit-state your mind's eye: a reflective retinal double of your lens. It reflects the reconvergent rays back down on the situations, illuminating them in a flat white light. Forget the upwardly projective refraction. Retain the retrojective downward beaming. Now you see, you feel you think you really see, from a distance. And from that little god's-eye view, the plane of the actual looks, well, okay. Your concern turns to discerning comfort as your eye sees patterns on the illuminated plane. Structure. Parallel and perpendicular lines from situation to situation, in full bloom, separate from and outside each other. Orders of juxtaposition and succession arrayed before your eye like so many flowered paths to choose from. The void now seems pleasantly doable. Forget it ever was a void. Cleave to the structure. Make it function. In moments of grandeur, you can even consider the structure of the actual to be yours, as if it was your own mind's eye that projected the order rather than retrojecting it. Yes, it was you, little idealist, who "constructed" it. Or maybe your "culture." Or maybe it wasn't constructed at all. Maybe you found it. Maybe you did reflect it, but accurately, not deformationally. Good work, you budding realist. Or maybe you're less a realist than a realizer. Maybe you "realized" all this, maybe it was you who brought it to fruition. Your viewpoint after all is at the pinnacle. Maybe you are the tree the acorn in the flower bed grew into. That's progress. So go for it. Put your self in the reflection of your eye and try idealism, realism, and progressivism on for size. Oscillate between them as you please. Don't take any one to an extreme. Keep your perspective. Keep your equilibrium. Cleave to the golden, entropic mean of common, habitual sense. Own it. Share it. Be it.

But every once in awhile, shed a tear for the void and the veer of the snap to intensity—for the virtual and the potential you habitually only see-think to be, your own self-referential actuality. Fall with a tear back down the cone. Imagine, synaesthetically, where that takes you. Plunge through sensation to the insensate. Think-feel that. Alone, in the cosmos. Impassive turbulence. Continue still to suffer (the void of becoming). Monad it.

[End topological phantasm]

NOTES

This text is excerpted from the essay "Parables for the Virtual," forthcoming in Brian Massumi, *The Critique of Pure Feeling*. It is published here with the permission of Harvard University Press.

1. Gilles Deleuze, *Francis Bacon: Logique de la sensation* (Paris: Editions de la Différence, 1981), chaps. 3, 15, 18.

2. See C. S. Peirce's topological diagrammaticism, *The Essential Peirce*, vol. 1, ed. Nathan Houser and Christian Kloesel (Indianapolis: University of Indiana Press, 1992), 2, 71–2, 246–68. See also Deleuze, *Francis Bacon*, 65–71; and Gilles Deleuze and Félix Guattari, *A Thousand Plateaus*, trans. Brian Massumi (Minneapolis: University of Minnesota Press, 1987), 91, 140–2, 510, 513.

3. Gilles Deleuze, *Kant's Critical Philosophy*, trans. Hugh Tomlinson and Barbara Habberjam (Minneapolis: University of Minnesota Press, 1984), 17–8, 50–2; and Gilles Deleuze, *Difference and Repetition*, trans. Paul Patton (New York: Columbia University Press, 1994), 320–1.

4. René Thom, interview, *Le Monde*, 22–23 January 1995.

5. Deleuze, *Francis Bacon*, 73–8.

6. Gilles Deleuze and Félix Guattari, *What Is Philosophy?*, trans. Hugh Tomlinson and Graham Burchill (London: Verso, 1994), 37–8.

7. Gilles Deleuze, *The Logic of Sense*, trans. Mark Lester with Charles Stivale, ed. Constantin Boundas

(New York: Columbia University Press, 1990), 210–6.

8. William James, "The Feeling of Effort," *Collected Essays and Reviews* (New York: Russell & Russell, 1969), 151–219.

9. Henri Bergson, *Matter and Memory*, trans. Nancy Margaret Paul and W. Scott Palmer (New York: Zone Books, 1988), 68–9.

10. Nicholas Negroponte, *Being Digital* (New York: Knopf, 1995).

11. Deleuze, *Difference and Repetition*, 138–41.

12. C. S. Peirce, *Selected Writings*, ed. Philip P. Wiener (New York: Dover, 1958), 381–93.

13. James, "The Feeling of Effort," 203.

14. Brian Massumi, "The Autonomy of Affect," in *Deleuze: A Critical Reader*, ed. Paul Patton (Oxford: Blackwell, 1996), 217–39.

15. Deleuze and Guattari, *What is Philosophy?*, 118; Deleuze and Guattari, *A Thousand Plateaus*, 267, 381.

16. Deleuze and Guattari, *What is Philosophy?*, 21, 132.

17. David Bohm, *Wholeness and the Implicate Order* (London: Ark, 1983), 85–8.

Immersive technology represents both the grail at the end of the history of cinema and the beacon that draws creative energies toward the culmination of computing. It replaces the traditional ethos of comput- ing—bodiless minds communicating via keyboard and screen—with the notion that the senses are primary causes of how and what we know, think and imagine....In the world of total immersion, authorship is no longer the transmission of experience, but rather the construction of utterly personal experiences.

—Brenda Laurel

The Desire to Be Wired

GARETH BRANWYN

WILL WE LIVE to see our brains wired to gadgets? How about today? Just mention "neural interfacing" (being wired directly to a machine) on a computer bulletin board or newsgroup related to the subject, and you might receive a comment like the following:

> I am interested in becoming a guinea pig (if you will) for any cyber-punkish experiment from a true medicine/military/cyber/neuro place. New limbs, sight/hearing improvements, bio-monitors, etc. Or even things as simple as under the skin time pieces.[1]

On-line conversants will often pour forth such cybernetic dreams as computers driven by thoughts, implanted memory chips, bionic limbs and, of course, the full-blown desire to have one's brain patched directly into "cyberspace," the globally-connected computer networks. The romantic allure of the "cyborg" seems to captivate the fringes of digital culture.

Neural interfacing fantasies have mainly grown out of science fiction, where "add-on" technologies turn people into powerful hybrids of flesh and steel. Since so much of our contemporary mythology comes from sci-fi, an inherent confusion between fantasy and reality is to be expected. This already has happened in the field of virtual reality. Today's crude systems in no way reflect the media hype and "Cyberspace NOW" mentality of the impatient computerized masses. Neuroscientists and engineers in the area of implant technologies offer a similar tale of woe. Science fiction has fed us so many images of technologically souped-up humans that the current work in neural prosthesis (devices that supplement or replace neurological function) and mind-driven computers seems almost retro by comparison.

Images of human-machine courtship are omnipresent in pop culture. Albums by digital artists Brian Eno, Clock DVA, and Front Line Assembly sport names like *Nerve Net*, *Man Amplified*, and *Tactical Neural Implant*. A recent *Time* magazine article on the cyberpunk movement made a number of dubious references to the near-future tech of brain implants, offering "instant fluency in a foreign language or arcane subject." Role-playing games based on bionic, post-apocalyptic sci-fi are gobbling up market share once reserved for...

DUNGEONS & DRAGONS

Computer network and hacker slang is filled with references to "being wired" or "jacking in" (to a computer network), "wetware" (the brain), and "meat" (the body). Science fiction films, from *Robocop* to the recent Japanese cult film *Tetsuo: The Iron Man*, imprint our imaginations with images of the new, increasingly adaptable human-cum-cyborg who can exfoliate one body and instantly construct another. One might even speculate a link between the surprising popularity of modern primitivism (piercing, tattooing, body modification) and the emerging techno mythology of "morphing" the human body to the demands and opportunities of a post-human age. The human body is becoming a hack site, the mythology goes, a nexus where humanity and technology are forging new and powerful relationships.

Academic discourse is also rife with talk of cyborg bodies and the need to rethink the postmodern relationship between humans and machines. "There's a rapt, mindless fascination with these disembodying or ability augmenting technologies," says Allucquere Rosanne Stone, director of the Advanced Communications Technology Lab at the University of Texas. "I think of it as a kind of cyborg envy.... The desire to be wired is part of the larger fantasy of disembodiment, the deep childlike desire to go beyond one's body. This is not necessarily a bad thing. Certainly for the handicapped, it can be very liberating. For others, who have the desire without the need, there can be problems. Political power still exists inside the body and being out of one's body or extending one's body through technology doesn't change that."[2]

"People want the power without paying the attendant costs," says Don Ihde, professor of the Philosophy of Technology at SUNY, Stonybrook. "It's a Faustian bargain."[3]

Is the desire to be wired a fantasy born of our relationship with increasingly personalized and miniaturized technology? Will neural interfacing be commonplace in a future we will live to see? If so, what biomedical and bioengineering feats will be necessary? Most important, what function-restoring neural prostheses are being researched that show promise for the disabled, and may eventually lead to function-amplifying implants?

BIONIC HARDWARE

In her influential essay "A Cyborg Manifesto," science historian Donna Haraway suggests that the severely disabled are often the first to appreciate the fruitful couplings of humans and machines.[4] A brief conversation with anyone who has a pacemaker, a new hip, a (good) hearing aid, an artificial heart, or any one of a host of bionic devices will bear this out.

The neural prosthetic and interface technologies of today can be broken down into three major areas: auditory and visual prosthesis, functional neuromuscular stimulation (FNS), and prosthetic limb control via implanted neural interfaces. So far, the most successful implants have been in the realm of hearing. Larry Orloff, a scientist who has suffered hearing loss since childhood, and is the editor of *Contact*, a newsletter for people with hearing implants, reports that there are more than seven thousand people worldwide outfitted with cochlear implants. These devices work through tiny electrodes placed in the cochlea region of the inner ear to compensate for the lack of cochlear hair cells, which transduce sound waves into bioelectrical impulses in ears that function normally. Although current versions of these devices may not match the fidelity of normal ears, they have proven very useful. Dr. Terry Hambrecht, a chief researcher in neural prosthetics at the National Institutes of Health, reports that implanted patients had "significantly higher scores on tests of lip-reading and recognition of environmental sounds, as well as increased intelligibility of some of the subjects' speech."[5]

The hearing-implant patients and family members I interviewed spoke of their desperation during their deaf years, and emphasized how much they appreciated the technology that had changed their lives. John Anderson, a forty-three-year-old implant recipient from Massachusetts offered his views via electronic mail (he still has trouble communicating by phone): "The silence of those three years when I was totally deaf is still deafening to me these many years later. My life was in the hearing world and it was critical for me to be able to hear like 'everyone else.' "[6] Orloff spoke movingly of hearing things like crickets, birds, and church bells for the first time. He also points out that computer networking was instrumental in his getting the implant: he first learned of the technology on CompuServe.

An even more radical type of auditory prosthesis now under development snakes hair-thin wires deep into the brain stem, linking it with an external speech processor. But don't expect to see it soon. Likewise, visual prosthetics are still a long way from offering any major breakthroughs, though several promising directions are being explored. The goal of most of these schemes is to implant electrodes into the visual cortex of the brain to stimulate discernible patterns of phosphenes which can then be interpreted by the user. Phosphenes are those tiny dots (the proverbial stars) that can be seen after rubbing one's eyes or getting beaned on the head. These phosphenes originate in the brain and are responsive to electrocortical stimulation. Recently, Dr. Hambrecht and fellow researchers at the National Institutes of Health (NIH) implanted a thirty-eight-electrode array into the visual cortex of a blind woman's brain. She was able to see simple light patterns and to make out crude letters when the electrodes were stimulated.

Richard Alan Normann, professor of bioengineering at the University of Utah, has been developing similar "artificial eyes" that would use denser phosphene arrays (one hundred electrodes). The long-range goal of his research is the development of vision hardware that "will consist of a miniature video camera mounted on a pair of sunglasses, signal processing electronics, a transdermal connector to pass across the skin, and an array of…microelectrodes permanently implanted in the visual cortex."[7] The development timetable for these systems is still long-term; advances have been slow. Often years pass between experiments as researchers painstakingly assemble the required miniature electronics.

Beyond sight and sound, functional neuromuscular stimulation systems are in experimental use in cases where spinal cord damage or a stroke has severed the link between the brain and the peripheral nervous system. These systems usually combine implanted electrodes and an external battery-powered microprocessor. The system is controlled by switches, either triggered manually or through movement of some body part (an elbow or shoulder) that is still operational. These types of systems are likely to be used clinically one day to restore movement in legs, arms, and hands. Similar electrical stimulation schemes to restore bladder control and respiratory functions are also in experimental and even clinical use.

Some of the most compelling research in the area of neural interfacing is being done at Stanford University. A recent paper reports that "a microelectrode array capable of recording from and stimulating peripheral nerves at prolonged intervals after surgical implantation has been demonstrated."[8] These tiny silicon-based arrays were implanted into the peroneal nerves of rats and remained operative for up to thirteen months. The ingeniously designed chip is placed in the pathway of the surgically severed nerve. The regenerating nerve grows through a matrix of holes in the chip, while the regenerating tissue surrounding it anchors the device in place. Although this research is very preliminary and there are still many intimidating technical and biological hurdles (on-board signal processing, radio transmutability, learning how to translate neuronal communications), the long-term future of this technology is exciting. Within several decades, "active" versions of these chips could provide a direct neural interface with prosthetic limbs, and by extension, a direct human-computer interface.

While a composite image of all these technologies might hint at the bionic humans of sci-fi, the practical limitations and technological obstacles are sobering. Very few of these technologies are in approved clinical use, and most of them will not be for a decade or two. One of the main things frustrating this research is finding (or developing) materials that are not toxic to the host organism and that will not be degraded by that organism. The human body has formidable defenses against invading hardware.

Besides the material and physical hurdles, this technology raises tremendous ethical and social issues. Many critics say that neural implants are impractical at best, if not downright irresponsible. These critics contend that implants are bioengineering marvels looking for a justifiable use, rather than appropriate technology for the disabled. Other naysayers argue that these unproved prosthetic devices give experimental subjects unreasonable expectations of sight, sound, and independence. Scott Bally, assistant professor of audiology at Gallaudet University, points out that auditory implants are very controversial in the deaf community. "Many deaf people feel as though deafness is not a handicap. They are culturally deaf individuals who have successfully adapted themselves to being deaf and feel as though things like cochlear implants would take them out of their deaf culture, a culture which provides a significant degree of support."[9]

William Sauter, head of prosthetics at MacMillian Medical Center in Toronto, also has reservations. "A patient must go into surgery again, and I think most amputees don't like to be opened up," he observed in a 1990 article on the Stanford research.[10] In thinking of a future populated by machine-grafted humans, questions are raised as to how society as a whole will relate to people walking around with plugs and wires sprouting out of their heads. And who will decide which segments of the society become the wire-heads? "People are just not ready for cyborgs," says the implanted John Anderson.

And the moral issue of animal testing cannot be overlooked. Society as a whole, and armchair "neuronauts" in particular, should be aware that this research is totally dependent on the extensive use of laboratory animals. Legions of cats, monkeys, rats, rabbits, bullfrogs, and guinea pigs have been poked, prodded, zapped, and stuffed full of experimental hardware in the name of progress.

BASEMENT NEUROHACKERS

Perhaps more within the realm of science fiction than science fact, "neurohackers" fancy themselves to be do-it-yourself brain tinkerers who've decided to take matters into their own heads. "There is quite an underground of neurohackers beaming just about every type of field imaginable into their heads to stimulate certain neurological structures (usually the pleasure centers)," a neurohacker wrote to me via email. Several of these basement experimenters were willing to talk.

Meet Zorn. I got his name (which has been changed) from another neurohacker who told me a wild tale about a device that Zorn had recently built. "It's got an electrode ring situated over the pleasure centers of the brain. I know someone who tried it and he said it was like having a continuous orgasm." My God, you mean this guy's invented the Orgasmatron? I immediately called Zorn, but at the suggestion of the other hacker, I only talked to him generally about basement brain tech.

Zorn's a psychologist by trade and a weekend electronics hobbyist. He tells me about several sound and vision devices (brain toys) he's built, similar to those now commercially available. He seems entirely sane; he's full of cautions. When I tell him about some of the other neurohacks I've heard about, he expresses deep concern. "If these people are going to mess with neuroelectric or neuromagnetic stimulation, they should build in more safety devices. There's a tremendous potential for harm: brain damage." When I ask him what he's been doing recently, he becomes quiet. "Well, it's something I'd rather not talk about. It's a device I built that could very easily be abused." (Hmmm…My mind flashes with perverse images of twitching orgasmojunkies permanently jacked into The Zorn Device.)

"Why would it be abused?" I ask.

"I really can't say anything more about it. It would be a disaster if it got out into the world." Definitely an Orgasmatron…or perhaps just another cybernetic wet dream.

David Cole of the nonprofit group AquaThought is another independent researcher willing to explore the inside of his own cranium. Over the years, he's been working on several schemes to transfer EEG patterns from one person's brain to another. The patterns of recorded brainwaves from the source subject are amplified many thousands of times and then transferred to a target subject (in this case, Cole himself). The first tests on this device, dubbed the Montage Amplifier, were done using conventional EEG electrodes placed on the scalp. The lab notes from one of the first sessions with the Amplifier report that the target (Cole) experienced visual effects, including a "hot spot" in the very location where the source subject's eyes were being illuminated with a flashlight. Cole experienced a general state of "nervousness, alarm, agitation, and flushed face" during the procedure. The results of these initial experiments made Cole skittish about attempting others using electrical stimulation. He has since done several sessions using deep magnetic stimulation via mounted solenoids built from conventional iron nails wrapped with twenty-two-gauge wire. "The results are not as dramatic, but they are consistent enough to warrant more study," he says.[12]

Part of the danger of monkeying with one's brain, especially with little or no knowledge of neuroscience, is that most individuals do not have access to the sophisticated testing and feedback devices that are available to legitimate researchers. Through devices like the Mindset, a "desktop EEG,"

Cole and other researchers hope to change that. "It is imperative that neuro-science research is not limited to large organizations with big budgets," insists Cole.[13] The further I got out on the fringes of neurohacking, the more noise overcame signal. I heard rumors of brain-power amplification devices, wire-heading (recreational shock therapy), and most disturbing of all, claims that people are actually poking holes in their heads and directly stimulating their brains. (Kids, don't try this at home.)

JACKING IN? PLEASE STAND BY...

We know the future will be wired. Hardwiring of neural prosthe-sis is already here and will continue to develop toward completely implantable systems controlled by the user's brain. Most researchers contend that these advanced systems are at least ten to twenty years in the future. Whatever the date, this technology will eventually become a common enabling option for the disabled, and at that point, people will surely start talking about using sim-ilar technologies for elective human augmentation.

But when that day comes, many questions will remain. Will peo-ple really want to have their bodies opened and wired? How will they pay for what will certainly be expensive procedures? And what about obsolescence? Technology moves at light speed now. How fast will it move decades from now? In that accelerated future, today's hot neural interface could become tomorrow's neuro-trash. "Look, Jimmy's still got the version 1.1 Cranium Jack" (titter, titter). Even the most enthusiastic neuronauts will not want to subject themselves to repeated brain surgery in the pursuit of the latest hard-ware upgrade.

For the near future, the bulk of elective interface options will continue to be softwired ones, mainly via the sophisticated neural transducers we already have: our five senses. Likely directions include more immersive three-dimensional environments, voice input/output, and a whole wardrobe of VR work and leisure suits. The most sci-fi-like interfaces of the next decade will include EEG controlled/radio transmitted input devices.

Certainly the mythic desire for the bionic human, whether to restore what was lost or to add on what is desired, will continue to drive much of this inquiry. What direction such desires take is anyone's guess. Don Idhe: "I think a lot of this is conceptualist stuff, wishful thinking. These are fantasies that may have nothing to do with what eventually gets developed and used." As Avital Ronell points out in *The Telephone Book: Technology, Schizophrenia, Electric Speech*, the phone was originally intended as a prosthetic device for the hard of hearing.[14] Technology will always develop as society decides what it's to be used for, not necessarily what the designer or visionary had in mind.

NOTES

1. Anonymous, email to author, 8 February 1993.

2. Allucquere Rosanne Stone, telephone interview with author, 7 April 1990.

3. Don Ihde, telephone telephone interview with author, 14 April 1993.

4. Donna Haraway, "A Cyborg Manifesto," in *Simians, Cyborgs, and Woman* (New York: Routledge 1991).

5. Terry F. Hambrecht, "Neural Prosthesis," in *Annual Review of Biophysics and Bioengineering*, ed. L. J. Mullins (New York: Pergammon Press, 1979).

6. John Anderson, email to author, 27 April 1993.

7. Richard Alan Normann, telephone interview with author, 7 August 1993.

8. Gregory T. A. Kovacs, C. W. Storment, and J. M. Rosen, "Regeneration Microelectrode Array for Peripheral Nerve Recording and Stimulation," *IEEE Transactions on Biomedical Engineering* 39, no. 9 (September, 1992): 893–902.

9. Scott Balley, telephone interview with author, 14 April 1993.

10. Sarah Williams, "Tapping into Nerve Conversations" *Science* (May 1980): 555.

11 Anderson, email to author.

12. David Cole, telephone interview with author, 2 April 1993.

13. Ibid.

14. Avital Ronell, *The Telephone Book: Technology, Schizophrenia, Electric Speech* (Lincoln NB: University of Nebraska Press, 1989).

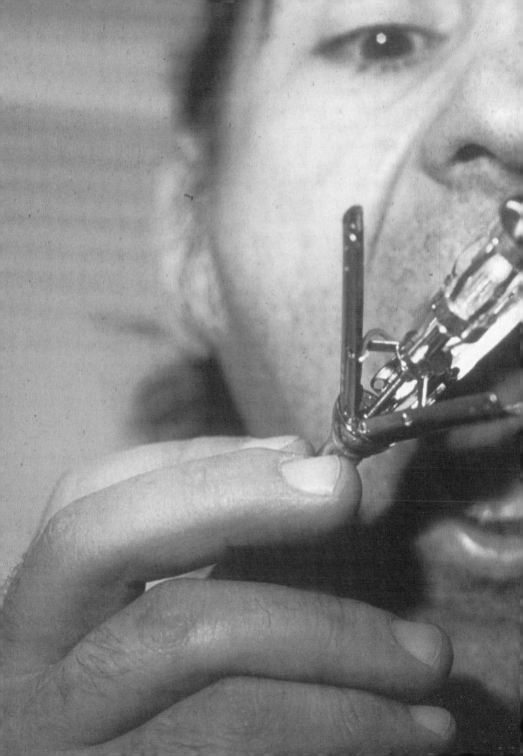

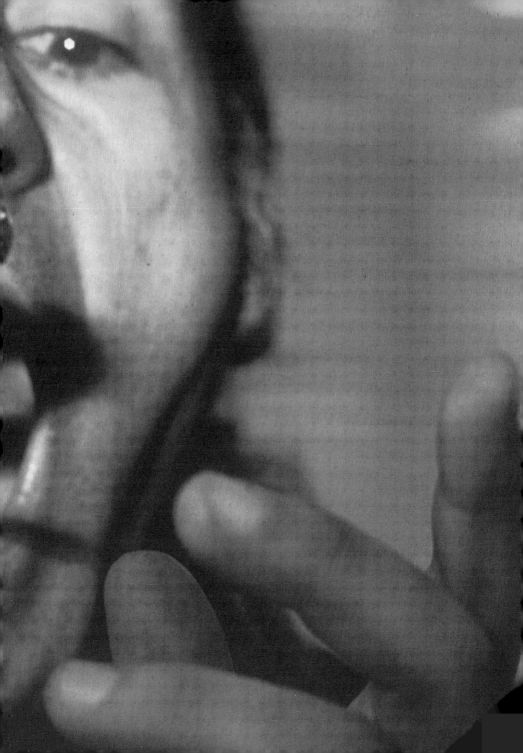

Stelarc: The Evolutionary

Alchemy of Reason *(AN EXCERPT)*

BRIAN MASSUMI

"What is important is the body as an object, not a subject—not being a particular someone but rather becoming something else."

"Information is the prosthesis that props up the obsolete body."

—Stelarc

BODY SUSPENSIONS EVENTS (1976–88)
Stelarc's early body suspensions were careful, calculated, literally antiseptic. They weren't shamanistic or mystical or ecstatic. And they most certainly weren't masochistic. The pain wasn't sought after or reveled in. It was a soberly accepted byproduct of the project. The point was never to awe the audience with the artist's courage or hubris. Neither was it to treat the audience to a dramatic staging of symbolic suffering in order to shed light on or heal some supposedly founding agony of the human subject.

Stelarc applies instrumental reason—careful, calculated, medically-assisted procedure—to the body, taken as an object, in order to extend intelligence into space, by means of a suspension. Now how does suspending the body-object extend intelligence? And what is the something else the body becomes, beyond its objectivity and subjectivity?

above left: Rock Suspension, Tokyo

above right: Sculpture Space Suspension, UNAM, Mexico City

facing page: The Third Hand, Yokohama

To begin to answer these questions, it is necessary to clarify what precisely is suspended. It is not simply the actual body of the artist. By targeting the body as object, Stelarc is targeting the generality of the body. The suspended body is a sensible concept: the implications of the event are felt first, before being thought out. The apparatus of suspension set up the body's relation to itself as a problem, a compulsion, and construed that problem in terms of force. The basic device employed was, after all, an interruption of the body's necessary relation to the grounding force of human action: gravity. The hooks turned the skin into a counter-gravity machine.

THIRD ARM EVENTS (1981–94)

The operation in play in this project is about extension as opposed to substitution, or what is commonly called prosthesis. The robotic Third Arm attaches to the right flesh arm. It does not replace it. It is a "prosthesis" in the etymological sense of the word, "to put in addition to." As an addition, it belongs to an order of superposition. The tendency of Stelarc's events is toward superposition. The body is probed so that its inside is also an exterior. The body inputs information into the computer in order to express it or relay it as a force: the body places itself between information and force. The left side of the body receives programmed gestures fed in from a machine, which it then transduces into involuntary gestures: programmed and

The Third Hand, Yokohama

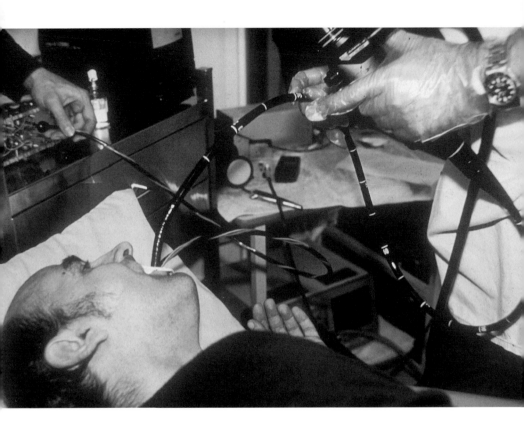

above: Microfilm Image of Inside of My Stomach

right: Stomach Sculpture

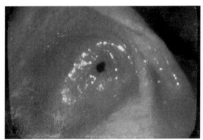

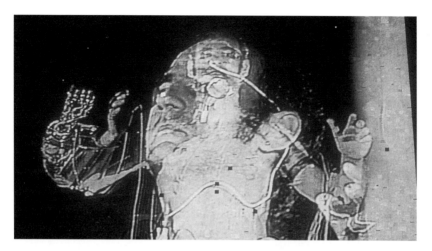

Amplified Body/Enhanced Image

involuntary. The right side of the body relays muscular movement into mechanical movement: organism and machine. Computer and robotic arm. Sensation and purposive functioning.

AMPLIFIED BODY EVENTS (1970–94)

The body performs in a structured and interactive lighting installation that flickers and flares in response to the electrical discharges of the body. Light is treated not as an external illumination of the body but as a manifestation of the body's rhythms.

HOLLOW BODY EVENTS (1994)

In the Hollow Body Events, the interior of the stomach, colon, and lungs are filmed with a miniature video camera. The probes disable the default envelope of intensity by following the infolding of the skin into the body, through the orifices. The extension into visibility of the body's inside reveals its sensitive-intensive, palpitating interiority to be an infolded—and

Fractal Flesh Telepolis (Helsinki–Luxembourg)

unfoldable—exteriority that is as susceptible to transductive connection as any sampling of body-substance. The body is hollow. There is nothing inside— there is no inside as such for anything to be in, interiority being only a particular relationship of the exterior to itself.

FRACTAL FLESH-SPLIT BODY: VOLTAGE IN/VOLTAGE OUT (1995)

Here, the body was plugged into the World Wide Web via electrodes connected to the body. The body and Third Arm were situated in Luxembourg, and people in seven cities around the world were invited to gather at specially networked terminals where they could remotely control the body's gestures. Others were encouraged to log in through their regular Internet connections. The audience is let into the loop. It becomes part of the performance. The distance between the performer and the spectator is abolished. Sensation has unfolded into a transindividual feedback loop of action-reaction, stimulus-response. The performance potentializes a material interconnection of bodies.

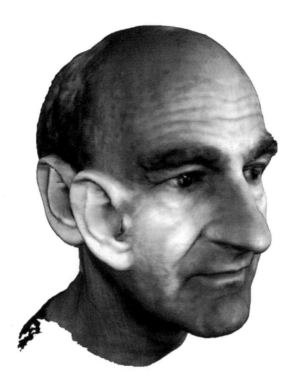

EXTRA EAR (1997–98)

Having a Third Hand, the body will construct an extra ear. This will be positioned on the side of the face beside the right ear. A balloon will be inserted beneath the skin and gradually inflated for an estimated four-to-six weeks until an adequate bubble of stretched skin is formed. The balloon is then removed and a cartilage or plastic ear framework is inserted in the excess bag of skin. A cosmetic or plastic surgeon will then cut, nip, tuck, and sew the skin over the underlying ear structure. The Extra Ear will retain feeling, but, of course, it will not be able to hear. It is intended that this ear will speak. An implanted sound chip will be actuated by a proximity sensor whenever another body gets close enough. Ultimately, the aim will be for one ear to whisper sweet nothings into the other ear. —*STELARC*

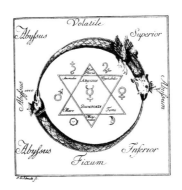

The technologies of VR, therefore, are post-medieval surfaces where we merge with the aesthetic *trompe l'oeil* of anamorphosis, go liquid and become spinning tops, silver cones on glittering surfaces, a liquid array matrix. This is a way of breaking through to the nonspace of the third body: that virtual space where reality-function dissolves into a perverted image, and where reflecting surfaces are signs of that which never was. In the anamorphic space of virtual reality, we become the nonspace of the perverted image.　　—Arthur Kroker

Seeing with your Eyes:

An Email Discussion between

Vivian Sobchack and John Beckmann

DECEMBER 1996–MARCH 1997

JOHN BECKMANN: In your 1994 essay "The Scene of the Screen: Envisioning Cinematic and Electronic Presence," you discuss how electronic representation "denies the human body its fleshly presence and the world its dimensions" and how at this particular moment in culture, "the lived-body is in crisis."[1] Since that essay was written just prior to the explosion of the Web, I was curious to know if you feel that the Web further intensifies this crisis of the "lived-body," if so how, and what can we do about it?

VIVIAN SOBCHACK: Given when "Scene of the Screen" was written and where we are now, I find myself a bit uncomfortable with some of the overarching assertions I made in that piece. I now think the issues of embodiment and dimension need more specific interrogation. The explosion of the Web as a site for the fulfillment (or disappointment) of many and multiform desires certainly demonstrates this—that is, its diversity of function and actual use raise questions about what kinds of fleshly presence or worldly dimension become available through electronic transmission and digital representation. In terms of embodiment, of course one immediately thinks of Web sex, which throws the "lurker" into a flagrant interactive relationship at the level of desire, but creates a body that must—and I pun here quite purposely—turn on itself. This, in a way (like autism, like masturbation), leads to an intensified sense of one's body and an isolated sense of one's self, a heightening of one's fleshly presence, not its denial. What is denied here is the desire and the body of the other.

This, though, is only one form of embodiment. There are many others, I'm sure. I just saw an advertisement on television promoting the child-friendly "interface" of Fischer-Price toys and Compaq computers. We see a little boy (no more than five years old) in front of a computer screen that seems to show a Web site, but instead of a mouse, he is using a big plastic steering wheel and what looks like a big plastic car phone to direct his travels through the Net. It is, if you think about it, quite telling: what's familiar here, what's user-friendly, is the heightened dramatization of the "cocooned" body, the kind of body we first sensed (long before computing) in our cars, where we felt protected and unseen and snug—and, of course, in control. This is a body that is not denied, but rather "nested." Thus, there is a certain double cocooning or nesting going on in that Fischer-Price-Compaq drama: comfy and snug within one's own home, one can get more comfy and snugger still—and all while seeming to move outward into the world.

In "Scene," I talk about the "crisis" of the lived-body as it fears becoming merely a ghost in the machine. It's been going on now for so long, it doesn't feel like a crisis anymore. The body's "hysterical" attempts to reassert itself as a physical capacity are by now normalized. Everybody (at least just about everybody who has access to computing) belongs to a gym or has a personal trainer. What remains frightening is the kind of body that is reasserting itself: rather than putting flesh on the ghost in the machine, it is transforming—or, more aptly, morphing—the ghost into the machine. Informed and guided by digital manipulation of an effortless and seamless kind, as a culture we believe deep-down we can truly sculpt ourselves into immortality, erase the labors of being and the very un-special effects of human mortality by religiously (and I mean religiously) going to the gym or the cosmetic surgeon. This is delusional.

> JB: Well, I guess I'm one of the last hold outs, as I don't have a personal trainer yet. But seriously, I agree with you that it seems that we are led to believe that we can now reconfigure our bodies as easily as touching up some pixels on an image in Photoshop.
>
> To me the real question is, is it even possible now to "move outward into the world," or is that urge delusional in itself? For example, previously we moved through space, now space moves through us. Accelerated digital technologies in many ways have surpassed reality, and thus our very bodies and gene structures are becoming more and more transparent to our human gaze.

VS: I love your making a distinction between us moving through space and now space moving through us. I've just had an epiphanetic experience that confirms this latter experience and it's not all bad. After just having come back from the Armand Hammer museum (here in Los Angeles) which is having a show of René Magritte painting and sculpture, I started looking at (a description I will shortly put in suspension) a CD-Rom I bought called *The Mystery of Magritte*. It's quite wonderful in various ways, but what really startled me since I don't normally look at painting on CD was when I would magnify one of the Magritte paintings to fill the screen. There was this really uncanny sense of being in, *inhabiting* the space of the painting, or of the space of the painting *coming out to envelop me*. That's almost impossible to do walking in and inhabiting the physical space of the museum with the physical gravity of my body keeping me *outside* the painting. Only intense focus allows me a way into the painting in the museum—and then it's a space of attention, not exteriorized or possibly homogenized as a space my body can occupy. The computer allows a really extraordinary extroversion that is at one and the same time an introversion. This, perhaps, is the transparency—or easy reversibility—of inside/outside of which you speak.

On the other hand, I do believe it's possible that we can electronically still move outward into the world. I haven't had an intense experience of it, but have spoken to a friend whose use of the Web truly extends his being—in this instance to his home country of Hungary. He is truly excited by the fact that he is able to connect to his home city and explore what's going on and feel connected. I remember him telling me with great pleasure and pride that when he actually went back to visit this past summer, he felt more at home and embedded in what was going on than a friend who had only been away for a month and was "out of touch." This was not merely a matter of "information" (like getting a weather report from a city you're going to visit), but an adding of lived dimension that he experienced over distance as proximity.

JB: Yet this semblance of information as knowledge (quantitative information or even phenomenological experience), represents an illusionary or dream-like position, because in a sense this new "real-time" shift is a move toward a kind of virtual cannibalization of space, as information now devours itself as quickly as it can be produced (i.e., the Web, whirling stock market quotes, etc.). So in a very real way, we now float in a digital ouroboros, as what seems to be real becomes a substitute for what is truly real. And this is the issue, because the problem with digital technology is that we can not yet simulate soulfullness. So these "lived dimensions" of which you speak are, sadly, already instantaneously dead. They represent a vortex of "dead signs" that circulate in a data cloud that is adrift on a membrane of hypertext links that is further disguised as an "architecture of information." So, I suggest, that it is now impossible, or close to impossible, to move outward into the world of "real events." Or, by pushing this metaphor even further, I suggest that "real-time" is an extension of "dream-time"—that is, a "dream-time" that cannot possibly exist because there is no "real space" for it.

vs: I am sitting here smiling at the fact that I (as a near-luddite, definite skeptic, and someone who is usually outright hostile to the Web) am somehow in the position of devil's advocate. (In that regard I do want to get in my negative say about the Web here somewhere, but you'll have to remind me.) You say what I would call our "lived dimension" or, as you would call it, "soulfullness," is dead (it used to be God, didn't it?), and what remains is merely quantitative information devouring itself and us along with it. In many ways I agree with you. Certainly, a lot of people have bought into the illusion that if you somehow have enough quantitative information, it will somehow magically take on *value* and transform itself into qualitative understanding. But it is also true that for each of us, to use a cliché, the buck stops here—here both at the interface and in our real chairs (pace the hypothetical chairs of philosophers) where each of us is embodied and situated, where we have to make choices and act, where we (even those of us who need to get one) have a life. Given our personal and social situations, whether we admit it or not, want to or not, we do take and, often more importantly, leave that information and always already confer upon it or deny it qualitative value. The problem here is that we too often forget this inescapable fact; the solution (and it needs continual resolving) is to consciously remember it and make it explicit and not just thoughtlessly act it out. In sum, what provides us at least the possibility of an "out" from the self-cannibalizing "digital ouroboros" is that we ultimately *feel* the digital bites we take of our own fleshy and mortal tails.

For me (and here I'm reminding myself of why I really hate the Web), I feel that digital bite on my very mortality. I sit there in front of that computer shell and feel like I'm the victim of a shell game, like I'm being conned (or, maybe, "commed"). The Web is the one place where I am acutely aware of being offered infinite space while being robbed of finite time. The interface doesn't help—nor will, despite all techie protests, a "faster" modem. No modem will ever be fast enough to overcome the digital version of Zeno's paradox.

JB: You're referring to Zeno's bisection paradox, right? If a person must walk a mile, they must first walk half a mile, then they must walk half of what remains, or one-fourth of a mile, so it is never possible for their journey to come to an end.

What I call the digital ouroboros (remember the alchemical symbol of the snake biting its own tail?), refers to a condition whereby we've fallen into infinity. An infinity of dead information and obese images. This is the vicious paradox of the digital age, it is the height of masochism and hunger. Content has now been replaced with metacontent, physical attributes have been replaced with meta-attributes and so on. So we're really slipping quite quickly out of any kind of gravitational pull and at the same time, and this is the point that I think is very interesting, the world is seizing up on itself.

Forget all the hype about a new frontier, it's far too late for that kind of utopian spin. We're out to colonize cyberspace because there's simply no place left for us to go. The space program hasn't quite worked out.

So indeed, it is a shell game. But it cannot be stopped—there's too much money at stake. Our "New World" economy is absolutely dependent on it's success, the digital revolution I mean. And it is quite addictive, the Web—look there's even Web TV (silly idea)! I'm predicting an increase in divorce rates.

VS: An infinity of dead information and obese information? Mostly, you're right. But luckily, we're finite and it is in that fact—the materiality of the bodies that sit at the computer and their phenomenological sense of having to ultimately live and suffer in mortal time—that gravity reasserts itself. I don't believe in the new frontier crap, either. (Indeed, I've written an article titled "Democratic Franchise and the Electronic Frontier" for a British journal called *Futures* that definitely quashes those notions that cyberspace is somehow inherently democratic.)[2] And I agree with you that our insertion/immersion in electronic culture can't be stopped. But insofar as that culture will never be entirely electronic, insofar as human bodies are involved ultimately, at the terminal ends so to speak, there remains at least the possibility of gravity rather than free fall, of responsibility rather than of seemingly consequence-less play, of value rather than quantity. So it's not a question of stopping anything here, but rather one of foregrounding those aspects of human existence that are not served or satisfied by the Web (or Web TV) and redressing the imbalances that fascination with the novel always causes. That is, we need to pinpoint with greater specificity what we get and what we lose engaging the Web, or playing computer killing games, or getting to "know" people through email. (I've a friend who just completed writing a book called *e-mail trouble: love and addiction @ the matrix* that critiques in very moving and personal ways our easy belief in the intimacy and community one finds so easily on line.)[3] In sum, I think we're past the "blanket condemnation" we all practiced to varying degrees as a counter to the utopian hype that's attached to "new" media. Now, we need to get really specific about the specificities of our engagements with electronic culture and digital media. Quick Time is not email is not the Web is not a CD is not a chat room and I don't think they're equivalent in terms of what we might specifically gain or lose in engaging any of them. On the Web (which I hate), for instance, I am always acutely aware of losing or wasting time—my own mortal time. I find, however, that watching certain Quick Time movies that do not attempt to approximate "real time" movies, I feel immersed in a kind of timelessness, their hovering somewhere between stillness and movement and their miniaturosity (laugh: no such word, but it fits) reminding me of Cornell (Joseph) boxes. Anyway, I think we have to be careful not to reduce everything to Doom (pun intended).

JB: It's not a question of condemnation, it has more to do with realizing, or accepting the distortion inherent in any form of medium at this point in time. From my point of view, it's no longer possible to examine value or content, it's only possible to examine the relative functions between signs and their referents.

What is the societal function of corporate CEOs earning 150 times the average "Joe Blow" worker, basketball players earning $3 million a year, teenagers committing suicide at unprecedented rates, young girls suffering from anorexia because they want to look like Kate Moss? Granted, these are surely not just end of the millennium problems, but they *will be* further compounded by immersion into the illusionary quagmire of virtual images and desires.

So it's not at all surprising that we feel that we have no time, or that we're more aware of our own mortality—it's partially because the former Cartesian coordinates of x, y, and z are being shanghaied. It is a loss we all feel in some way.

Similarly, the superpostcapitalist condition (in which the digital revolution now plays a very large role) is in effect rewriting history. It is rewriting history from a vantage point that has turned inside out—this is what concerns me, this is what is specifically problematic. If the "information superhighway" is potentially democratic, it is perhaps because it's the only thing that is. Though I don't think it will last very long, because the new prototype or metaphor being developed is the notion of the Internet as a channel, meaning it is being seen as an extension of broadcast media, so again, you've got huge companies (i.e.; Microsoft, GM's Hughes Corporation, AT&T, Philips Maganovox, Sony) salivating all over one another, in a kind of feeding frenzy, over how to make use of the Web medium, so it can be packaged, consumed, and quickly reduced to another form of TV.

As with most things, the real work will be done at the edges, this in and of itself is nothing new, but the possibilities are there for artists, film makers, writers to create new conditions. This was not the case when TV was first introduced, everyone was effectively locked out from the get-go. And of course one cannot participate with a television set, it's one way.

vs: Why single out "this moment in time" relative to realizing and accepting the distortion inherent in, to use your words, "any form of medium"? It was *never* possible to examine value or content apart from the "relative functions between signs and their referents"—except insofar as one was ignorant of signs as signs and really thought the map was the territory. Indeed, one could argue that it is the very scope of this electronic "empire of signs" that has brought representation and simulation to the foreground, that has made everyone (not just postmodern academics) aware of mediation and the relativity of sign functions. The question, then, is not one about the refusal of this condition, but about the relation between an endlessly relative continuum of deferred signification (all that info out there is meaningless in its circulation) and the individuals who, because they are situated materially and physically in a particular time and space and culture, stop that circulation and make meaning by giving value to some of the circulating signs and not to others. This ascription of value and meaning does not undo relativity, but it also does not undo value or meaning: what it asserts in the human situation is that values and meanings are always contingent. This is Derridean "differance" lived by people whose actual phenomenological choices always mark a "difference" as real because it has both material consequences and meaning in their moment.

 You're right in being generally pessimistic, though. The "real work," as you call it, will be done at the edges and, yes, by artists and filmmakers, and writers—and even critics and theorists. In general, though, the institutionalization of this glut of information and stimulation (whether the info superhighway or Web TV) and its reification as capital will reduce our capacity to recognize our possibilities for choice and the ascription of value and obfuscate our responsibility for our actions and their consequences. But even television, which you say locked out possibilities from the get-go, had its Ernie Kovacs! He was able, even if only briefly, to make television dialogic rather than unidirectional.

You have to know, by the way, how both funny and peculiar it is to me that I am not the one here laying out all the negative stuff *vis à vis* electronic culture. You've co-opted my usual position and forced me to think (as Fredric Jameson suggests it is necessary for us to do even when it seems impossible) about the progressive possibilities, or at least to reassert human possibilities. I guess I'm not so much defending the Net as defending the existential conditions that allow for and indeed mandate choice and value as contingent, multiple, and always really ambiguous, which then allows an opening (however tiny) through which the progressive can emerge.

> J B : Do you think it's possible to still shock people by creating works that connect "directly to the nervous system," as Francis Bacon would say, thereby triggering transcendental sensations, recognitions of the virtual, (I'm using the Deleuzian notion of the virtual here), of the sublime? Surely film presents the most suitable medium for pulling this off.

v s : It seems to me that today it's all but impossible to shock people—whether through painting, sculpture, literature, or electronic works. Offend, disgust, thrill, yes, but really shock, I think not. The reason? If, as Benjamin as well as others suggest, one of the essential characteristics of modern life (and hence modernity) that marked it off from what came before was the novelty and increasing dominance of shock as a phenomenological experience, then perhaps what we call postmodernity is such a familiarity with shock that it has become "naturalized" and "normalized"—which, paradoxically, neutralizes its phenomenological effects. Shock takes on the banal quality of the merely novel.

Given this, perhaps artists and, for that matter, all of us "regular" people, might be most shocked by a lack of shock. Here's a radical idea (and I definitely don't want to suggest a return to the "flower child" and "make love, not shock" generation): maybe the big social and aesthetic problem is how to refigure the disjunctive and discontinuous within a contingent unity and continuity—one that denies difference as abrupt, but nonetheless promotes differentiation. Now that would be shocking!

It would also refigure our notions of the sublime. I've written a piece called "The Passion of the Material: Prolegomenon to a Phenomenology of Interobjectivity" that suggests the sublime is misunderstood as a transcendental experience that, in olden days, bespoke the spiritual and, today, evokes the virtual.[4] This is continuing a tradition that sees the sublime experience as metaphysical. I would argue just the opposite: that it is a transcendent experience of our own materiality, of experiencing being as not different but differentiated in the world and in relation to others, of being as what Merleau-Ponty calls a "fold" in the world's matter and, hence, its mattering. This is not the same sense in which we are presently cultivating "the body" as both a complement and countermeasure to the virtual—in the first instance fantasizing ourselves as immortal cyborgs, in the second trying to do the equivalent of "pinching ourselves" to see if we're real. Rather, apprehending oneself as living a material existence that is in excess of consciousness (and the unconscious) is to apprehend "the difference that *doesn't* make a difference"; it is to recognize one's being as nonoppositional, however differentiated; this is a transcendent nontranscendental sublime, a sublime grounded in the materiality of our being and not its virtuality. Maybe artists and writers and critics ought to look for ways to tap into this formation of the sublime as a way to counter the normalization of shock.

JB: Let's talk about the cloning of the ewe in Scotland by Dr. Ian Wilmut and company. Let's talk about Dolly. Dolly the double is world famous. The boundaries of science fiction have been crossed. President Clinton is scrambling to organize committees to study the legal, moral and ethical consequences of cloning. What's your take on it ?

v s : Well, first of all, I do find it really funny that—of all animals—it is a sheep that has been cloned. Metaphorically, isn't that "meta"? After all, in our culture we have been using the image of the sheep for a very long time to connote conformity, sameness. And now, as seems so apposite to the current moment, we've taken the metaphor and realized it concretely.

Furthermore, is it so surprising that we're currently fascinated by cloning? After all, cloning is to time as fractal images are to space. That is, where fractal imaging figures self-similarity across scale, cloning figures self-similarity across time. Thus, it seems part of a cultural gestalt in which difference of both subjectivity and situation is—in each case—written out of the picture. As such, culture and history disappear or are made meaningless. I'm reminded here of Jorge Luis Borges's wonderful story in *Ficciones*, "Pierre Menard: Author of *Don Quixote*."[5] In it, a critic celebrates writer Pierre Menard for his much more nuanced and significant writing of *Don Quixote* and goes on to compare a passage from Cervantes with a passage from Menard. They are word for word exactly the same. What Borges plays with here is the very way that culture and history constitute difference and deny the existential possibility of sameness. Our fascination with fractals and Dolly would do the opposite; it's yet again a fascination with, a longing for, transcendence from (or in?) existence.

By the way, although I often trash him, Jean Baudrillard is frequently prescient. He's written a very good essay on cloning in *The Transparency of Evil* called "The Hell of the Same." He tells us: "Cloning is thus the last stage in the history of the modeling of the body—the stage at which the individual, having been reduced to his abstract and genetic formula, is destined for serial propagation." Citing Walter Benjamin on the work of art in the age of mechanical reproduction and the consequent loss of "aura," he suggests that now human bodies "are conceived from the outset" as having no originality, but rather "in terms of their limitless reproduction."[6]

So, we're back not only to Baudrillard and the postmodern, but immersed in what already is a tired term: the posthuman.

JB: Oh no! I think the general concern with regard to the cloning scenario is fear of replacement, rather than transcendence. On the most paranoid fringe, people are fearful of the development of a black market; a kind of off-shore body part slave bazaar.

If I may add an ironic note, at a recent congressional hearing on cloning, Tom Harkin (D-Iowa) urged against any bans on cloning, "What nonsense—what utter nonsense—to think that we can hold up our hands and say, Stop....Human cloning will take place, and it will take place in my lifetime. I don't fear it at all. I welcome it." Harkin is clearly not in the majority with this position.

Speaking of black markets—I'd like to return to your interest in science fiction for a moment. I'm curious, what was your reaction to the film *Strange Days*. Did you find it a believable scenario for the future? Were you entertained by it?

VS: What interests me most about *Strange Days*—and remember that I'm a film scholar who has written not only on sci-fi cinema but also on technologically-mediated perception—is less the millennial moment it is supposedly representing than the perceptual technology it envisions. Although I've only seen the film once, what I found most engaging and what makes me want to go back and look at it much more closely (if I can ever dig myself out from under) are the convoluted and extremely complex relationships that occur between perceivers and perceived. The imbrication of vision in the film makes a Moebius strip of what is already quite complex in *Blade Runner*'s interrogation of mediated vision: i.e., Roy Baty's ironic gloss on photography and cinema as a whole: "If you could only see what I've seen with your eyes."

1. "The Scene of the Screen: Envisioning Cinematic and Electronic 'Presence'," in *Materials of Communication*, ed. Hans Ulrich Gumbrecht and K. Ludwig Pfeiffer (Palo Alto, CA: Stanford University Press, 1994), 105.

2. "Democratic Franchise and Electronic Frontier," *Futures* 27 (1995): 725–34.

3. S. Paige Baty, *e-mail trouble: love and addiction @ the matrix* (Austin: University of Texas Press, forthcoming).

4. "Die Materie und ihre Passion: Prolegomenazu einer Phänomenologie der Interobjektivtät" (The Pas-

sion of the Material: Prologomena to a Phenomenology of Interobjectivity), in *Ethik der Ästhetik*, ed. Christolph Wulf, Dietmar Kamper, and Hans Ulrich Gumbrecht (Berlin: Akademie Verlag, 1994), 195–205.

5. Jorge Luis Borges, "Pierre Menard, Author of *Don Quixote*," in *Ficciones*, trans. Anthony Bonner (New York: Grove Press, 1962), 45–55.

6. Jean Baudrillard, "The Hell of the Same," in *The Transparency of Evil: Essays on Extreme Phenomena*, trans. James Benedict (London: Verso, 1993), 118.

STAN ALLEN is an architect who practices in New York City and teaches at the Columbia University Graduate School of Architecture, Planning and Preservation. A monograph of his work, *Points + Lines: Diagrams and Projects for the City*, will be published by Princeton Architectural Press in 1998.

PETER ANDERS is a practicing architect and principal of Anders Associates, a firm specializing in physical and simulated information space. He has been a visiting professor at the University of Michigan School of Architecture and Special Lecturer at the School of Architecture at the New Jersey Institute of Technology. He is currently writing a book on spatializing cyberspace environments.

ASYMPTOTE was formed in New York in 1987 by Hani Rashid and Lise Anne Couture. The studio's work includes building designs, urban planning, installations, objects, and computer-generated architecture. Asymptote's projects examine the position of architectural production within a broad range of cultural practices, and its work has been featured in many publications and has been widely exhibited.

ERICA BAUM is an artist living and working in New York City. Her photographs explore the transformation of ordinary facts in an absurdist archaeology of the everyday. She is represented by the New York gallery D'Amelio Terras.

JOHN BECKMANN is a practicing architect and designer, and is the founder of the interdisciplinary design firm Axis Mundi in New York. His architectural and design projects have been published in *The New York Times*, *Progressive Architecture*, *Casa Vogue*, and other international design journals. He is currently developing another book with the photographer Barry Perlus on the eighteenth-century astronomical observatories in India colloquially known as the *Jantar Mantar*.

GARETH BRANWYN is a contributing editor to *Wired* and co-author of *The Happy Mutant Handbook* and *Jamming the Media: A Citizen's Guide*. He has written widely about the Internet and is currently writing a book on amateur/subversive media.

BEN VAN BERKEL and **CAROLINE BOS** established an architectural practice in Amsterdam in 1988. Among the many projects they have realized is the Erasmus Bridge in Rotterdam. They teach and lecture widely on theoretical aspects of architecture.

BERNARD CACHE is an independent architect and furniture designer living in Paris. He is currently under contract with the French government to explore software elaborations of his ideas and is preparing a series of furniture prototypes for production. He is the author of *Earth Moves* (1995).

CHAR DAVIES is an artist and Director of Visual Research at Softimage in Montreal. Her work has been exhibited at the Musee d'art contemporain in Montreal and at the Ricco/ Maresca Gallery in New York. Her work has been the subject of articles in publications including *Wired, Metropolis,* and *Art in America.*

MANUEL DE LANDA is the author of *War in the Age of Intelligent Machines* (1991) and *A Thousand Years of Nonlinear History* (1997). His philosophical essays have appeared in many journals, and he lectures extensively in the United States and Europe on nonlinear dynamics, theories of self-organization, artificial intelligence, and artificial life.

FRANCES DYSON is a media artist and theorist who specializes in sound. Her audio artwork has been aired internationally, and she has exhibited media installation works in North America, Australia, and Japan.

MICHAEL HEIM directs a Tai Chi group and teaches Internet and new media design at the Art Center College of Design in Pasadena, California. His writing and lecturing center around the human body in its relation to the computer. He is the author of *Electric Language: A Philosophical Study of Word Processing* (1987), *The Metaphysics of Virtual Reality* (1993), and and *Virtual Realism* (1998).

KNOWBOTIC RESEARCH is a Cologne based media art and research group founded by Yvonne Wilhelm, Alexander Tuchacek, and Christian Huebler. In partnership with the Academy for Media Arts, Knowbotic Research has founded Mem_brane, a laboratory for media strategies.

BRIAN MASSUMI is the author of *A User's Guide to Capitalism and Schizophrenia: Deviations from Deleuze and Guattari* (1992) and (with Kenneth Dean) *First and Last Emperors: The Absolute State and the Body of the Despot* (1992). He is the editor of *The Politics of Everyday Fear* (1993), and co-editor of the University of Minnesota Press book series "Theory Out of Bounds." His translations from the French include Gilles Deleuze and Felix Guattari's *A Thousand Plateaus* (1987).

WILLIAM J. MITCHELL is Professor of Architecture and Media Arts and Sciences and Dean of the School of Architecture and Planning at the Massachusetts Institute of Technology. He teaches courses and conducts research in design theory, computer applications in architecture and urban design, and imaging and image synthesis. His most recent book, *City of Bits: Space, Place, and the Infobahn* (1995), examines architecture and urbanism in the context of the digital telecommunications revolution and the growing domination of software over materialized form.

HANS MORAVEC built his first robot at age ten. Since 1980, he has been Director of the Carnegie Mellon University Mobile Robot Laboratory, birthplace of mobile robots deriving three-dimensional spatial awareness from cameras, sonar, and other sensors. His books, *Mind Children: The Future of Robot and Human Intelligence* (1988), and the forthcoming *Robot: Mere Machine to Transcendent Mind*, consider the future prospects for humans, robots, and intelligence.

STEPHEN PERRELLA is an architect and editor/designer of *Newsline* and *Columbia Documents* at the Columbia University Graduate School of Architecture Planning and Preservation. He is also president of HyperSurface Systems, Inc. an Internet technology design firm created to explore broader architectural interfaces. He recently guest-edited an issue of *Architectural Design* titled *Hypersurface Architecture* (1998). He has taught architecture at various universities in the U.S. and has lectured internationally.

FLORIAN RÖETZER is a theorist and art critic who lives in Munich. He is the author of several books on electronic art and the digital era. He prepared five special issues of the cultural journal *Kunstforum* and was editor of the communications magazine *Tumult*. Currently, he is editor of the electronic journal *Telepolis*.

ANDREAS RUBY is a widely published architectural critic, theorist, and curator based in Cologne, Germany. He lectures regularly in Europe and North America. He is currently preparing a book on the Viennese architects Coop Himmelb(l)au.

VIVIAN SOBCHACK is Associate Dean and Professor of Film Studies at the University of California, Los Angeles School of Theater, Film and Television. She was the first woman elected president of the Society for Cinema Studies and is currently a Trustee of the American Film Institute. Her articles and reviews have appeared in journals such as *Artforum* and

Film Quarterly. She is editor of the anthology *The Persistence of History: Cinema, Television and the Modern Event* (1996) and author of numerous books. She is currently at work on a volume of her essays, *Carnal Thoughts: Bodies, Texts, Scenes and Screens* (forthcoming).

MICHAEL SPEAKS is a critic and lecturer in New York City. He has taught in the architecture departments at the Harvard University Graduate School of Design, the Parsons School of Design, and the Columbia University Graduate School of Architecture, Planning and Preservation.

CLAUDIA SPRINGER is a Professor in the English Department and Film Studies Program at Rhode Island College, and is the author of *Electronic Eros: Bodies and Desire in the Postindustrial Age* (1996).

LARS SPUYBROEK is an architect and one of the founders of NOX, a design office with a multidisciplinary approach to architecture and design. He lectures extensively in the Netherlands and abroad, and has taught at numerous universities.

STAHL STENSLIE is a media artist and media researcher working on the development of different interface technologies within the fields of art, media, and network research. He lectures frequently and his work has been exhibited internationally. He is presently working on cognition- and perception-manipulation projects.

STELARC is an Australian-based performance artist whose work explores and extends the concept of the body and its relationship with technology through human-machine interfaces incorporating the Internet and the Web, sound, music, video, and computers. He has performed extensively in international art events. Stelarc's artwork is represented by The Sherman Galleries in Sydney, Australia.

ARNE SVENSON is a New York based photographer whose work has been exhibited internationally. His first book, *Prisoners*, was published in 1997. He is represented by the Julie Saul Gallery in New York

MARK C. TAYLOR is Cluett Professor of Humanities and director of the Center for Technology in the Arts and Humanities at Williams College. He also serves as director of the Critical Issues Forum at the Guggenheim Museum in New York. He is the author of numerous books, including *Disfiguring Art, Architecture, Religion* (1992), *Nots* (1993), and *Hiding* (1997).

MATTHEW AARON TAYLOR is Visiting Associate Professor of English at Kinjo Gakuin University. He is working on a series of essays relating artificial life to fiction.

PAUL VIRILIO is the Director of the Ecole Speciale d'Architecture, and an editor of Esprit, Cause Commune and Critiques. He is a founding member of CIRPES, the Center for Interdisciplinary Research in Peace Studies and Military Strategy. His many books include *Pure War* (1985), *War and Cinema: The Logistics of Perception* (1989), *Bunker Archaeology* (Princeton Architectural Press, 1994), *The Art of the Motor* (1995), and *Open Sky* (1997).

MARGARET WERTHEIM is an Australian science writer now living in New York City. She has written extensively about science and technology for magazines, television, and radio. She is the author of *Pythagoras' Trousers: God, Physics and the Gender Wars* (1995) and is currently working on her next book, *The Pearly Gates of Cyberspace* (1998). Her articles have appeared in many magazines and newspapers, including the *New York Times*, *Vogue*, *Elle*, *Glamour*, *World Art*, and *Metropolis*.